Permanent Exclusion from School ˏ Institutional Prejudice

STUDIES IN INCLUSIVE EDUCATION
Volume 20

Scope
This series addresses the many different forms of exclusion that occur in schooling across a range of international contexts and considers strategies for increasing the inclusion and success of all students. In many school jurisdictions the most reliable predictors of educational failure include poverty, Aboriginality and disability. Traditionally schools have not been pressed to deal with exclusion and failure. Failing students were blamed for their lack of attainment and were either placed in segregated educational settings or encouraged to leave and enter the unskilled labour market. The crisis in the labor market and the call by parents for the inclusion of their children in their neighborhood school has made visible the failure of schools to include all children.

Drawing from a range of researchers and educators from around the world, Studies in Inclusive Education will demonstrate the ways in which schools contribute to the failure of different student identities on the basis of gender, race, language, sexuality, disability, socio-economic status and geographic isolation. This series differs from existing work in inclusive education by expanding the focus from a narrow consideration of what has been traditionally referred to as special educational needs to understand school failure and exclusion in all its forms. Moreover, the series will consider exclusion and inclusion across all sectors of education: early years, elementary and secondary schooling, and higher education.

Permanent Exclusion from School and Institutional Prejudice

Creating Change Through Critical Bureaucracy

Anna Carlile
Goldsmiths, University of London, UK

SENSE PUBLISHERS
ROTTERDAM/BOSTON/TAIPEI

A C.I.P. record for this book is available from the Library of Congress.

ISBN: 978-94-6209-180-1 (paperback)
ISBN: 978-94-6209-181-8 (hardback)
ISBN: 978-94-6209-182-5 (e-book)

Published by: Sense Publishers,
P.O. Box 21858,
3001 AW Rotterdam,
The Netherlands
https://www.sensepublishers.com/

Printed on acid-free paper

DEDICATION

This book is for the young people of Enway.

TABLE OF CONTENTS

PREFACE

This book deals with the administration of permanent exclusion from school within an urban children's services department. It focuses on two areas: what contributes to instances of permanent exclusion from school, and what the effects are of its existence as a disciplinary option. I suspected that the existence of permanent exclusion from school might limit the realm of the possible, and I was particularly interested in how and why local government officers made particular decisions about children and young people. In other words, I wondered whether professionals might be negatively affected by the fact that at some point they would have the option of excluding a young person rather than either continuing to try to help them or to attempt to change the institution's approach to educating them. Rather than focussing on what children and young people 'did' behaviourally to 'get excluded', the book adopts a Foucauldian analysis to concentrate on their place within a larger 'policy community' which includes professionals and policy makers.

The research was undertaken through an ethnographic methodology conducted within my place of work as a pupil support officer, and the fieldwork itself lasted two years. Because I was participant-observing within a group of local authority[1] staff, and was interested in local government decision-making, I have largely framed my approach as a 'critical-bureaucratic' exercise in 'studying up' on powerful organisations. So in order to support an informed approach to ameliorating social inequity, the book looks at the ways in which powerful institutions work.

The findings described here suggest a broad, deep and opaque seam of institutional prejudice in a range of areas. They point towards the idea that instances of permanent exclusion from school are partially caused or exacerbated by institutional prejudice. Permanent exclusion from school can also be seen to intensify the effects of institutional prejudice.

This has implications for the 'voices' of the young people subject to or at the risk of permanent exclusion from school both in school and in the research, and the final chapter outlines a Foucauldian/Freirian 'student voice' project, offering one idea about how schools might tackle this.

NOTE

[1] Local city or rural administrative bodies responsible for managing provision of everything from waste management and local taxes to transport strategies and education.

ACKNOWLEDGEMENTS

I have to thank my children Jimi and Tallula for putting up with me going on *ad nauseum* about Michel Foucault for the last six years. Their encouragement and unconditional positive regard has sustained me. And they are fantastic lovely people: if I have contributed to that, it's my best achievement. My PhD supervisors, Professor Rosalyn George, Dr Heather Mendick and Professor Dennis Atkinson were immensely insightful, supportive and thoughtful. Everyone at the Educational Studies Department at Goldsmiths has supported me in so many ways- thank you especially to Dr Chris Kearney for being there at the beginning, and to Sue Dixon, Maggie Pitfield, and Lynsey Salt for help during my study leave. Thanks too to my students at Goldsmiths. They have consistently encouraged and challenged the development of my thinking- I've learned so much from all of them. I would also like to thank students and staff at Coopers Technology College for their engaging and creative discussions and hard work on the Illuminate project. It was a privilege to be part of that learning community for a short while, and I have developed my understanding a great deal as a result of our collaboration. All four of my parents and my various siblings assisted me variously with hot meals, tea and sympathy. Thanks to my mum for the cover illustration. Thank you to Jo, for her astounding love, and to Louis, for his lovely smile. And to Sheryl, Liza, Dona and the fantastic people at 'Enway' of all ages, who I wish I could name: You know what you've done. I can't thank you enough.

INTRODUCTION

Excavating Silence

This book aims to deconstruct some of the problems around disciplinary practise in schools and to offer both local and systemic solutions. It is based on an ethnography addressing the causes of permanent exclusion from school (what used to be called 'being expelled'), and its impacts as a disciplinary option. It also looks at permanent exclusion as a critical incident capable of illuminating weaknesses in a system[1] which consists of 'inclusive' schooling, discipline, and supporting children and young people. As such, it is focused fundamentally on the tangled imbalances of power; representation; how representation is experienced; and the privileged or unprivileged 'voices' behind these issues. It is also, on a macro level, an ethnography which uses permanent exclusion from school to illustrate the way in which a relationship between the individual and the state is mediated by the technologies of policies and policy-making.

The book rests on a set of ethnographic data gathered within the 'shared social space' (Atkinson and Hammersley 1994: 256) of a local authority children's services department during two years of work as a pupil support officer. My job during this time was to support young people who had been permanently excluded from school in an urban local authority ('Enway')[2] through a combination of multi-agency support planning meetings, advice to schools and parents, and importantly, through listening to children and young people and trying to privilege their concerns in the midst of a series of complex discussions and decisions.

To begin, it is important to trace the roots of my concerns about how voices might become less-privileged. This chapter thus simultaneously tracks my journey to the questions on which this book is based, before situating the topic within its policy and academic contexts, and clarifying my own positioning. I am hoping that the narrative approach which follows will serve to evoke the importance of the inclusion and exclusion of children's and young people's voices, both to me and as an issue embedded and threaded throughout children's educational experience in an urban English education system. Perhaps it is apt, then, to begin with my own.

JOURNEY'S BEGINNING

When I was seven, my family moved from the quiet Roman town of Chester to a large rented red brick house set in farmland in the Welsh hills just across the border from Shropshire. My peers at the tiny Welsh school I attended were the children of rich owner-farmers and financially struggling tenant farmers, and had known each other since birth. I was an English outsider, and found it difficult to connect in terms of accent, language, history, lifestyle and looks. I was a pale, skinny town child; they were red-cheeked country children who ate giant Welsh teas and leapt off huge piles of bales in the straw barn. I struggled to make friends and in fact did not do so until I met another middle-class English misfit, the daughter of a communist British Broadcasting Corporation (BBC) Russian Service correspondent in the second year of high school, when I was thirteen years old.

My primary school was a small Church of Wales school serving between eighteen and twenty-five children. We sat in one of two classrooms, 'The Infants' and 'The Juniors', and copied flags out of a Ladybird book for 'Topic' lessons or wrote furiously for three days to fill our empty Religious Education (RE) books in preparation for the local vicar's pre-OFSTED[3] inspection.[4] The school taught maths well; all the local mothers congregated by the gate for their daily chat; the local Women's Institute used the school hall for its meetings, and its Summer and Christmas fetes were attended by most of the local community. However, it was not a happy place.

The real trouble was rooted in the fact that our teacher – the teacher of 'The Juniors', and the head teacher of the school – was a dangerous, unbalanced person. The RE marathons were frightening enough; he would stand at the board, slapping it with a long wooden ruler, flashing red-faced and filling and refilling each of the three boards in succession in tiny looped handwriting in yellow chalk, often for hours at a stretch, erasing each one as we finished copying it, our hands aching, desperate to keep up for fear of reprisal. But the teacher could be physically violent, too. Once, as I sat at a large, blonde wood trestle table in the hall and giggled through the Topic lesson with another outsider, a girl from Northern Ireland, he strode furiously towards us and without breaking his stride, purple veins popping out terrifyingly on his forehead, frightening tufts of grey-black hair on each sides of his swollen skull, our teacher smashed his fist down on the table between us and we watched, horrified, as a crack spread along the edge of the table, the centre of the tabletop splintering and buckling with a crash down onto the floor as we leapt backwards, knocking our chairs over as we moved out of the way. This man was also inappropriate with personal space and with sexual boundaries, and no girl in 'The Juniors' was safe from his daily advances. My sister and I told our parents, but they struggled with the fact that our lack of friends, a result of our status as émigrés, meant that they had no other parents to call and verify the story with. After eighteen months of this, the daughter of a new English family told her parents, and they finally telephoned mine. The teacher was invited to our home and my sister and I peeped through the banisters and saw that he was crying as he crossed the rough stone-flagged hallway into the living room. When we were finally questioned, my sister spoke as I could not, and hid my face in a cushion. A few days later, my mother went to visit the teacher and warned him, on behalf of the Parent-Teacher Association (PTA), to leave our school. Teaching in another school, he finally did something far more violent, and was sent to prison.

The trouble was that the law at that time would only accept a child's word as evidence if there was an adult's word to corroborate it. I had always assumed that there was no such evidence. But I discovered later that 'The Infants'' teacher had told the lunchtime supervisor that she had seen the head teacher acting inappropriately with the children, and the lunchtime supervisor verified this. They were chatting in the sun at a village Summer Fete when my mother overheard them, and she told me years later, when I was processing the experience with her at the kitchen table, my own children throwing toy cars at my ankles across the floor. It felt too late for corroboration by then; a fear of the legal construction of truth had obliterated the telling of the story of the very real experiences of around twenty children.

My village school experience left me with the feelings that some teachers could be seduced by a dangerous power; that children were not listened to in life or in law; that parents were vulnerable in relation to the trust they placed in teachers to safeguard their children. It established in me a kernel of empathy around the experiences of children who found themselves experiencing the state of being an outsider, and this kernel grew and became the core around which I grew into rebellious adolescence, and later on, a teacher myself.

My early teenage years were spent at a small high school in the Welsh hills. Some of the teachers at the high school were very good, and left a lasting impression on me. My English teacher was genuinely interested in what we had to say; he had high expectations and his lessons were intellectually stimulating. However, there were some strange and difficult characters. Mr Evans' nickname was 'Och', Welsh for 'goat' to reflect his white goatee beard and terrible temper. Och was the Physics teacher and did not believe that girls should be studying science. He placed the girls in a row, their backs to the blackboard, and placed the boys opposite, facing it. We were not permitted to turn around to view what he was writing. We once entered the room on a Friday afternoon, a low orange autumn sun streaming through the high windows and warming the long wooden lab benches, to find our books on the floor, footprints over their torn covers: a statement of our teacher's disgusted, self-righteous misogyny. My embryonic socialist-feminist sensibilities were outraged; I would rush down to the head teacher's office and stride in, demanding that Och be sacked, only to be told not to worry; that he would retire in a year or two. Once again, my voice was not heard, and we girls had been disregarded, disrespected and effectively rendered less than worthless in the classroom. Despite getting a good set of GCSEs[5] and having significant family encouragement to continue my education into post-compulsory courses, my experiences dissuaded me, and I left school at sixteen years old.

Five years later, after the birth of my own two children, and living in London, I signed up for an Access course in Anthropology, Social Policy and Film Studies, placing my children in the on-site nursery downstairs from the classroom. On this Access course, I began to glimpse the potential for education to address (rather than cause) social inequity. The Northern Irish social policy teacher taught us that policy was constructed by and imposed upon mere humans. One of his assignments was to collect an education-focused oral history of someone we knew. I chose my mother, and grew to know her more profoundly as she talked about her painful experiences of being dyslexic at a Catholic boarding school during a time when dyslexia was not recognised. The anthropology tutor introduced me to ethnography through a book about the nomadic !Kung people (Shostak 2000). And the film studies teacher, a (male) Marxist feminist, showed me that there were fascinating lateral views of the world that could cut across the unsatisfying rhetoric I had struggled against during my time at secondary school.

The Access course opened the door to a law degree, which clarified my research and writing skills and built my academic confidence. On the degree, I came across the idea of narrative as a counterbalance to the positivist theories of truth and rationality on which the legal system rests. My degree-level introduction to 'narrative truth' came when a feminist lecturer gave us an article to read written by a woman criminal lawyer and academic researcher (Estrich 1986). Like many woman lawyers, Susan Estrich was often given work concerned with women and children, and this meant that she had become an expert on evidence and consent issues in rape cases. She had also become somewhat case-hardened.[6] Estrich had been writing a dry academic article about the law relating to rape, and was halfway through it when she herself was raped. It was an anonymous, violent attack, and she found herself going through all the processes she had been describing in her article. She gained insight into the experiences of the many women she had worked with, and decided to tell her own story. Restructuring her original article, she divided it into two parts. The first part became a richly described, evocative narrative of her experience, including the ways in which she was treated by police, the evidence-gathering process, and her time in court as a victim-witness. The second part of the article was an academic discussion of the experience in the old, dry style Estrich was accustomed to reading and writing in law journals. The comparison was shocking: the power of narrative again became glowingly apparent to me. I became frustrated with the ideas of constructed truth inherent in the practice of law, and with the delusional, partitioning 'doublethink' (Orwell 1949) process involved in the growing of the professional carapace I knew might be required to continue to carry out the job.

In order to find out if I could cope with working in the field of law, I spent the summer between the second and third years of my law degree as a legal clerk for two solicitors dealing with criminal cases. On arrival at their office, drenched in a summer storm as I crossed the city, and star-struck at working with a (somewhat famous) human rights lawyer, I was shown into a large office room with one full wall of shelves. The room was stuffed with piles of paper and boxes. They covered three large tables and every piece of shelf space available. I was told that these were case files: the case had been taken over from another solicitor, and the files had just been couriered over. There were several duplications and anomalies, and my job was to sift through the paperwork, shred the duplications, and arrange the remainder into some kind of sensible structure. As I read the piles of transcribed interviews and reports, I pieced together a complex and shocking story. The client was accused of taking a team of men armed with Kalashnikovs, hijacking a plane from Afghanistan and landing it in Russia (BBC 2000). Turned away by the Russian authorities, the plane flew to England where it stood for five days on the runway in blistering heat before the British authorities allowed the men, women and children to disembark and move through the airport into holding centres and temporary accommodation. The authorities saw the move as an act of terrorism against the Taliban regime – at that time, a political ally of Britain and the United States. The hijacked plane had been shown on television, shimmering on the hot tarmac at Stansted Airport, and the parliamentary opposition was uneasy about what the media reported to be the government's 'soft touch' (BBC 2000a) in the face of 'piracy' and 'terror' (BBC 2000). The client had a very different story. I saw him one day as he came in to speak to the famous lawyer. He was tall but stooped and softly spoken. He had a moustache and smiling, intelligent eyes, and sighed with patient exhaustion as he told his story yet again. At the end of the interview he engaged in small-talk with the blasé, case-hardened lawyer; his little one was learning to walk, he explained, and he also had an older toddler at home in his flat in North London. Yes, he had landed in a plane near the city of London illegally and carrying automatic weapons. But it seemed that the plane-load of 'captured hostages' were actually family members and friends. He explained that the pilot was also a friend and had risked his life to fly fifty-two people away from imminent and specific threats from the Taliban regime. Stumbling out of the slightly dank document room into the broad afternoon sunlight that day, I was struck by the way that the world looked slightly skewed to me since I had entered the building only a few hours before. The effect was strange; in my distress, everything even *looked* 'out-of-true'. On the news that night, people were still discussing the 'terrorist hijackers'. The difference between the man's own story and the media and legal stories was vast. Again, the personal narrative shone a new light on a situation that accepted public frameworks of discourse, driven by current foreign policy, were not able to cope with. The experience taught me much about the relationship between the individual and the state; between policy rhetoric and personal lives.

Later that summer I spent several weeks in court-room cells and prison interview rooms, talking to new clients and gathering their stories on behalf of my solicitor employer. It was a new world for me: the walk down dark stairs to the cells; the uniformed guards and their keys; talking to young people at scratched, grey tables behind locked and barred gates. The clients always asked me if I had any cigarettes. They were usually young men who had been in the wrong place at the wrong time; who had made the wrong decision. They were boys who could often not read very much, who had often grown up with alcoholic parents or in the care of the local authority,[7] who had problems with impulsive behaviour and who found it hard to make the right choice when someone more wily said, 'Hold this stuff for me for a couple of weeks, there's a good lad', or 'Just pick me up at the corner, don't worry, no one will know it was stolen.' And outside the cells were mothers and girlfriends and sisters crying tears of frustration. I began to think that these boys had complex stories that did not have a place or space to be told within the legal system. I thought that some of them may have some kind of learning disability, but I did not know enough about learning disabilities to find out. I wanted to be there earlier in their stories, to try to help them avoid the same mistakes. I did not know if I would be able to make any effective difference to the potentially devastating futures facing other, similar boys. But this is why I went from law into teaching. For me, it was on the same continuum.

After my law degree I travelled to California to become qualified as a teacher. The programme was delivered at a prestigious college with a strong history of teaching social justice and political awareness. I thrived on the feminist and queer theories we were given to play with; my teaching identity began to blossom and I ventured with ethical courage under the blistering Californian sun to my teaching placements. The course was heavy and exhausting; we taught in school every morning and studied for our postgraduate diplomas every afternoon. The readings in educational philosophy and theory were consistently challenging and the writing assignments relentlessly self-reflective; we formed discussion groups to talk about how to deal with internalised and institutionalised racism, homophobia and sexism. We read the African American educational theorist Lisa Delpit (1995) on 'white teachers' teaching 'black children'; we asked along with Beverley Tatum Daniels (1999) 'Why ... the black kids all sit together in the cafeteria'; we crossed cultural borders with Gloria Andalzua (1987) and 'read the world' with Paulo Freire (1987). We spent three days on a traumatic retreat at the Elie Weisel Museum of Tolerance in Los Angeles, listening to the harrowing narratives of ex-white supremacists and Jewish Holocaust survivors. Our mantra was that teaching is a political act; an ethic of care; an agent of change. And we were reminded and coached and trained into understanding that we were being sent as change makers, possibly alone in our political awareness, into 'a system' still mostly ignorant of its epidemic of institutional racism and other prejudices. Now, as an adult, I could see reflections in the education system that reminded me of my own experiences. Could it be that children's voices were still being ignored in schools on both sides of the Atlantic? Was the system so innately inequitable, still, that a prestigious college was training us to go in undercover?

Armed with my renewed understandings and an excellent grounding in empathic, responsive strategies for curriculum writing and lesson delivery, I advanced into my first full time teaching job in a school for young people with Asperger's Syndrome. Teaching these students involved explicit lessons on social skills; about building relationships and reading human interaction. In this post, I learned much about myself and crystallised some of my technical skills through writing a curriculum tailored to the specific needs of my students.

As part of my role, I had been asked to design and deliver an English Language curriculum in line with the California State Standards. These Standards were fairly prescriptive, much like the English National Curriculum at the time, so I needed to design a programme of study that catered to the needs of my pupils whilst fulfilling the state criteria. With a hindsight which prefers to challenge the deficit model,

I now understand how Asperger's Syndrome can bring with it a brilliant, quirky sense of humour; an amazing level of empathy; startling skills, particularly in maths or computer science; and an incredible focussed energy which can result in important academic advances. But as a new teacher researching the syndrome, I discovered that it often causes a feeling of depression rooted in unsociable obsessions and a series of comprehension and personal barriers to interacting constructively with others (Stewart 2002; Sacks 1996). Many of these children felt like outsiders everywhere they went: awkward, tongue-tied, and irritated by the illogical reactions and understandings around them. Many people with Asperger's Syndrome identify with the Star Trek (Paramount Television 1964) character 'Mr Spock', or as something akin to 'An Anthropologist on Mars' (Sacks 1996), baffled and questioning about other people's apparently unfounded thinking processes. I wanted desperately to try to facilitate both the voice and the sense of belonging which I, with my relative advantages, felt I had been denied at school. I wanted to address this directly through the curriculum, so basing my approach in the 'backwards design' (Wiggins and McTighe 2006) methods I had learnt on my teacher education programme, the curriculum I finally put together was called 'Who am I and what is my place in the world?' It began with an autobiography project. Each pupil wrote his or her story, and we shared them in class. They were poignant, sad, and movingly courageous, and they helped to build a trusting classroom community. The autobiographies also enabled me to further tailor the curriculum to jigsaw with and respond constructively to these children's experiences, needs and interests. It enabled me to try to keep delivering what I hoped were relevant, interesting lessons, which helped somewhat with behaviour management. I hoped that my students would feel heard, and more confident that people might understand them better.

Despite the promises of the curriculum, however, I was frustrated. I was learning about the inexorability of institutional frameworks. School rules and state testing requirements meant that in practice these young people's stories were only seen as relevant by those of us sitting in the English classroom. We published some of them in the school magazine, but the school's Principal limited this, feeling that they were not 'literary' enough.

I felt a bit stifled by the Principal's outlook, so when local school district staff (the California equivalent of an education authority) came to look around the school to model some of its practices for their new Asperger's inclusion programme, I asked them if they had any work for me. I was given a class of pupils with BESD (behavioural, emotional, or social disorder or difficulties).

This job was an enormous challenge. The students were aged between fourteen and nineteen (in California, pupils retake each failed year of high school until they graduate or get too old) and needed to have a 'dual mental health diagnosis' to qualify for a place in the class. This meant that their diagnoses had to fit within the American Psychiatric Association's X- and Y- diagnostic axes: both a 'mental illness' and a 'personality disorder'. I was introduced to my new students when the class's resident social worker showed me their case files. These files offered me the official view of the students - their categorised, diagnosed identities - and constituted my first proper understanding of what Foucault (1977) describes as official documentation's propensity to 'capture and fix' (189) identities. This was the start of my deep interest in the effects of the documentation of children's lives, and I refer to permanent exclusion-related documentation, forms, work-notes and records in detail in chapter eight of this book. The case files described, for example, Lisa, a girl said to have 'bipolar disorder' and 'a personality disorder'; another with 'schizophrenic-type personality disorder and pathological paranoia'; and a boy with a 'serious learning delay' and 'a history of arson, sexual harassment and kleptomania'. I wondered with intense curiosity what these young people's own stories about themselves might reveal. When I finally met them, their classroom behaviour was a real test to my lofty college ideas of teaching as 'an ethic of care'. We had our differences to overcome: I was a middle-class white English teacher; they were African American teenagers living in decrepit housing estates and surrounded by drugs and guns. Their lives were in their lexicon, their topics of discussion, their music, their dress, and their outlook. I had to swap stories with them to gain their trust. And the school system just had no place for them. The US Bush administration's 'No Child Left Behind' (NCLB) policy[8] meant that they were offered 'a mainstream school place'. But these pupils had been placed in my programme in an effort to get them out of the mainstream classroom. My class was merely located on the mainstream campus, and was tucked away in a decrepit mobile classroom at the edge of the site. It was so out of the way that during the summer, on very hot, quiet days, we were told to take steps to ensure that we were not vulnerable to attack by mountain lions coming onto the school campus from the surrounding woods. The mainstream curriculum I was supposed to teach them excluded them further. The Californian History presented in the standard textbook, for example, did not feel very relevant to many of these pupils; it concerned battles from long ago and far away and did not address any possible links with their current life battles. State-prescribed English lessons demonstrated a constant, accusatory tension between the pupils' accent and dialect (described by some local professionals as 'Ebonics') and the required Standard English grammatical rules. My programme was a function of the Special Education provision in the district; I taught all the subjects and the students were in my classroom all day. But they needed Spanish to graduate from high school (through a set of examinations), and without a Special Needs Spanish teacher, I had to try to persuade mainstream Spanish teachers to take them. It was a disaster. The students' identities as 'delinquent' preceded them and the one Spanish teacher who agreed to 'try' could hardly bear their presence for more than two or three lessons before sending them back to me to fill out worksheets in my room.

I had to get to know my students, fast, before I lost all hope of a meaningful interaction with them. I really got a chance to know Lisa when I delivered the autobiography curriculum I had developed in my previous post. At fifteen years old, she was a very butch 'out' lesbian, and was seen as frightening by many members of the teaching staff. Her father was Tongan and she was built very stocky, with a serious, angry face and an aggressive stance; her curly hair was gelled viciously against her head. She was thrown out of one mainstream class after another before landing in mine. Her dad was doing a long prison sentence and her mother kicked her out of the house on a regular basis. Lisa sometimes had to sleep rough, and had found solace in the home of a much older woman. Her girlfriend was thirty-two and had a two-year-old daughter. Lisa had told her that she was eighteen years old. She could pass for that and had taken a part-time job at the local fairground, selling hotdogs and sodas from a small booth to help support her girlfriend and the child. She never knew Lisa was young enough to attend school. Encouraging Lisa to write her autobiography meant that all of these conflicting and difficult circumstances became known to me, and I was able to begin to build a positive mentoring relationship with her. If she came into class and threw a desk across the room, I would have the benefit of what I knew about the stresses she was under, and ask one of the counsellors to take her for a walk to calm down. I also knew that Lisa loved rap music, like all the students in the class, and she learned to spell through writing hiphop 'flows' (rhymes). Lisa needed this extra help with spelling; her dyslexia was not picked up until later in her fifteenth year when the Educational Psychologist was finally persuaded to test her for it. Her behaviour and 'bad girl' identity had always precluded consideration for the test, which would have led to her American legal right to 'free, appropriate public education (FAPE)'.[9] Instead of a useful early dyslexia intervention, however, Lisa had spent years in frustration, hating herself because she thought she was 'stupid'. Allowing her to tell her own story enabled me to understand her behaviour, to give her space when necessary, to structure curriculum to interest her, and to refer her for social services and child protection intervention when she needed it. It was not always easy: Lisa had a tendency to change her story according to how she thought people might react, and sometimes made accusations; because of this, I learned a lot about professional integrity and teamwork. The social worker, educational psychologist, district psychiatrist and I managed to collaborate successfully, though, and Lisa ended the year with decent grades and in a relationship with a young woman of her own age. However, I was still frustrated with the fact that outside my classroom – for example, in the mainstream Spanish class – Lisa's story was barely audible and almost completely irrelevant.

At the end of the year, I returned to England. My own children wanted to be near our family, and we all felt that it was time to come home. I took a job as a pupil support officer in the Children's Services department of a local authority on the outskirts of a large British conurbation: 'Enway', working with pupils who had been permanently excluded (expelled) from school. I was very happy to be working in local education administration, as I was anxious to find out about how decisions were made about children and young people at that level. In California I had seen things from the point of view of a teacher unfamiliar with the local governmental administrative system, and I had been extremely frustrated by the mismatch between the various and bureaucratic graduation requirements and students' actual life opportunities. For example, my Californian pupils would have been excluded from graduation through the inaccessibility of the Spanish requirement (described above) had the team not spent many lunchtimes and planning periods begging, pleading, persuading and supporting the mainstream language staff in behaviour management or in the production of a few worksheets and study guides. And because many of my pupils were in foster care or otherwise mobile, their records had been lost during placement moves and this meant that even if they had spent the summer in catch-up classes, on paper, the required classes had not been taken. I came into conflict with the administrative staff because I refused to accept that despite all the students' hard work the records would just stay lost and that it didn't matter if these young people did not graduate from high school. So I was concerned to see the inside of a Children's Services office. I wanted to hear how people working in local government administration discussed the students and to know whether they were aware of the multiplicity of experiences and feelings affecting their educational chances.

At first, my new job was extremely frustrating. I had to sit impotently in cramped school meeting rooms, inspecting the paint peeling off battered cupboards, hearing children described by tired teachers as 'troublesome', 'dangerous' and 'disruptive'. I noticed that in Enway at that time, both primary and secondary school head teachers routinely permanently excluded children and young people for a list of low-level 'persistent disruptive behaviour'. Teaching staff would come to meetings armed to justify an imminent permanent exclusion with a list of behaviour faults. The behaviour logs, often proudly displayed as dedicated school database system printouts, would contain such decontextualised entries as 'Monday April 4: swore at teacher, kicked door on way out. Tuesday April 5: pushed Becky Smith in playground, refused to look at head teacher when being reprimanded. Wednesday April 6: sent home for disrespecting head teacher'. There was no word of de-escalation or distraction strategies, nor any attempt to record the pupil's view of a situation, mitigating circumstances, home life, or context clues to behaviours (see chapter eight for a detailed description of this process and the use of documentation). I would ask whether the children had seen an Educational Psychologist (EP), hoping that this respected professional would be able to talk with the parents; to offer the school some alternative behaviour management and empathy skills; to throw some light on the reasons behind children's behaviours. But several schools would complain that they had paid for a limited amount of EP time and that the dyslexic children 'needed it more'. Permanently excluded children were often talked of as having 'BESD',[10] seemingly without an understanding for the catch-all nature of the term. Their stories were unheard or dismissively gossiped about in meeting rooms and school staff rooms as the result of 'bad parenting'. It was common to hear, for example, the confident phrase 'well, I blame the parents.' And in the meantime, the children were missing weeks and months of education because new schools dragged their feet in the enrolment process, reluctant to take on a child with such a reputation. The head teachers would cite attendance figures, league table[11] and falling SAT[12] scores and OFSTED inspections as reasons for not immediately welcoming these children onto their rolls. I was the messenger-confessor, and I spent many hours earning my wage sitting on uncomfortable chairs in head teachers' sun-dappled offices, nodding sagely and trying to remember to breathe as they told me their stories, barely able to avoid directing their vitriol towards me as an officer of the local authority and thus representative of these children who were in the lacuna between one school and another and who might be expensive and difficult to educate.

I was very occasionally able to unearth the personal versions of the stories of children and families at the centre of exclusion meetings. These emerged during the course of a home visit or a discussion with a social worker, attendance advisory officer or youth offending team officer who had taken the time to carefully listen to those they were supporting. The time (although not the inclination) available to do this careful listening was scarce for many staff-members, rather than embedded into most people's work. But when their stories were available, it was clear that the families' experiences and the school system of exclusion and reintegration were fundamentally mismatched. For example, I once spent the morning listening to a parent as she talked about how her son was so frustrated at home that he could not sleep any more and was walking around looking pale with dark rings under his eyes; that she had begun to drink and throw shoes across the musty living room at her ten-year-old because she was so frustrated with him being at home. In a chilly room at the local school the following afternoon, trying to persuade a head teacher to take the child on roll, I heard again and again about league tables[13] and attendance figures. Back at the office, the hierarchical structure of the local authority and the national government's DfES (Department for Education and Skills)[14] meant that my views, and the concerns of teachers who felt unprepared for 'difficult' pupils, were also unheard.

Towards the middle of the first school year I was at Enway, I began to feel wholly disheartened. I felt that I could not condone the practices of my own employer. I recognised that everyone was operating under stress and against the pressures of policy, financial, and other institutional constraints, but I could not bear the casehardened attitudes of some of the higher officers and head teachers.

FROM EXPERIENCE TO ACTION

Running through my experiences since childhood were themes of silence, privilege and disempowerment. In my new job as an officer in local government, I felt that I was in danger of perpetuating the imbalance I could see in the relationship between individuals and the state. I was beginning to feel that in order to counteract this, I had to describe what I was seeing in order to try to address the inequalities which I suspected were rooted deep in the education system itself. I began to see my workplace as a potential ethnographic research field (discussed further in chapter two) and formulated a working focus for research which seemed to draw together what I was thinking about: the inequitable and ultimately exclusionary disconnect between the experiences of pupils who are exhibiting behaviour which is perceived as challenging, and the systems in which they are trapped. One of the things I kept asking my Enway colleagues was why, in our '*Inclusion* Department', a subsection of Enway Children's Services, was one of my colleagues called an '*Exclusions* Officer'? And why did disciplinary permanent exclusion exist as an option for head teachers in a system framed around a discourse of 'inclusion'? These became the questions around which I framed my early reading around the subject. I was looking for a history of permanent exclusion, but what I found was a shifting definition of 'inclusion', instead. The next section of this introduction will situate this book within a recent policy history and definition of 'inclusive education'.

POLICY HISTORY OF 'INCLUSIVE EDUCATION'

During the Conservative administration prior to New Labour's coming to power in England in 1997, the government's policy relating to Special Educational Needs was based on a concept of 'integration' in schools. New Labour, however, with its focus on education as a vehicle for social justice, suggested that this placed the onus on the child to assimilate (Cooper 2002), so chose a new (political) concept: 'inclusive education'. This promoted the narrative that a New Labour government provided good quality schools which opened their doors to all, not only to promote social inclusion, regardless of differences in ethnicity and ability, but to actively celebrate diversity (Ball 2001; Macrae *et al.* 2003). To many parents of physically or learning disabled and 'behaviourally disordered' children, this meant that for the first time they would be able to attend mainstream school with appropriate support. The systematic inclusion in mainstream education of pupils with 'behaviour management issues' and the linked closure of some 'special schools' thus focused central government and local authority attention on the effects of actual or threatened permanent exclusion from school.

In 1998, the New Labour government acknowledged the 'direct link between exclusion from school and longer-term social exclusion' (Osler and Vincent 2003: 33; see also Rendall and Stuart 2005; Cooper 2002; Slee 2001), and produced corresponding policy declarations regarding the reduction of school exclusions. In England and Wales, permanent exclusion is known to be problematic on a national level, partly because it has been confirmed that there are links to long-lasting negative effects, damaging social, financial and emotional progress beyond school and into adulthood (Macrae *et al.* 2003; Cooper 2002; Wright *et al.* 2000; Rendall and Stuart 2005; Osler and Vincent 2003; Slee 1995). In response to this (and in the wake of the death by neglect of a child called Victoria Adjo Climbié and the subsequent Laming Enquiry),[15] the DfES promoted 'multi-agency' or 'joined-up' work between professionals such as social workers and teachers (Meo and Parker 2004:104; Macrae *et al.* 2003:95-99; Rendall and Stuart 2005). This constituted an attempt to ameliorate the interlinked social and emotional issues behind instances of permanent exclusion, among other things, by promoting collaborative working between social work, medical, education and other support services. However, as I discuss throughout this book (especially in chapter four), the processes and pressures involved in interagency working are varied and intricate. A multitude of tensions affect whether professionals choose to collaborate or negotiate within this complex, stressful landscape, and whether these collaborations actually help or hinder children and young people.

Perhaps partially because of this interagency disconnect and despite the recognition that it was potentially damaging, by the time I came to work at Enway in 2005, many of the young people with whom I was working were still at risk of being officially subjected to a disciplinary permanent exclusion from school. But as Osler and Vincent (2003) explain, the government had by 2002 transformed their 'social inclusion' discourse to an official 'consequences' discourse (34). The goal to reduce numbers of permanent exclusions had, they explain, 'been replaced by a growing official concern about the need to address youth violence and criminal behaviour, in which exclusion from school was seen as an essential policy tool' (34). Twenty-seven children were recorded as being excluded permanently from school in Enway in 2005. However, official permanent exclusion statistics do not account for those children and young people who are out of school due to the kinds of unofficial and temporary exclusions (Osler and Vincent 2003) and processes that they often travel through before being permanently excluded (addressed throughout this book). So, as well as the overarching research question, which sought to investigate in detail the institutional causes of permanent exclusion from secondary school in Enway, I was also interested in the impact of the journey towards a potential permanent exclusion. I felt that the mere existence of an official permanent exclusion *option* must have a significant negative effect on pupils and professionals. As Searle (1996) explains,

> The abolition of corporal punishment gave teachers the opportunity to develop skills in alternative approaches and strategies of counselling and community liaison that they had not thought possible hitherto. An end to 'permanent exclusion' (except in the most dire and unavoidable circumstances) would have the same positive effect.

(41)

I would align myself with Searle (1996) here: with the idea that the existence of permanent exclusion from school limits the realm of the possible. Along with this, I am interested in what a focus on permanent exclusion can tell us more generally about the cracks and weaknesses in an educational system which is nominally dedicated to 'full inclusion'.

Defining 'Inclusion'

It may be useful here to define 'inclusion' in the context of schooling. It is a concept which shifts in its nature according to context and policy (Slee 2001). Lunt and Norwich (1999) challenge a reductive understanding of what they see as this value-laden concept arguing that it is inherently complex and context-sensitive.

'Inclusion', for example, may refer to the idea that all children must be educated on the same school-site (as with my second class of Californian students); their ability to participate in decision-making; an open choice of education for all; or the provision of differentiated teaching strategies enabling universal access to the same taught material (80) – which my Californian students did not have access to in Spanish, for example. OFSTED has stated that:

> Educational inclusion is more than a concern about any one group of pupils such as those pupils who have been or who are likely to be excluded from school. Its scope is broad. It is about equal opportunities for all pupils, whatever their age, gender, ethnicity, attainment and background. It pays particular attention to the provision made for and the achievement of different groups of pupils within a school.

> (Ellis et al 2008:30)

So the idea of 'inclusion' in education is subject to a variety of wide ranging and sometimes contradictory views. It is flexible, fluid and difficult to clarify. Whilst a flexible definition offers a useful space for local interpretation and debate, a lack of agreement poses problems for the practical creation and implementation of cohesive policies.[16] What is clear from the importance given to it in international law is that inclusive education has been conceived as a civil and human rights issue. For example, Article 24 (Education) of the United Nations Convention on the Rights of Persons with Disabilities (2006) emphasizes disabled children's rights to an inclusive education; the UNESCO Salamanca agreement (1994) framed inclusive education as a world human rights issue; and Articles 23, 28 and 29 of the UN Convention on the Rights of the Child (1989) require education for all children, and promote the participation in all areas of life for children with disabilities. This broader approach is also reflected in the *Index for Inclusion* (Booth and Ainscow 2000) which views inclusion as an aspirational goal for schools, being concerned with fields as broad as culture, policy and practice. I address these issues in this book, investigating professional culture, education and inclusion policy, and the practice underpinning disciplinary structures in schools.

It is important to understand the potential effects of the adoption of varied conceptions of 'inclusion', and to establish my own stance. Viet-Wilson (1998 cited in Macrae *et al*. 2003: 90) discusses this, arguing 'that a 'weak' version [of inclusion] merely intends to include the excluded; a 'strong' version addresses the mechanisms through which powerful constituencies exercise their capacity to exclude'. In describing this strong conception of 'inclusion', Macrae *et al*. (2003) advocate attention to a Foucauldian (1977) concept: 'the capillaries of power that forge connections between the excluded and the excluders' (Macrae *et al*. 2003: 90). Slee (1995) and Cooper (2002) also view issues of school inclusion and exclusion through a Foucauldian perspective, adopting an understanding of those subject to disciplinary exclusion as constituting 'docile bodies' trapped within a web of authoritarian power, a theoretical framework built on in chapter three, and which is at the heart of my analysis.

In seeking out details of these 'mechanisms through which powerful constituencies exercise their capacities to exclude' (Viet-Wilson 1998 in Macrae *et al.* 2003: 90) and the 'capillaries of power' (Foucault 1997; Macrae *et al.* 2003: 90) through which they operate, my sub-foci investigate the links between permanent exclusion from school and institutional or systemic prejudice on the basis of gender and sexuality (chapter five); social class (chapter six); and 'race', culture and ethnicity (chapter seven). In investigating how permanent exclusion and institutional norming through the expression of prejudice 'works', I look in chapter eight at how policy is developed, disseminated, and implemented.

THE ECHOING ABSENCE OF 'PUPIL VOICE' IN AN AUDIT CULTURE

Running through this book is the idea that '[c]hildren can be permanently excluded from school without having any opportunity to defend themselves, highlight an injustice, or challenge the decision' (Osler and Vincent 2003: 36). In chapter eight, for example, I look in detail for spaces for children's 'voices' or opinions within the avalanche of documentation surrounding instances of school exclusion. The echoing absence of 'pupil voice', and a desire not to essentialise their experience, constitutes some of the reasoning behind why I chose to critically analyse the practices of the excluders, rather than collect personal views of the experiences of the excluded- and why, in chapter nine, I offer recommendations on the development of a specific set of strategies for the privileging of the 'pupil voice' through teacher awareness and empathic policy.

At the same time, mainly in chapter eight, I locate some of the institutional pressures leading to instances of exclusion within the schema of an 'audit culture' (Strathern 2000a). I explain how young people's opinions are largely absent in the administration of a government marketisation of schooling; and of a surveillance model of school effectiveness which focuses on target-setting and league tables.

Because league tables measure 'attainment', leading to the detriment of a school focus on 'inclusion' (Osler and Vincent 2003; Cooper 2002; Rendall and Stuart 2005; Ball 2001), I adopt Viet-Wilson's (1998 in Macrae *et al.* 2003: 90) conception of a 'strong' version of inclusion which addresses 'the mechanisms through which powerful constituencies exercise their capacities to exclude' (ibid). This enables an investigation of the surveillance techniques involved. It will be seen that they pay great attention to particular selected details whilst excluding the perceptions and self-representations of children and young people.

THE FOCUS OF RESEARCH INTO PERMANENT EXCLUSION

In looking at the 'constituencies' (Viet-Wilson 1998 in Macrae *et al.* 2003: 90; Nader 1972) which implement the technologies of exclusion from school, it is hoped that this book will contribute new findings and recommendations to the field of exclusion and inclusion in education. This will be achieved through an in-depth incorporation of the opinions of staff from across a range of agencies (what I call in chapter eight 'policy-implementers') and the use of these findings to illuminate elements of the relationship between the state and the individual.

Important research has been undertaken into disciplinary exclusion from school, hitherto largely involving research with pupils, parents and school staff (Osler and Vincent 2003; Cooper 2002). One of the issues addressed in this canon is gender, and this is addressed in chapter five. There has been a recent rebalancing emerging from feminist research to focus on girls. Girls had hitherto been somewhat neglected in exclusion studies due to the fact that they constitute a minority of those pupils excluded and tend to perform and resist their disadvantages more quietly than boys (Archer and Yamashita 2003; Tomlinson 2005; Wright 2005; Osler and Vincent 2003). However, girls' perceived propensity to truant or self-harm, for example, rather than directly confront teachers with loud aggression, has concealed the importance of the need to focus on their experiences of school exclusion (Lloyd 2005; Francis 2005; Osler and Vincent 2003). In any case, girls form a substantial minority of those excluded from school, and because of this, their stories, as well as those of boys, can shed light on some of the gender-related issues and heteronormative biases which may lead to disciplinary permanent exclusion from school. In addition to this, the book will address the ways in which boys in Enway are also under heteronormative pressure, and how this can sometime erupt into sexual violence (see chapter five).

The role of social class is discussed in chapter six. The chapter is theoretically rooted both in the idea that formal education systems reproduce social class (Bourdieu and Passeron 1977) but also have the converse potential to transcend these constraints and facilitate critical reflection and social equity (Freire 1996). Skeggs (1997), Arnot (2003), Walkerdine et al. (2001), and Reay (1998) develop the theory around class and schooling, whilst Rendall and Stuart (2005), Maguire et al. (2006), Wright et al. (2000), and Gerwitz et al. (1995) focus particularly on the relationship between social class and exclusion. Chapter six is aligned with the way in which most of these theorists situate the problem within a neoliberal context. This serves to identify the marketisation of schooling as a key feature in understanding how schools choose to retain or exclude children.

Institutional racism and its relationship with permanent exclusion from school are dealt with in chapter seven. As with gender, school exclusion in terms of elements of 'race' and ethnicity has been researched extensively, with Gillborn (2009) speaking from within a Critical Race Theory perspective. Christian (2005), Parsons (2008), Izekor (2007), Graham and Robinson (2004), Gordon (2001) and Blair (2001) all look at the relationship between ethnicity and exclusion from school on the basis of the institutional pathologising of racial stereotypes, teachers' expectations, and the relationship between this and young people's self-actualisation. Blair (2001) places the problem within a blend of institutional and historical socio-economic and Critical Race Theory frameworks.

Several researchers address the complex interactions between gender, class and 'race' in social and disciplinary exclusion from school (Archer and Yamashita 2003; Ball *et al.* 2002; Skeggs 1997; Tomlinson 2005; Wright *et al.* 1999; Wright 2005). I have attempted to address these interactions throughout chapters five, six and seven.

The Multi-Agency 'Systemic' Approach

There has also been a range of research looking at school exclusion from a 'systemic' point of view, triangulating the perspectives of pupils, families, and schools as interlinked systems (Cooper 2002; Rendall and Stuart, 2005; Wright *et al.*, 2000; George 2007). The problem of exclusion in these pieces of research is generally situated within 'the education system', a useful approach but one which omits a view of the effects other professional and interlocking 'systems' (such as the social services element of children's services, and the wider policy context) can have on a child at risk of a disciplinary exclusion from school. Some researchers do acknowledge the need to make recommendations which have multi-agency implications (Rendall and Stuart, 2005). How multi-agency collaboration would work in practice was discussed in the 2003 Green Paper *Every Child Matters* and the subsequent Children Act 2004. Massive upheaval was experienced in local authorities following this government advice, with children's social services and education services being united under larger 'Children's Services' departments, such as the department in Enway where this research was conducted. The Common Assessment Framework (CAF) form was introduced as a strategy to facilitate and guide the inter-agency work. It was designed to draw together a cross-agency narrative about children in need of support. Contact Point, a searchable database constructed to fulfil a similar function, was also mooted.

However, as I detail throughout this book, multi-agency or inter-agency work is not easy. This is partially due to long-established work cultures, opposing policy goals, and what many Enway staff referred to as people 'being stuck in their silos'. There are detailed descriptions of incidents evidencing this throughout the book. All of this seems to have partially eroded the potential benefits of the *Every Child Matters* framework and the Children Act 2004. The wearing-down of the multi-agency preventative/collaborative approach since 2002 has been noted elsewhere, with Osler and Vincent (2003) linking it to a new policy focus on dealing with anti-social behaviour. Rendall and Stuart (2005) identify a reduction of resources behind the refocusing of teachers, educational psychologists, and social workers into taking a 'firefighting'[17] crisis-response stance rather than once focussed on preventative work. This problem became evident in the 2009 'Baby P' case in the London Borough of Haringey, where an infant was said to have lost his life because of a failure of professionals from different agencies to collaborate adequately. This case echoed the claims made during the Victoria Climbie case mentioned above, but came after the changes made to prevent such cases. Sharon Shoesmith, director of the children's services department at Haringey, lost her job over the incident (Williams 2010).

A professional stress, similar to that under which Baby P's social and other support workers may have been operating, has been identified amongst professionals working with children at risk of permanent exclusion, and described in this book. There are occasions when decisions are made about children and young people under the pressure of staff exhaustion in the face of chronically stressful circumstances, such as 'persistent disruptive behaviour'; or distressing incidents, such as sexual or domestic violence. This, and the different policy and ethical directions from which the various professions emerge (Normington 1996), can lead to work-related stress and conflict (Heath *et al.* 2006), as well as 'frustration with and between the professions, and a lowering of professional morale' (Rendall and Stuart 2005: 174).

STATE POLICY-IMPLEMENTERS, THE INDIVIDUAL CHILD, AND THE 'EXTENDED BODY'

A key finding in this book is that inter-professional stress in Enway was often misunderstood as deriving solely from a child or family. It is suggested that this problem is rooted in the propensity of authoritarian power to divert attention away from whatever is wrong with a state institution (Foucault 1977; Thomas and Loxley 2001; Rendall and Stuart 2005; Cooper 2002; Slee 1995; Rose 1989). Cooper, coming from a Foucauldian theoretical standpoint, explains,

> Even though a child's 'non-compliance' is invariably a response to conflict situations or personal difficulties, the education system, due to its primary concern with managerialist targets, is unable to accommodate this behaviour. Consequently, the system pathologises such ways of behaving as 'abnormal', in need of treatment or punishment. (2002: 120)

This mode of understanding is then played out to the detriment of the child or young person at the centre of the work. This book draws on a model, developed in chapter three, which attempts to establish the space which acknowledges the interaction with the biological[18] (Blackman 2001: 182) and the experienced into one integrated subject (see also Blackman and Venn 2010; Butler 1999). The model developed in this book thus places the personal/institutional conflict identified by Cooper (2002, above) within the 'contested space' of the child's 'extended body'.

The 'extended body' is an experienced representation of a person combining embodied, projected, chosen and conflicting assumptions and identities. I hope that the 'extended body' will constitute a theoretical contribution to thinking about authoritarian power, particularly around the relationship between the individual and the state. A serious caveat here is that I must acknowledge that professionals also have their own extended bodies, and that there is scope for further research on this basis. In this book, however, I have used the 'extended body' model to look at how children and young people in particular are constructed by others, and how this construction affects them and interacts with their own self-identification and the embodiment of their own experiences. A note on my positioning, below, illustrates my approach to this task.

POSITIONING

When I started the research which forms the basis of this book, I wanted, following many researchers on the subject of school exclusion (Pomeroy 2000; Slee 1995; Cooper 2002), to focus on foregrounding the less privileged (young) 'voices' in the ethnography, in an attempt to 'challenge ... the assumptions of education professionals concerning these groups' (Osler and Vincent 2003: 13). As the research progressed, I experienced a growing awareness of the complications of representation (Skeggs 1997; Hall 1992), for example in the case of identifying and describing a 'group' of people with special educational needs, where 'the particularity of individuals is in fact not of themselves, but themselves reconstructed within the space of new simultaneously descriptive and judgmental criteria' (Slee 1995: 69). So I had to confront the fact that I, as narrator, had the power to choose the voices I included in the ethnography. In this acknowledgement, I was attempting to avoid the assumption that 'knowledge comes from nowhere allowing knowledge makers to abdicate responsibility for their productions and representations' (Skeggs 1997:17).

In addition to my concerns about unwitting misrepresentation, I had an unsettling ethical issue to confront in the design of this research. I wanted the 'youth voice' which I felt was underprivileged in school to be foregrounded in my research. Many researchers have very validly sought out and interviewed children and young people in order to collect their views on social and disciplinary exclusion (for example, Cooper 2002; Lawrence-Lightfoot 2003; Lloyd (Ed.) 2005; Pomeroy 2000; Lloyd-Smith and Davies (Eds) 1995; Rendell and Stuart 2005; Skeggs 1997; Slee 1995). However, these researchers were not usually employed to work with their interviewees as anything other than a researcher. Because I was so embedded in a range of permanent exclusion cases as a professional,[19] I did not feel that it was ethically appropriate to switch back and forth between being a support worker and an academic investigator. I did not want to alter the dynamic between myself and the children and families (Rendall and Stuart 2005). I was also reluctant to set up a situation which might cause my colleagues to question my motives in actively seeking 'the other side of the story'.[20] An 'acceptable' attempt to gather young people's opinions through the foregrounding of 'pupil voice' may have provoked an ethical tension in this research between the kind of pupil voice that underpins the hegemony and that which forces the hegemony to rethink its own structures. And sadly, with my main method being participant observation as a member of children's services staff, I found that it was very difficult to access young people's spoken voices. I was not, after all, participant-observing as a young person. The young people I worked with were definitely expressing a view through their silence or their behaviour. But this lack of privilege for young people's 'officially spoken' voices has become a central finding of this book and testament to the significant power imbalance between pupils and the systems which educate them. I have responded to this problem in the methodology (chapter two) and in chapters nine and ten of this book, making some recommendations as to the foregrounding of young people's participation in planning, implementing and evaluating local authority and school policy.

So my own experiences as a professional and those of my colleagues were much more tangible. Because they were tangible, they were perhaps, accepting that my own version of events might be privileged through dint of my authorial status, also less susceptible to misrepresentation by me. I wrestle with this paradox throughout the book. In chapters five (on gender and school exclusion), six (on social class), and seven (on 'race' and ethnicity), I discuss the idea that it is difficult to talk about any group of people without essentialising and therefore misrepresenting the experience of those discussed (Solomos and Back 2000; Butler 1999; Hall 1992; Gilroy 1998; Ball *et al.* 2002). I hope that it is therefore a less objectifying approach to focus on the 'perpetrators' of, for example, racism, sexism or classism (Solomos and Back 2000); to describe the institutional prejudice directed towards young people and their parents in the midst of an experience of actual or threatened permanent exclusion. This is based in a methodological ethic, which I will explain further in chapter two, of what some anthropologists call 'studying up' (Nader 1972). Nader explains that 'we have to describe the bureaucracy and its culture' (295) in order to analyse 'the cultural dimensions involved in the failure of national programmes ostensibly geared to reintegrate society' (293).

I acknowledge, however, that a focus on the 'perpetrators'' experience can be essentialising too, and that not all professionals have the same amount of power. As I have mentioned above, professionals have their own extended bodies. In chapters six, seven and eight, I refer to and attempt to develop the idea that institutional prejudice does not, therefore, necessarily constitute the chosen actions of individuals, but is enacted through those individuals (Sivananden 2005).

Thus, I attempt to deconstruct the filters that lie across every perspective (such as that of each member of staff, including my own). At the same time, I tell stories which address inequity in the intersection between the personal and the political. So I attempt in this book to operate from what might be called a postmodern feminist perspective. In this respect I must, as Skeggs (1997: 18) explains, acknowledge my own constructed position in terms of its 'history, nation, gender, sexuality, class, race, age, and so on', whilst remembering that 'we are positioned in but not determined by our locations' (ibid). In describing my journey to the conception of this book (above), I hoped to locate some of my understandings within a more lucent, explanatory personal context. Further, by focusing partially on my own experiences as a participant-observer, I hoped to go some small way towards addressing 'that disjuncture between the observer and the observed' (Atkinson and Hammersley 1994:256). The style of writing in this book is thus an ethical choice. My orientation is towards equity and social justice in education, so I wanted to try to avoid the same kinds of misrepresentations I criticise by 'evoking' rather than describing a flat (mis) representation of a 'shared social world' (Atkinson and Hammersley 1994: 256). At the same time, I attempted to at least be aware of my own 'privileged gaze' and the tensions between my 'authorial omniscience' (ibid.) and my ethic of social justice.

SOCIAL JUSTICE IN EDUCATION: EVOKING THE RELATIONSHIP
BETWEEN INDIVIDUAL AND STATE POWER THOUGH THE LENS OF
DISCIPLINARY EXCLUSION

A permanent exclusion incident is a rupture in both the smooth running of 'the system' and the life of the person excluded. As such, it represents a critical, high-stakes moment with the potential to shed light on more than simply the causes and effects of disciplinary permanent exclusion from school. Concerns in schooling about professional stress and conflict, institutional prejudice and (mis)representation, and a lack of pupil 'voice' can, I hope, be illuminated and resolved through an exercise in unravelling the causes of permanent exclusion from school. My focus on the multi-agency experience and its responses to policy and work pressures is an attempt to broaden this task from within an 'education system' to embrace an entire 'policy community'. The book therefore refers to the opinions, words and actions of social workers, school nurses, educational psychologists, admissions officers, inclusion managers, teachers, youth offending team officers, administrators, school receptionists and police officers, as well as, where possible, parents and pupils. This 'policy community' model is developed as a 'field' for research in chapter two, laying out in more detail the reasoning behind my choice of an ethnographic methodology.

As I have explained above, the ethnographic style of this book is an ethical choice, reflecting my orientation towards equity and social justice in education. In looking in detail across a whole 'policy community', I am attempting to describe a 'shared social world' (Atkinson and Hammersley 1994: 256) subject to authoritarian power. This world, although in this book analysed through conceptions of local nation state authority, is part of, influenced by and entangled with a global corporate and popular culture-influenced world. I hope that the ideas I develop can be thought of as *part of* 'a model of the state that is sensitive to both its durability and its permeability, a model that can account for the massive interconnections between local and global forces and different material and discursive sites' (McCarthy and Dimitriadis 2005: 322). The institutional prejudices I unearth are analysed here as tools of a normative state. But they should not be limited to this analysis; the people using these tools are also influenced by global corporate, political and media tropes.

Within the corner of the field on which I have concentrated, this study of what permanent exclusion from school can tell us about weaknesses in 'the system' might reveal spaces where change could be effected. This focus on advocating social justice within the context of school exclusion is well-established, sometimes through ethnographic or empirical means within the 'education system' (Osler and Vincent 2003; Cooper 2002; Blair 2001; Gillborn 2009); and sometimes through detailed analyses of educational policy (Slee 2001; Ball 2001). I believe that my role as a researcher oriented to social justice can go some way to informing 'the control that citizens must have to harness managerial manipulation' (Nader 1972: 294) - or what I develop in chapters eight and nine as a form of what I call 'critical bureaucracy'. I hope that by investigating the causes and impacts of permanent exclusion from within a multi-agency framework and from both an ethnographic and a policy-implementation point of view, I might contribute to this goal. This requires a broadening of the study of disciplinary school exclusion beyond the field of school and family to encompass the workings of a 'policy community'.

NOTES

[1] When I mention 'the system' or 'the education system', I am referring to the whole framework of schooling, discipline and support for children and young people implemented through the children's services across England in the 1990s and 2000s, and in this case, through the Enway Children's Services department, including social services and the inclusion department (see chapter four for a description of an integral part of this, the Pupil Placement Panel) as well as the schools.

[2] 'Enway' is a pseudonym, designed to protect the confidentiality of the local authority, children, families and staff represented in the book.

[3] Office for Standards in Education: the body tasked by government to visit and inspect many aspects of education, including schools, teacher education programmes, nurseries and child-minders.

[4] Even then I could see the teachers' desperate attempts to concoct an acceptable reality for the visiting assessor.

[5] General Certificate of Secondary Education: a standard set of exams across subjects taken at the end of year 11 when students are sixteen years old, and the end of compulsory education.

[6] This happens when lawyers see too much of the same thing and no longer react with the kind of horror the rest of us might when confronted with graphic descriptions of rape or murder; a blasé response is developed, perhaps to protect oneself from deeper emotional effects.

[7] That is, in foster care or a children's home.

[8] Similar to the British 'Every Child Matters' or ECM framework.

[9] Section 504, Rehabilitation Act 1973 (United States of America).

[10] Behavioural, emotional, or social disorder/disabilities.

[11] These published tables are taken very seriously by politicians, parents and in the media. They measure 'attainment', leading to the detriment of a school focus on 'inclusion' (Osler and Vincent 2003; Cooper 2002; Rendall and Stuart 2005; Ball 2001).

[12] Standard Assessment Tasks; normed tests administered universally to pupils at the ages of six and ten years old (at the time of writing).

[13] As mentioned earlier, these measure 'attainment', leading to the detriment of a school focus on 'inclusion' (Osler and Vincent 2003; Cooper 2002; Rendall and Stuart 2005; Ball 2001).

[14] This became the DCSF (Department for Children, Schools and Families) and is now the DfE (Department for Education).

[15] Victoria Climbie died aged eight after being abused and neglected by the adults in whose care she was living; a lack of collaboration between professionals such as social workers, doctors and teachers was thought to be partially to blame for her death (Batty 2003).

[16] See chapter eight for a discussion on the role and status of policy which illustrates this problem.

[17] Another Enway term, widely recognised in other local authorities.

[18] What one might call the physical body and its workings. For example, in chapter five, I discuss the case of a young woman whose diagnosis of PMS affected her experience and the development of appropriate support.

[19] 'Professional', 'staff' or 'worker' in this book refers to teachers, social workers, support workers, administrators, and local authority officers; anyone employed by the schools or local authority in the task of schooling, supporting and/or disciplining children and young people.

[20] See chapter two for a discussion on whether ethnography might be viewed by its subjects as surveillance.

CHANNELLING ETHNOGRAPHIC REFLEXIVITY

A Tool for Inclusive Practice in Education and Children's Services

INTRODUCTION

From a practitioner's point of view, it is accepted practice to try to be reflective. Certainly it is anathema to claim to prefer ignorance to self awareness. Doing an ethnography on my own work, within my own workplace, I came to view the task as an enhanced form of reflective practice. An ethnography is a piece of writing- a literary form- which investigates and describes themes arising from spending a protracted amount of time (usually at least one cycle, and in this case, two years) embedded as a participant-observer. As such, I think that the ethnographic sensibility could validly form part of any children's services or education practitioner's toolkit. This chapter explains how this might work, but begins by developing the reasoning behind the use of a methodology based around ethnography to investigate the causes of permanent exclusion from school. I also begin to look at how this could work within a field of research framed as what I have called a 'policy community', a concept derived from Shore and Wright's (1997) ideas about an 'anthropology of policy'.

The chapter begins with an explanation about how this research started with the telling of the disparate stories of those whose voices had been less-privileged within the 'education system', but moved towards a more holistic ethnographic methodological framework. The capacity for ethnographic approaches to support social change and social justice (Redfield 1963; Nader 1972; Shore and Wright 1997) is then discussed. The chapter proceeds to describe facets of conducting ethnographic research in the children's services workplace, including the functions of ethnographic reflexivity (Cohen *et al.* 2000) in promoting reflective practice; its role in supporting work with young people in crisis; and the intersecting uses of field-notes and work-notes. In terms of its potential sensitivity to power hierarchies, ethnography is then discussed as a valid tool for looking at 'those who have responsibility by virtue of being delegated power' (Nader 1972: 290) as a check on authoritarian surveillance (Foucault 1977).

An ethnographic methodology is also assessed in this chapter in terms of its amenability to the pragmatic application of research findings. The chapter will discuss its potential for cross-fertilisation in interdisciplinary approaches both to practice and to research and theoretical analysis (Rendall and Stuart 2005). Schools, as one of the main delivery-places of children's services, are discussed as particularly important places to conduct ethnographic research in that they mirror and crystallise societal pressures (Lawrence-Lightfoot 2003). Schools are formulated in this chapter as 'borderland' places (Anzaldua 1987), representing what we might call one of the main 'intersection locations' of the 'policy community' on which the ethnography is based.

FROM STROYTELLING TO ETHNOGRAPHY

As I described in chapter one, I embarked on this piece of research as a participant observer in my own workplace. Initially, I had considered using a narrative methodology, collecting and contrasting the stories of head teachers, pastoral staff, families and pupils in a few isolated case studies of permanent exclusion from school. I intended to obtain multiple views of each 'instance' of permanent exclusion and expected to find that people's views of each instance were often radically different. With this in mind, I started the research by recording unstructured interviews with two head teachers. However, I found that I was often supplementing, in my mind, what the interviewees were telling me with details of my own experiences in working with permanently excluded pupils in Enway. In fact, my very first interview went some considerable way towards setting the context for this whole book, helping me think about the complicated issues involved in researching the subject of permanent exclusion. The head teacher I interviewed told me:

This young man came to my attention about two weeks ago. He was clearly a boy who needed some attention. He dived onto another child and tried to attack him … for a Year Seven boy he seemed to be displaying characteristics that were abnormal. This boy's in care and I think he just started with his second carer, first carer clearly couldn't cope with him. He was not attending school regularly, and those times when he has been here he has been problematic, refusing to go to lessons and was just wandering around the school. This boy was entitled to 25 hours full time support … I suspected that there was something wrong with him; this is somebody who is very needy. I got his report from his primary school … he had a social worker, I found out, I think he was known to CAMHS,[1] the mental health people, and I thought yes all this is making sense now and I want to know why he came here in the first place. I then made a decision that I was going to give him a fixed period exclusion for ten days, and in that ten days I hoped that somebody would get him some appropriate provision. School, in my opinion, was totally inappropriate and mainstream school, totally inappropriate, any mainstream school, was inappropriate, and I would have fought against him being placed anywhere. This was a chance to move things on.

Interview with Head Teacher at Forrest Boys School, November 6 2006

Listening back to this interview on my voice recorder, I found myself answering back in my mind. I took issue with the head teacher's use of the words 'abnormal' and 'problematic'; I felt he was lacking in empathy around the pupil's status as a child in foster care; I objected to the bald refusal to accept that school, 'any mainstream school', might be an appropriate place for him; and I felt that the head teacher's goal was to move the pupil on; not to take responsibility for trying to work out a way in which he could remain at Forrest Boys School, or even to access an appropriately supportive alternative education placement. I felt that this head teacher wanted to pass this eleven year old boy on to other people: to get him out of the way.

In my notes, I wrote that 'I left the meeting bemused as [the head teacher] spoke about the pupil for four minutes and about his own marvellous strategies and background for 39 minutes' (Field-notes, November 7 2006). But when I listened to the recording again some time later, I realised that the head teacher had only started to talk about himself following my own (slightly wheedling) prompt about his work advising on government policy. Reflecting on this, I realised that my own anti-authoritarian biases, derived, as I described in chapter one, in part from my own experiences and education, were heavily filtering my investigations. A broader ethnographic approach, I felt, with myself as a participant observer, subject to the reflexivity necessary in ethnographic research (Cohen *et al.* 2000), and including a cautious awareness of my 'privileged gaze' (Atkinson and Hammersley 1994: 256) might prove a better methodology. At the same time, I agreed with Atkinson and Hammersley's caveat that 'there is no perfectly transparent or neutral way to represent … the social world' (254). I have thus acknowledged my orientation towards social justice, and like Conteh *et al.* (2005), I 'question the notion of educational research as neutral and objective and argue for a recognition of personal experience as a starting-point' (173).

In these initial stages of research, as well as experiencing a crisis of self awareness, I was beginning to feel that I could be less disruptive as a researcher if I observed and listened carefully to what people were communicating about their experiences both in their actions and in their words, without setting up the additionally distracting context of an interview. I was also starting to understand the complex interactivity and embeddedness of policy, activity, personality, narrative, culture, and environment in instances of permanent exclusion.

Nader (1972) discusses the effects of remote 'policy makers' as a feature of interacting relationships sometimes omitted from localised ethnographies, and so I have tried to include these policy makers (throughout the book but especially in chapter eight). A level of complexity seemed to exist which was not adequately illuminated by the disparate stories of individuals. I also felt that the lack of privilege given to young people's voiced (offered or solicited) input into the situations surrounding disciplinary exclusion, such as parent-teacher meetings, was important information in itself. Nader (1972) does not advocate 'studying up' to the detriment of information gathered through 'studying down'; she explains, 'we are not dealing with an either/or proposition' (292). So I wanted to problematise the notion of 'voice', going beyond the spoken word and its receiver and decoder and contextualising it by the inclusion of my own professional and personal hunches and emotional responses: 'somatic modes of attention' (Csordas 1999: 153). I felt that I could acknowledge young people's demonstrated (behavioural) input and pay attention to the significance of the 'gaps, silences and contradictions' (Blackman 2001) and to my own responses to things in piecing together the permanent exclusion 'picture'. I stopped recording interviews, and came to focus on an ethnographic methodology enacted mainly through participant-observation and document analysis.[2]

ETHNOGRAPHY AS A TOOL FOR SOCIAL CHANGE

Ethnography emerged from a colonial past through the practice of travel writing and the discipline of anthropology as a literary, analytical and evocative means to describe unfamiliar and exoticised distant cultures. Perhaps because of this past, and anthropology's focus on social hierarchies and power relations, it has become a self-conscious methodology, attracting '*Ideologiekritik* unmaskings of anthropological writings as the continuation of imperialism by other means; clarion calls to reflexivity, dialogue, … verbatim recording, and first-person narrative as forms of cure' (Geertz 1988: 131).

Following this ethnographic movement, a goal of my methodological approach was therefore to problematise and deconstruct rather than essentialise the ways in which people were represented (Butler 1993, 1999; Hall 1992; Gilroy 1998; Ball *et al.* 2002). In adopting this goal, I recognised that 'men [sic] … every last one of them, are cultural artifacts' (Geertz 1973: 51). In other words, I needed to remember that the people I would encounter during the ethnographic research would constitute the embodiment of a morass of learned, projected, experienced, chosen and conflicting assumptions and identities: something I have developed into the concept of the 'extended body' (see chapter three). I knew that I had a researcher's responsibility in describing the hierarchical power-processes (such as heteronormativity and institutional racism)[3] that ordered what went into the construction of these 'cultural artifacts', and which often resulted in inequitable but normed representations of young people. If I was to avoid misrepresenting young people affected by permanent exclusion from school, and to uncover misrepresentations generated by institutional practices, it was not just a methodological requirement but an ethical imperative that I pay attention to detail (Back 2007).

I also wanted to take the opportunity, through conducting ethnographic research, to be immersed as a worker in children's services in a process of detailed reflexivity; to submit myself to a similar scrutiny and through this to become self-aware rather than just 'self-conscious'. I was through this process considering or 'trying out' ethnography as a tool for developing empathy and understanding in education. This chapter develops some of my findings in this respect, below.

Ethnographic strategies have found their way from the discipline of anthropology into the methodological toolkits of a range of disciplines within the social sciences, including education (Conteh *et al.* 2005; Cohen *et al.* 2000; Hammersley 1995; Redfield 1963; Spindler and Spindler 1987). Robert Redfield, at the University of Chicago's School of Sociology, was involved with the development of the idea of ethnography as a tool of useful *local* discovery of what he called 'social problems' and of how they could be 'surmounted' (1963:92).[4] For example, Redfield talked about the uses of this qualitative methodological branch of social sciences specifically for teachers:

> Being established in the viewpoint of culture as an organic unity, anthropologists seem to be calling upon the teacher to understand ... the community in which the teaching takes place. The real nature of effective teaching ... lies, not in ways of preparing instruction units ... but rather in the part played by the school and by what goes on in the school in the cultural life of the children's community.

> (1963: 97–8)

Because I was interested in the extent to which an instance of official permanent exclusion was caused by a school's institutional and normative practices as opposed to pathologised within-child 'problems' (Slee 1995), Redfield's conception of the use of ethnography in education underpins the basis for my decision to use it as a methodological framework. I hope that this book will demonstrate its efficacy and enable teachers and other people who work with children and young people to consider borrowing its techniques to underpin reflective and inclusive practice.

Lawrence-Lightfoot (2003) used ethnographic fieldwork strategies in her study of parent-teacher conferences in North America. She describes schools as 'the arena where the cultural and historical dramas of our society get played out...' (216). So looking at the causes and effects of permanent exclusion from school might not only illuminate weaknesses in 'the education system', but also the broader causes and effects of the relationship between the individual and the state- and what might be done to redress inequities in this relationship.

An Ethnography of a 'Policy Community'

I needed to find a way to think about the people experiencing these inequitable relationships; a way that encapsulated their mutual experience and recognised their common subjectivity. So the people I encountered in Enway who were affected by the existence of permanent exclusion from school as a disciplinary option, implemented within a system politically committed to a policy of *inclusion,* have come in this ethnography to constitute what I have called 'a policy community'.[5] This approach is theoretically based on what Shore and Wright (1997) introduce as an 'anthropology of policy', explaining that whilst policy is often accepted as 'fact', it is in fact a 'cultural text' (15): a dynamic entity, being produced by one set of people (in this case, the DFES and DCSF), implemented or contested by another (here, children's services workers like myself), and directed as an expression of authoritarian power at a third group (children and schools), which in turn reacts and interacts with it.

My focus on policy-makers and policy-implementers represents an attempt '[t]o get behind the facelessness of a bureaucratic society ... at the mechanisms whereby (it is) directing the everyday aspects of our lives (in order to) raise important questions as to responsibility, accountability, self-regulation' (Nader 1972: 288). Schools and children's services departments are 'borderland' places[6] in which groups are brought together as policies are developed, interpreted and implemented, making an identifiable field of the policy community of workers, pupils and families at the centre of this ethnography.

Conducting Ethnographic Research in the Workplace

Reflexive ethnography as reflective practice: managing the representation of vulnerable young people   Who are the people that make up this policy community? I want now to introduce some of these characters and their relationships in order to demonstrate how the reflexivity inherent in an ethnographic approach can support the development of deeply reflective practice in working with young people affected by permanent exclusion from school.

As a pupil support officer in Enway, my work involved helping vulnerable young people who had been or who were engaged in some stage of their school's disciplinary procedures. Many of these children were either at risk of- or already subject to- a permanent exclusion from school. Across the two years of the ethnography, I interacted with the cases of around six hundred secondary school aged children and young people;[7] attended around six hundred school meetings at twelve mainstream secondary schools and six alternative education provisions; and collaborated with nine different services and agencies. It was my job to organise and facilitate the school meetings. My goal was 'reintegrate' the excluded or at-risk young person into a new school or other education placement. This meant that I needed to ensure that the head of year, staff from related services, the pupil and the parents or carers were doing what they could to empathise with each other and to collaboratively develop a plan of support that would enable the pupil to benefit from his or her education without unduly disrupting that of other pupils.

Because professionals from the multiple agencies were present at the meetings, pastoral support planning for one young person might be developed with input from people as diverse as a housing support worker, an educational psychologist, a police officer or support worker from the Youth Offending Team, and a social worker. Because of the conflicting and often authoritative opinions and cultural-professional approaches of these people, it was crucial that I remained reflective and alert in planning for support. On one occasion, for example, I heard the same pupil described as 'very dangerous' by the police officer; 'learning disabled' by the educational psychologist; 'a nasty piece of work' by the head of year; 'a young person with a lot of potential, caring for her alcoholic father' by the social worker; and 'in need of an ASBO' by the housing officer (Field notes, January 14 2007). In this situation, it was important to try to ensure that the collective and conflicting 'knowledge' engendered by my colleagues' years in each of their professions contributed to the process of constructive support planning for the pupil. So part of my task was to attempt to manage the professionals' composite description and engender an empathic and supportive representation of these vulnerable young people. Perhaps because of this, the 'extended body' theory,[8] being a way to analyse the experienced representation of people, combining embodied, projected, experienced, chosen and conflicting assumptions and identities, emerged early in the research period.

Complementing what is required for this kind of work with vulnerable young people, the ethnographic approach requires detailed observation and description, and a protracted amount of time spent consciously in the field. This offers 'insights that the structures, discourses, and agencies though which policy operates can offer on the workings of power' (Shore and Wright 1997: 7). I found that there were significant opportunities afforded by the detailed participant-observation inherent in an ethnographic approach to trace the complicated workings of relationships of power. It proved to be particularly apt for understanding the very complicated inter-professional conflicts described above. For example, its ability to synthesise all the little details of documentation, the voice timbre of a head of year, the placing of chairs (and the type of chair given to each participant) in a school intake interview, and the difficulties in finding a time for a reintegration meeting helped me to piece together evidence of a strong sense of resistance towards the reintegration of previously excluded pupils. Heads of year often talked of these new students as 'outside (their) remit of responsibility'. School receptionists, heads of year, and inclusion managers rolled their eyes when they saw me arriving at their school, often telling me, 'Oh, god what have you brought us this time?' When I told these stories back in our scratched and cramped grey office, my colleagues laughed at this; the high stress nature of the work often descended into morbid humour. The fact that the strategies of an ethnographic approach enabled me to incorporate details such as these helped me to illustrate the deeply embedded nature of the problems I was unearthing.

Field-notes and work-notes   Just as they have enabled me to include office jokes, the rolling of a receptionist's eyes, environmental details, words, objects, actions, and silences in order to understand some of the causes and effects of permanent exclusion, the textual conventions of ethnography (Atkinson and Hammersley 1994) have also allowed space for my own agenda to be clarified. Those who work with children and schools usually find that reflective practice is crucial in order to maintain a balance between compassionate empathy and professionalism. In a similar effort of reflexivity, I needed in this piece of research space to acknowledge, as I explain in detail in chapter one, that I tend towards a resistance against expressions of authority.

'Reflexivity' could be understood as reflective practice in action, as it 'requires researchers to monitor closely and continually their own interactions with participants...' (Cohen *et al.* 2000: 141). I found that my field-notes became the vehicle for this endeavour. My A5 spiral-bound notebooks became both work-notes- records of conversations and meetings, and lists of work actions I needed to take- and ethnographic field-notes. In my sometimes blended working and research roles, I did not differentiate between these notes. If meeting minutes were late or incomplete, my manager often directed colleagues to me, as she knew I had a detailed record of what had been said. I always explained that my notes had this dual purpose, and that confidentiality and anonymity were assured where the research was concerned,[9] although this did not apply where the very same notes were used as 'back-up' minutes in the work context. I wrote before, during, and after meetings, and my colleagues always gave me A5 spiral-bound notebooks for my birthday and as Christmas presents. Interwoven with my meeting and observation notes were notes made whilst I was reading. I was thus able to both incorporate my academic readings as tools for reflection within my ethnographic musings and descriptions, and to help my work become more thoughtful; to question accepted practices in the administration of exclusion from school and to gather the words and reasoning to challenge them with a considered set of arguments where necessary.

I decorated the fronts of my notebooks with small bits of paper detritus from my workday, to remind me of the periods of time during which I had been making those notes, and to maintain the feeling of 'being there' for the benefit of my writing. These decorations incorporated 'Authorised Visitor' stickers and security passes from school visits; sweet wrappers from the Christmas sweet collection in the office; bits of poems and graffiti designs made by the young people I worked with; aspirational policy leaflets from department conferences; and the business cards of colleagues and of people who had escaped the local authorities to become 'consultants', resplendent with inspirational taglines. These bits and pieces constituted a collection of cultural artefacts from the places, people and organisations with whom I interacted in my role as a pupil support officer. They all contributed to the interwoven density of somatic, literary, remembered, and observed detail I needed in order to evoke (Atkinson and Hammersley 1995) and construct my experience. To as accurately as possible evidence my ideas about permanent exclusion from school, I felt that I 'must ... descend into detail ... to grasp firmly the essential character of not only the various cultures but the various sorts of individuals within each culture' (Geertz 1973: 53). The office sweet-wrappers, for example, evoke the inclusion service team-members' exhausted and constant craving for sugar resulting from the high pressure and massive volume of work we encountered, and in the midst of which we were expected to make reasoned decisions about supporting young people with a vast and at times deeply distressing array of behavioural, emotional and social needs and experiences. They also remind me of the strong bond between people in the office, further cementing our service's cultural identity: working together under stress, we cared about each other and brought each other sugar-based gifts on a regular basis. So whilst I had to develop a sensitivity to the superimposition of a set of research ethics on top of a different set of work ethics, the ethnographic impulse to notice, listen, pay attention, and reflect became an indispensable strategy in my work with young people and families.

Ethnography as a check on authoritarian surveillance in local government   The ethnographic need to reflexively place the self within the field is thus congruent with the importance of maintaining an empathic approach to work with vulnerable and excluded young people. But what of my relationship with my colleagues? How would they feel about me describing the flurry of sweet wrappers in the office?

Reading for my research within my first year as a worker within local government - public administrative services - it was perhaps inevitable that I would find great resonances within the work of Michel Foucault. A growing awareness that my work could be viewed as that of a 'surveillance officer' within the panopticon (Foucault 1977)[10] arrangements of local government led me to a firm belief that I was ethically bound to interrogate my own practice- including my practice as a researcher.

All the people I encountered as part of my work day could have become part of the ethnographic research I was conducting. In order to ensure informed consent, I announced and discussed my dual role as worker and researcher as often as seemed appropriate. Nevertheless, a potential problem with conducting ongoing participant observation within my public workplace was that it might have been experienced as 'surveillance', a problem tackled by Nader (1972) in her discussion of 'studying up' (1972). In other words, I had a duty of ethical care to prevent my research from contributing to the functions of a panoptic system already dedicated to suffusing all activity with authoritarian power through the means of recording, classifying, and formalising the encounters of my workmates and pupils.[11] However, an ethnographic approach, with its requirement for empathy (Conteh in Conteh et al. 2005), revealed itself especially useful in the field of research as an antidote to the objective nature of panoptic surveillance techniques. My colleagues knew this, knowing me as a somewhat reluctant and critical bureaucrat, not given to swallowing policy pronouncements without question. I asked so many questions that my very first piece of official feedback at my job in Enway, during a 'Performance Review' meeting, was written in capitals on the record sheet: 'BE CIRCUMSPECT!' With its ability to 'make the familiar strange' (Atkinson et al. 2001: 188; Spindler and Spindler 1987); to illustrate in detail; to then deconstruct that which has hitherto been prima facie 'common sense' (such as a policy document: Shore and Wright 1997), ethnography is particularly appropriate as a tool for challenging accepted institutional 'wisdom' (Nader 1972). In its postmodern conception, its open-minded ethic can move beyond what is presented in the officially stated reports favoured within public services (Dyck in Amit 2005).

For an example of the space between the 'official' view and my own ethnographic reports of my experience, it is useful to consider the government's requirement, described in chapter one, that local authorities should reduce exclusions from school through multi-agency collaboration (Macrae et al. 2003; Heath et al. 2006). As I have described above, through a long period of participant-observation in multi-agency meetings, instead of seeing a holistic approach to helping pupils stay in school, I was able to detect a pattern of conflict between professionals, focussed within the pupil's 'extended body'.[12] This conflict, I found, tended to deflect constructive, support-based attention away from the pupil. Of course, there were situations where professionals collaborated very successfully to support young people at risk of exclusion. But what appeared to be a common-sense government policy[13] designed to help pupils appeared in many cases to result in discordance between professionals, often, as I will explain in the following chapters, screened behind an increased pathologising and experienced representation of the pupil (Thomas and Loxley 2001). I found the ethnographic methodology, with its requirements for reflexivity, participant-observation, a protracted amount of time spent in the field, and a commitment to attempting to read situations from informants' viewpoints (Malinowski 1923; Cohen *et al.* 2000; Conteh *et al.* 2005; Bell 2005; Back 2007), to be particularly suited to uncovering and describing this complicated inter-professional conflict and its departure from official views promoting more 'joined-up thinking' (Fielding 2001: 12). Where professionals did collude, it was often to apply normative and prejudiced understandings of the young people they were supporting (discussed in chapters five, six and seven).

PRIVILEGING THE VIEWS OF YOUNG PEOPLE: 'YOUTH VOICE'

One of the ideas explored in this book is that inter-agency conflict might be exacerbated by, among other things, competition between policy discourses[14] and by the emotional stress of working with the high-stakes, complicated and serious issues which can emerge during a permanent exclusion. This conflict can distract supportive attention from the socio-cultural contexts Redfield (1963) felt should be made visible by ethnography, such as community and family circumstances; and from institutional norms and prejudices (Nader 1972), instead focusing attention on a pathologised 'within-child' view of their behaviour (Thomas and Loxley 2001; Rendall and Stuart 2005; discussed further in chapter three). Working with young people excluded from school thus required a resolute effort to try to ensure that their opinions were heard and their living and experiential contexts were taken into account during school meetings: fundamentally, that they could represent themselves. Children's voices are especially important here because 'they are the only people who know both the family and the school domains...' (Lawrence-Lightfoot 2003: 224). However, as I have explained, these voices were not always apparent or privileged, and it became important to pay attention to the details implicit in the 'gaps, silences and contradictions' (Blackman 2001: 8) left by their absence, and the institutional mechanisms which led to these gaps and silences (Nader 1972).

The 'youth/pupil voice' agenda is a social justice-oriented stance which considers that in order to participate in a democracy, young people should be able to effectively voice their opinions, perhaps in order to effect positive local change and to improve services (Hart 1992). Hart (1992) offers a 'ladder of participation' model, advising on how to most effectively foreground the useful facilitation of youth voice within an organisation. There is a parallel to be drawn between this and the possibilities ethnography offers in providing space for the stories of people who do not usually have the opportunity to have their concerns heard (Conteh at al 2005; Caputo in Amit 2005). Gregory (in Conteh *et al.* 2005) conducted an ethnography comparing local government official spending statistics with the experiences of local people (what she calls 'JPFs' or 'Just Plain Folks') within schools in London's East End. She explains, '[b]y making visible the lives of people whose stories are not often told, (ethnography) gives a voice to all of us who are 'nothing special'' (ix). Because the points of view of the pupils with whom I worked were often omitted from the school documents and meetings held ostensibly to support their lives at school, an ethnographic approach to research became the basis of a useful working ethic within which to try to make their lives 'visible'- to investigate and foreground their points of view. This imperative has suffused this book and becomes the core of some of my recommendations in chapters eight, nine, and ten, addressing the need for 'a space for critical enunciation' through 'forms of politics and expressive practices which resist oppressive structures of the state and global capital' (Allen 2009).

Another group whose points of view often seemed to be absent from multi-agency support meetings constituted the subject teachers- those who spent hours in the classroom with the young people we were discussing. The teachers and other professionals I met as part of my work and research usually considered themselves lacking in agency or engaged in a hopeless struggle in the face of multiple and swiftly changing government education policies and numerous bureaucratic responsibilities. Their experiences of conflict under this pressure did find voice within my field-notes. Parents were occasionally happy to talk to me about their experiences, and I gathered useful information both as a worker and as a researcher from the 'doorknob' phenomenon (Lawrence-Lightfoot 2003), whereby a father might stand up from his chair to leave the meeting room, put his hand out towards the doorknob, and then suddenly 'unleash ... the anguish that he has managed to ignore and repress during the meeting' (218). However, it was only when I looked outside the schools and local authority offices and visited a youth-led programme focussed on diverting young people who were 'at risk of offending' that I was able to solicit more than two or three words from young people. I was still within the policy community insofar as I was following an ethnographic trail initially generated within my work as a local authority officer. But I found myself having to stretch the boundaries of what I could call my 'work' in order to spend time with this group. This suggests that ethnography in a public space must take into account which sector of the public 'owns' a space. In writing this ethnography, I have tried to remain aware that the hierarchical arrangements within schools and children's services departments privilege the voices of adults.

On 'Truth': Stitching Together the Ethnographic Narrative

I want here to introduce a cautionary note to my discussion of the concept of 'voice'. My concern is that representation 'depends upon the rationality and stability of writers and readers and upon noncontradictory subjects who say what they mean and mean what they say' (Britzman 1995: 230). And as Atkinson and Hammersley (1994) state, 'there is the danger of adopting ethnographic myths, such as that ... informants speak "cultural truths"' (253). Particularly because I have interpreted and given importance to gaps, silences and cultural artefacts as well as voiced and documented concerns, it is important to acknowledge the constructive textual work involved in the reporting, interpreting, synthesising and reading of a cohesive narrative out of a mass of ethnographic data. Britzman (1995) encapsulates the main source of my disquiet, explaining that '[f]or poststructuralists, representation is always in crisis ... subjects may well be the tellers of experience; but every telling is constrained, partial, and determined by the discourses and histories that prefigure ... representations' (231–232). This may partially be because discourses around representation are often dealing with fixed moments in time, and thus fail to capture the dynamic effects of the experience of being represented (Blackman and Venn 2010).

In considering the subjectivity of the one who represents - the ethnographer - Atkinson and Hammersley (1994) recall Clifford and Marcus's (1986) emphasis on 'the nature of the textual imposition that anthropology exerts over its subject matter', pointing out 'the complex interplay of literary and rhetorical, historical, and ideological influences on the production and reception of anthropological ethnographies' (254). However, Haigh (2006) explains that it is important to use 'stories to understand, in sociological terms, how an institution works' (26). He sees this approach as capable of moving perceptions towards a collaborative understanding, explaining that 'all of us in schools should ... consider the different stories that have brought us to where we are, and, more importantly, how we can work to make the rest of the narrative hang together' (26). This has been my goal in stitching together this ethnographic narrative.

This ethnography is, then, a construction of my truth based on the evidence drawn from my fieldwork. In order to redeem 'an articulation of the significance and meaning of my experience' (Ellis 1997: 129), I wanted to 'tell a good story'. But as Alheit (2005) suggests, 'the fact that we are narrative constructors of our world does not imply that the 'real world' has no influence on our constructions; and it does not mean that our constructions have no impact on the 'real world'' (202). This addresses Britzman's (1995) concerns by naming and positioning the fact of representation within the context of experience. What it does not address, however, is the fact that readers of this book will apply their own understandings to what they read.

FROM THE IVORY TOWER TO THE CHALKFACE: APPLIED RESEARCH

I have attempted to piece together a cohesive and meaningful narrative in order to illuminate the causes of permanent exclusion from school and the systemic inequities it reveals. At the same time, as I explained in chapter one, I wanted my research to be pragmatically useful to the young people with whom I worked: to address these inequities. There is a concern in schools that academic research is not 'in touch' with the day to day 'real' experience of schooling: that it is removed from 'the chalkface'. This was exemplified in a comment made to me by one of the heads of year with whom I had worked on an almost weekly basis for three years, reintegrating young people who had experienced the most trying of circumstances. When I went to tell him that I was leaving Enway children's services to work in a university as a lecturer in inclusive education he said, 'Have fun in your ivory tower!' The comment stung, as this could not have been further from my intentions. For I had found that doing an ethnography where I worked and combining it with reflective practice comprised a means for very immediately sharing and implementing ideas generated by my findings with my work colleagues.

The intensity and depth of the research I was conducting quite quickly raised recurring patterns, which enabled me to experience a degree of research saturation: when the same issues kept arising over and over again, I felt that I could reasonably identify them as worthy of inclusion as an answer to one of my questions on the causes and effects of permanent exclusion from school. One example of the immediate effects of conducting ethnographic research at work concerns my observation of a pattern concerning new government policies in education. I realised that these could involve a considerable amount of work whilst appearing to be hopelessly inapplicable to the actual experiences and needs of young people and school staff. I observed professional anxiety around this when I attended a conference in 2005 about 'helping young people back into mainstream services after a period of exclusion.'[15] During this conference, I attended a session delivered by a civil servant from the then DfES on the 'Common Assessment Framework' ('CAF').

The CAF, at that time a system which had not yet been implemented across the country, consists of a paper and online form intended to guide a holistic assessment of a child's needs, and then to prompt a multi-professional discussion called a 'Team Around the Child' ('TAC') meeting. It was designed to identify children who presented with a 'moderate level of need'- that is, immediately below that considered appropriate (for the funding necessary) for a referral for assessment by a social worker. The CAF was eventually supposed to replace the need to complete many of the referral forms designed by individual agencies. The 'TAC' procedure required the nomination of a Lead Professional whose task it was to coordinate the professionals and to encourage 'multi-agency working for the benefit of children and families'.[16] The conference-room was full of professionals from different children's services agencies all over the country, and they all had questions.

One professional asked: 'How much time and effort was put into managing change?' The civil servant answered, 'It's up to the local authorities to manage change and deliver to the front line.' Another suggested that without the new workload generated by what was seen as this radical way of working, services were already 'understaffed and under resourced', and the civil servant replied, 'It's got to be worked through locally'. Every question concerned how local implementation would work, and each time, the civil servant's reply was that problems would need to be solved on a local basis.

It was made clear by the 'local practice' discourse that the CAF was going to signal massive upheaval and a significant extra workload within children's services, without a promise of extra money from the government to support its implementation. Eventually, all agencies were expected to be using the CAF procedures. I knew that if I did not become involved in the way that CAF was rolled out within my children's services department at Enway, it would be imposed upon me from above. I volunteered to be involved with the CAF steering group for Enway, and agreed[17] to become a 'Lead Professional CAF Champion'. Almost a year after I first heard of the CAF, and because I was taking ethnographic field-notes, paying attention to the multi-agency anxieties, I was able to take control of the effect it had on my working practice.[18]

Another example of the immediate and pragmatic application of my ongoing research findings involved pupils who were referred to my section of children's services for a school move by their parents as a result of bullying. One of the effects of the dissonance between the policies of inclusion and exclusion was that that bullied children were often moved before the alleged 'bully' was excluded. Ostensibly, these pupils had been subject to horrific treatment at the hands of their peers. One Enway pupil I worked with was bundled into a car at knife-point and held, dangling, over a river bank. Another was taken to a secret location and beaten as a mobile phone was held to his mouth so that his father could hear his screams. A third pupil wanted to move schools because the head teacher had told his parents that 'the school could not guarantee his safety' as he moved through the corridors between lessons. So it seemed to be grossly unfair that 'the bullied child' had to move schools. However, after a year of tracking these pupils and their progress in the new schools in which they had been placed for a fresh start, I found that pupils who had been moved due to their status as 'victims of bullying' were more likely to receive long or multiple fixed-term exclusions (suspensions) than those who had moved because they were at risk of permanent exclusion. The ethnographic research I was conducting enabled me to pick up on the significance of this pattern, and to gather the information necessary to implement support plans more appropriate to the behavioural needs of these pupils. My research would be completed several months or years after the fieldwork was being conducted, and may not be published for a while after that, if at all. And yet, because of the sensitivity of the ethnographic methodology, as an academic conducting reflective research at work, I was able to immediately implement some of my findings in a way that benefited the children and families for whom we worked.

Cross-Fertilising Interdisciplinarity in Work and in Research

As well as facilitating positive and immediate impacts on my work as a pupil support officer, the ethnographic research seems to have the potential to not only describe but to resolve interdisciplinary conflict. As a qualified school teacher, conducting research with a policy community in a local authority's children's services department involved meeting other researchers, using techniques and reading reports developed within a multidisciplinary landscape. For example, other studies into permanent exclusion from school have been conducted by psychologists (Rendall and Stuart 2005) and sociologists (Cooper 2002), and understanding the literature provided me with the opportunity to learn about diverse disciplinary methodologies and theoretical approaches. I also attended conferences and symposia on a range of issues initiated by psychology, philosophy, anthropology and sociology departments, and read across these disciplines (for example, in sociology, Back 2007; in psychology, Rendall and Stuart 2005; in philosophy, Cooper 2002 and Rose 1999; and in anthropology, Geertz 1973, 1998; Shore and Wright 1997; and Nader 1972). The broad range of material generated by an ethnographic approach invited an integration of disciplinary knowledge which has served in this book to further inform a useful analysis and development of theory. The multidisciplinary effect inherent in ethnography has also been noted in work conducted by Lloyd-Smith and Davies (1995).

This theoretical interdisciplinarity complemented the empathy and knowledge necessary for working within a multi-agency environment. Understanding theories of psychology, for example, helped me to collaborate more effectively with educational psychologists.[19] This interdisciplinary engagement and empathy, embodied in ethnographic activity, exemplified the existence of a community of practice (Lave and Wenger 1991) across the disciplines, and in this way could potentially address some of the conflict that arises between the professions.

SCHOOL MIRRORS SOCIETY

Theoretical and professional interdisciplinarity, then, mirror and complement each other. Similarly, this book frames 'school' as an important reflection of societal and policy trends. This section will explain the amenity of schools to ethnographic analysis, and will try to explain, with an eye to Robert Redfield's (1963) sense for the social usefulness of ethnography, why school-based ethnography is important both within and beyond the school gates. The following is intended to exemplify the potential for ethnography to reveal information both broadly and immediately useful.

Why Ishaq '... Had to Hit the Kid with a Hockey Stick'.

Just as there is evidence of a hierarchy of value privileging the local authority's representations of children over their own efforts at self-representation,[20] school-based hierarchies between peers could be described as reflecting hierarchies from the neighbourhoods in which they are situated.

One family, for example, came to a school meeting to explain that their son, Ishaq, was justified in hitting another child with a hockey stick because it would protect his reputation, and therefore his safety, in the streets outside the school. The head of year found herself torn between asserting the school's basic behaviour code against the pupil's very real fear of retaliation outside school. Her initial response was 'we don't want that "gang stuff" in here …' But the pupil's grandfather replied, 'It's already here. That's why he had to hit the kid with a hockey stick'. The struggles this pupil was experiencing outside school in the face of peer pressure to fight on streets where police were in regular attendance was reflected in the same pressures at school- but instead of police, the surveillance and interrogation were being carried out by teachers.[21] Lawrence-Lightfoot (2003) recognises this phenomenon, considering schools to be particularly important sites for research because they are public places which 'in vivid microcosm … mirror societal priorities, values, and conflicts [and] … magnify and intensify them' (216). Because of this, ethnography in the public space inhabited by a policy community (in Ishaq's case, a school) could be seen to offer the potential to reveal a crystallised narrative reflecting the condensed experience of the diverse group of people across the home/school/community boundaries.

Understanding Borderland Conflict: Interconnected Relationships in a Multiplicity of Contexts

If, as in Ishaq's situation, in-school behaviour is affected by behaviour out of school, working with pupils requires an understanding of the diverse communities served by a school or a local authority (Redfield 1963). This kind of context needs to be taken into consideration where a researcher decides to conduct an ethnography on a policy community within the public space of schooling: can the diverse groups of children and adults in a school amount to a community? For that matter, do the social workers, pupil support officers, housing support workers and educational psychologists within a local authority amount to a community? And does an ethnography need to identify a community in order to describe the group of people it is investigating? Is the 'policy community' concept solid enough to warrant an ethnographic approach?

Anzaldua (1987) recognises places 'wherever two or more cultures edge each other' as 'borderlands' (26).[22] I should acknowledge here that Anzaldua (1987) is talking about the experiences of a colonised people living on the Texas-Mexican border, and this ethnography is situated in another culture and another time, which is, to a large degree, a post-colonial context. However, the power relations in colonial borderlands resonate strongly, and I am here employing this idea to frame the group being researched as a policy community. Schools, with their multiple adult and youth peer-groups, their home-school liaison efforts, and their existence as a site for multi-agency meetings between professionals who may not always agree, could be described as 'borderland' spaces. I consider 'policy' - the effects of absent 'policy-makers' - to insinuate itself right across this borderland location, seeping into work practices and the gaps and spaces between them; this has lead to my interest in the benefits of 'studying up' as well as 'studying down' (Nader 1972). I am, then, looking at 'a policy community of borderland people'.

In this book, I will describe pupils at risk of permanent exclusion as having 'extended bodies' which function as contested space (and which could similarly be described as a borderland) in which professionals unwittingly battle for authoritarian power and young people battle for self-representation. With its focus on 'encounters and relationships' (Caputo in Amit 2005: 21), ethnography has the capacity to address these 'borderland' or contested spaces, and the work which is the focus of this ethnography is indeed a series of encounters and relationships conducted in multiple intersection locations: formal meeting rooms, collaborative support planning sessions, school corridor negotiations, behaviour logs, computer databases, reports, and informal interactions in car parks and waiting rooms.

An ethnographic methodology has allowed me to gather information from the places in which inter-professional negotiations are conducted and where the private lives of pupils and parents erupt into the public physical and virtual spaces of local authority institutions. It has worked here because it benefits from 'the capacity to connect diverse and even contradictory discourses to patterned activities, institutional interests and personal relationships that span a variety of social realms ...' (Dyck in Amit 2005: 41). A public institutional space, such as a school, can be defined as an intersection location where 'diverse' borderland peoples - here, teachers, social workers, pupils, parents, and local authority officers - come together to interface with a common authority (that is, government, national and local), as a policy community. Ultimately, it is the fact that all the people in this ethnography (including myself) were subject to the power exerted through central and local government policy that rendered us a group amenable to ethnographic description.

CONCLUSION

In two years of fieldwork across this complicated policy community, I interacted, as I have explained above, with around six hundred children and young people and perhaps fifty professionals. Those individuals whose stories are told in this book have been selected as a representative sample because they best illuminate the ideas I have generated in answer to my research foci: the causes of permanent exclusion from school; the impact of its existence as an option; and what a focus on it can tell us about some of the weaknesses in 'the education system'.

In this chapter, I have considered the idea that ethnography is an appropriate methodology with which to look collectively at the experiences of pupils, parents, and education professionals within a local authority, as a 'policy community'. Ethnography as a tool for reflective practice in the work-place was considered, and I also suggested that there is a danger that ethnography could be read as a technique of insidious surveillance. In response to this, I argued that it may, conversely, represent an antidote to panopticism. Focusing on the idea that ethnography can facilitate a hearing for those who do not usually have their stories heard, I argued that it is a useful tool for work with disadvantaged young people. I sought to clarify schools as 'borderland' places that mirror and crystallise the experiences of the complex societies they serve. Finally, I argued that an ethnographic study of schools can assist in understanding the conflict within the multiple relationships generated when a young person is permanently excluded from school.

CHAPTER 2

NOTES

1 Child and Adolescent Mental Health Services
2 Document analysis is especially addressed in chapter eight.
3 In chapters five and seven respectively.
4 This is as opposed to cultural anthropology ethnographies of the time which were often conducted with remote island peoples.
5 Chapter eight deals with the specific features of policy production and implementation, including through documentation.
6 The conception of schools as 'borderland spaces' is discussed in this chapter, below in the section entitled *Understanding borderland conflict: interconnected relationships in a multiplicity of contexts.*
7 In chapters four, five and seven, the details of the school population in Enway in terms of ethnicity and class will be described in more detail.
8 This is developed in detail in chapters three and four.
9 I have changed identifying details including names and some other elements of all organisations, places and people in this book in order to protect confidentiality.
10 Foucault (1977) traced the development of authoritarian power from the brute force of sovereignty to a modern version of authoritarian power (77) which he describes as 'the Panopticon' (18). This name originates with the architect Jeremy Bentham's design for a prison building in which the guards can see the prisoners at all times- but as the prisoners cannot see the guards, they can only assume they are being watched and so internalise the surveillance, behaving as if they are being watched even when they may not be. OFSTED's Self Evaluation Forms could be seen as a current version of this internalised surveillance, more of which is discussed later in this book, beginning in chapter three.
11 Chapter eight includes a section on documentation and official records and the way in which these function to 'capture and fix' (Foucault 1977:198) representations of actors and their actions.
12 As explained above, the 'extended body' is a experienced representation of a person, combining embodied, projected, chosen and conflicting assumptions and identities. This can constitute an entanglement (Blackman and Venn 2010) of a pupil's embodied, experienced and corporeal states and the set of identity traits, behaviours and intentions ascribed to a pupil and pathologised once he or she becomes the focus of intensified school observation implemented during a disciplinary exclusion, described in detail in chapters three and four.
13 As Shore and Wright (1997: 11) explain, and I expand upon in chapter eight, policy can hide 'highly 'irrational' goals in the guise of rational, collective, universalized objectives'.
14 An example of a competing discourse includes 'inclusion to support the child' versus 'exclusion to protect the school': see chapter eight.
15 Conference arranged by the Association for Professionals in Services for Adolescents (APSA), entitled 'Come back and move on: A conference on re-integration- helping young people back into mainstream services after a period of exclusion', September 6–7 2005, Reading University.
16 Ibid; 'Workshop Profiles' handout.
17 Bear in mind I was a slightly anarchic and reluctant bureaucrat.
18 It is also ironic that ethnography to some extent turned me into a self-surveilling bureaucrat. This is perhaps where the impetus came from to develop the concept of 'critical bureaucracy' (see chapter eight).
19 See, for example, *The story of Nama* in chapter five.
20 See, for example, *Bizarre, disturbed and weird* in chapter five and *Cultural attitudes to mental health services: Ibrahim* in chapter seven.
21 These peer-group struggles for hierarchy are described later in chapter three as 'horizontal violence' (Freire 1996).
22 This idea is developed further in chapter three.

THE EXTENDED BODY IN CONTESTED BORDERLANDS

Children in Schools

INTRODUCTION

In chapter two I established the field for my research into permanent exclusion from school as a 'policy community'. I also described schools as microcosms of society (Lawrence-Lightfoot 2003), reflecting more general societal concerns and implementing state policy, and therefore suitable for the investigation of wider conceptions of the relationship between the state and the individual. This chapter will lay out the theoretical framework underpinning my analysis of what research about the causes and effects of permanent exclusion from school can reveal about weaknesses in an 'inclusive education' system.

The chapter will begin by extending the discussion as to why I chose to focus on permanent exclusion from school. It will proceed to develop some of the reasons behind the multidisciplinary nature of the theoretical focus introduced earlier in chapter two. The 'extended body' theory introduced in the previous two chapters will then be explained in terms of its Foucauldian roots. Here the idea that authoritarian power has extended the body in order to better control it will be developed, and the extended body will be established as 'contested space'. Because it is often partially constituted through the representations of authoritarian forces, the extended body is vulnerable to being represented as transgressive, and so the chapter will progress to discuss the transgressive extended body's enhanced vulnerability to exclusion.

I am focussing here on how vulnerable young people's extended bodies are represented and experienced in disciplinary situations where permanent exclusion features as an option. 'Representation' in this context is concerned with a dynamic kaleidoscopic entanglement of identity and projection (sometimes by the state), and the extended body is an attempt to conceptualise these in their interaction with the biological[1] (Blackman 2001: 182) and the experienced into one integrated subject. The concept of a young person's 'needs' proffered as a rationale for excluding practises (Thomas and Loxley 2001; Slee 1995) is offered as an example of the application of the theory of the extended body to situations concerning permanent exclusion from school.

Having developed a theoretical framework for thinking about the subject (that is, the individual child or young person subjected to a school disciplinary framework), the chapter investigates the field of research and the professionals or staff (teachers, social workers, support workers, administrators, and local authority officers) who work in it. The idea of borderland space (Anzaldua 1987) as contested space, introduced in the previous chapter, will be developed here, and the framing of schools as microcosms of society (Lawrence-Lightfoot 2003) will be further explained as constituting crucibles for the reproduction of social hierarchies (Bourdieu and Passeron 1977). The final sections of the chapter return to the central question of the causes of permanent exclusion from school. Its roots are found in the idea that teaching and related work with young people constitutes a set of political acts influenced by institutional prejudice. Permanent exclusion is also found to occur where conflict between young people emerges as a manifestation of 'horizontal' and 'objective' violence between oppressed subjects (Freire 1996; Zizek 2008).

Exclusion: Illuminating Weaknesses in a System Framed Around 'Inclusion'

When I mention 'the system', I am referring to a whole framework of schooling, discipline and support for children and young people. This 'system' is implemented through the Enway Children's Services department, including social services and the inclusion department (see chapter four for a description of an integral part of this, the Pupil Placement Panel) as well as the schools. So why did I choose to focus, out of everything in the education and related systems, specifically on permanent exclusion? It was, of course, my area of work. But more importantly, I chose this area because its quality of exclusivity concentrates attention on what might need to change within the whole structure of schooling, discipline and support for children and young people. If, between 2002 and 2009 in the UK, between 8000 and 9200 of the pupils for whom the mainstream 'inclusive' system has been designed were permanently excluded from it, not to mention those that were 'unofficially excluded', (DfEE 1999c; DfEE 2001; DCSF 2009) then there must be something that could be done differently. I felt that the very existence of permanent exclusion as a disciplinary option might affect the ways in which professionals discuss, represent and make decisions about young people. In seeking a coherent set of evidence for this which would be comparable with and build upon current research trends (discussed in chapter one and below), I focussed on representations of young people in meetings, paperwork, and professional talk in terms of perceptions of their gender, ethnicity, and social class.

A MULTIDISCIPLINARY THEORETICAL FRAMEWORK

It is widely accepted that gender, ethnicity and social class are intertwined in terms of their effects on subjective experience in schooling environments (George 2007; Archer and Yamashita 2003; Ball *et al.* 2002; Gillborn 2009; Lloyd 2005; Lloyd-Smith and Davies 1995; Skeggs 1997; Wright *et al.* 2000). As with the methodological strategies employed in this research and described in the previous chapter, a theoretical framework which lends itself to thinking about the problem of permanent exclusion from school needs to take into account the intercontextual factors behind each exclusion story (Sellman *et al.* 2002). A permanent exclusion from school is what can be thought of as a 'high-stakes moment', but it does not exist in a vacuum. There are a multitude of circumstances which have intersected in order to bring that moment into existence. Because of this, it has not been sufficient to think about permanent exclusion purely in terms of behaviour management; or of theories of autonomy and power relations (Foucault 1977; Slee 1995; Blackman 2001; Rose 1999), the body, identity and self-representation (Butler 1999; Rose 2007; Phoenix 2009; Blackman 2010); of pedagogy (Freire 1996); of local and national policy (Ball 2001; Whitty 2002), or of gender (Francis 2005; Archer and Yamashita 2008), ethnicity (Hall 1992; Gilroy 1998), and class (Bourdieu and Passeron 1977): but in terms of all of these things.

To balance the prevailing pathologising view (described by Slee 1995; Thomas and Loxley 2001) of a pupil trapped within a school disciplinary procedure, who may for example be seen as 'abnormal' or 'in need of an ASBO' (both discussed in chapter two), requires an understanding of the multitude of pressures brought to bear on that pupil. These might consist of, for example, his or her family's history or refugee status; the family religion's view of gender and sexuality; and any school's capacity to empathise with all of this (discussed in detail in chapters five, six and seven). As I described in chapter two, an ethnographic methodology lends itself to an interdisciplinary blend of the theoretical strategies necessary to manage the elements of this complicated picture, providing each with an array of examples to discuss and deconstruct. It provides that the stories of the people in the ethnography are not merely compared with each other but as far as is possible (given the caveats around the constructed nature of such things in chapter two) are given their holistic theoretical due. In trying to avoid a reductive approach, this task requires an analysis which might be called 'postmodern', applied throughout, from the 'macro', wider world view associated with state/individual theories, to the 'micro' view associated with personal experience, and to the interactions and the real, documentary, and virtual gaps between them.

Extending the Body in Order to Control It

The link in this book between the state (here enacted through practices of schooling and the support and disciplining of young people) and the individual is central to a discussion about permanent exclusion from school. It begins with Foucault, whose conception of administrative power is at the foundation of this theoretical framework. Foucault (1977) begins his work *Discipline and Punish* with a graphic description of a man being hanged, drawn and quartered. The punishment he describes was designed to reflect the ferocity of sovereign power: a subject had to be literally torn apart by horses to demonstrate the seriousness of the crime. The problem with this model was that once the physical body had been torn apart, the direct effects of administrative power on that individual ended. So the locus of power shifted in the 19th Century from the sovereign and began to be expressed through the growth of institutional frameworks that contained new power and institutional structures, such as armies, then hospitals, prisons and schools (Foucault 1977).

Because armies, hospitals, prisons and schools contain, control and investigate people, powerful constructions of subjectivity were invoked in these state institutions. This meant, Foucault (1977) elucidates, that religious conceptions of the soul and psychological theories of mind and behaviour became the focus of the 'therapeutic' or 'educational' nature of these institutions. Whereas a criminal's physical body had originally been the repository for punishment, what Foucault (1977) calls panoptic (all-seeing) power began first to be applied to what the body *did* (which I understand to mean behaviour/sin) and then to what the person's behavioural *intent* might be (which I understand to mean psychology/soul). As Foucault (1977) explains, '[i]t would be wrong to say that the soul is an illusion, or an ideological effect. On the contrary, it exists, it has a reality, it is produced permanently on, around, within the body by the functioning of a power that is exercised on those punished' (29). Thus whilst punishment was originally limited to the perceived capacity for physical visibility: where a body has been torn apart- once the body's actual and intended behaviour became subject to control, even at the atomic level (where the body was dissected and inspected in microscopic detail under the 'medical gaze' (Foucault 1989), the limits of an individual's body were extended- initially through the means of the discipline of psychology (ibid)- out beyond her/his skin. This is what I will call the 'extended body', particularly vulnerable to the immanence of institutional power because of its shifting boundaries. In developing the concept of the extended body, I am, like Blackman (2001), seeking to move beyond the social constructionist approach to 'explore the intersection of the psychological, the biological and the social' (182).

As Rose (2007) has identified, it is important, when thinking about the administrative control of behaviour and responsibility, to challenge '...the sociological binary of biological reductionism versus social causation' (226). It is this biological reductionism which is behind the kinds of 'therapeutic interventions' (ibid) pinpointed by Thomas and Loxley (2001) in their warnings against the 'discourse of need', implemented as a justification for the removal or exclusion of certain pupils from school- 'their indefinite containment in the name of public safety' (Rose 2007: 226). But this issue is complex. Whilst Rose (2007) warns against biological reductionism- for example, in the eugenics- related genetic identification of a propensity for crime, Blackman and Venn (2010) warn against the privileging of social constructivism over corporeality. Rose's (2007) overview of American criminal court system responses to this binary are revealing. He explains that

> ...biological and genetic defences have largely failed to displace older conceptions of responsibility...(t)here has been rather more success in pleas for mitigation of sentence, but this has long been an aspect of the trial process more open to psychological, psychiatric, and social expertise.

However, Rose (2007) also acknowledges that the American legal system generally views personal responsibility and free will as a more apt basis on which to pass judgment than genetics, '…background, environment, or biography' (234). In fact, 'legal arguments deem it necessary to proceed as if human beings had free will, for reasons to do with prevailing moral and political order…', and so the development of thinking related to the administration of judicial and disciplinary technologies appears to be '…increasingly toward the protection of society rather than the mitigation of responsibility' (235). With this in mind, it is illuminating to consider Foucault's (1977) genealogical tracing of the control of bodies from torture and hanging via prisons to education institutions. His analysis exposes a possible reason behind the pathologising and institutional rejection of the excluded pupil at the expense of a critical look at institutional and systemic fault. Thus if the 'Western' judicial system is based on a deeply held belief in free will, neither biology nor sociology nor their intersecting cousin, psychology, can expect to be easily invoked. The task here is to try to draw all of these features together into one intelligible, dynamic, bodily process: the 'extended body'.

Thinking about school exclusion in terms of Foucault's (1977) analysis of disciplinary governance, the imperative behind the expression of authoritarian power is to do with the maintenance of the state through market forces. He explains that a body's 'constitution as labour power (in a free market economy)… is possible only if it is caught up in a system of subjection' (26). In this model, schooling functions to produce workers. Pupils who do not fit into the worker-producing model are surplus to requirements, and so are excluded (Slee 1995:64). As Slee (1995) explains, '[b]ecause the tyranny of punitive disposition could not be relied on exclusively, other forms of management needed to be devised. In this context the institutional requirement of 'dividing practices' becomes more urgent' (64). In order to select and divide off those to be excluded, when pupil support officers, heads of year, learning mentors, social workers, attendance advisory officers, and education psychologists are faced with support planning for pupils perceived as having 'behaviour management issues', aspects of the pupil's 'attitude'; 'behaviour'; 'intention'; and 'mental state'[2] become subject to this control. These aspects fall within the 'extended body'.

The extended body, vulnerable to positivist but nonetheless embodied and experienced representation, becomes what Foucault (1989) describes in his discussion of clinical positivism as 'the dark, but firm web of our experience' (246). It is the place where the individual and the state become entangled (Blackman and Venn 2010); an experienced representation of a person, combining embodied, projected, chosen and conflicting assumptions and identities.

Note the inclusion of the concept of 'choice'. Blackman and Venn (2010) state that 'bodies are characterised by their intercorporeality and trans-subjectivity' (8). So whilst Slee (1995:69) suggests that individuals subject to a constructed 'particularity'- which I understand to mean 'labelled'- are 'reconstructed … taken from their own space and relocated', the concept of the extended body, contested space in itself, provides for the inclusion of a subject's personally chosen and/ or embodied aspects of identity and representation, incorporating these into the experience of the shared, changing, and thus sometimes conflicted space of the extended body. Blackman and Venn (2010) suggest a focus on 'how bodies are always thoroughly entangled processes, and importantly defined by their capacities to affect and be affected. These capacities are mediated and afforded by practices and technologies which augment the body's potential for mediation' (9). Indeed, just as we begin to understand the importance of corporeality and its intersection with socially constructed effects in terms of subjectivity, the technologies of judicial control recognise potential in this intersectionality. As Rose (2007) explains,

> ...biological factors are now thought of as one set of risk factors for perpetration of violence, interacting with intrapersonal, familial, peer, community, and cultural factors...early detection and treatment aspirations of biological criminality are only one of a range of tactics within this widespread reshaping of control mechanisms in which the work of many professionals, from genetic researchers through psychiatrists, police, and social workers, has come to be understood in terms of the identification, assessment, communication, and management of risk.

This book will offer examples of these and other 'tactics' and 'control mechanisms' (ibid) through a focus on the machinery of permanent exclusion from school.

So the extended body incorporates, along with the physical body and its actions, its intentions and attitudes: what Foucault (1977) called 'the soul', being 'produced permanently on, around, within the body by the functioning of a power that is exercised on those punished' (29).

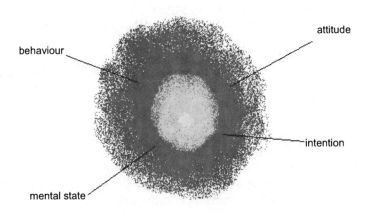

Figure 1. The 'Extended Body'.

In this diagram of the extended body, the lighter central part represents the 'physical body'. However, the boundary between that and the outer ring is blurred, emphasizing the absence of a dichotomy between the inner and extended elements. The boundary of the outer ring is also blurred, and this demonstrates the vulnerability of the extended body to further extension, providing more space within which a person can be 'supported' or controlled through the way it is represented or discussed. These discussions transform the pupil-subject's extended body into what I have described as a constituency of 'contested space'. In originally developing the theory of the extended body, I thought that it was 'docile', in a Foucauldian sense. That is, as I have explained above, 'the soul' can be conceived as being 'produced ... on, around, within the body by the functioning of a power that is exercised on those punished' (1977: 29). However, as Blackman (2001) explains, citing Walkerdine, there is 'a need to develop a 'psychology of survival' to explore the ways in which people 'live' and struggle with the competing ways in which they are addressed as subjects' (224).

The extended body is contested space   If the extended body is an experienced representation of a person, combining embodied, biological, projected, chosen and conflicting assumptions and identities, originating both from the subject and from others associated with the subject, then it follows that it is also contested space. An accurate account of the experience of constituting 'contested space' may not emerge from simply asking a subject questions, nor from observing their movements. Blackman and Venn (2010) challenge a reductive research approach understood to constitute 'representational thinking', suggesting that '[i]t is clear in the shift to bodies as processes (rather than fixed or unchanging objects or entities) that affect is invoked to gesture towards something that perhaps escapes or remains in excess of the practices of the 'speaking subject''. The extended body incorporates speech and observable action but includes intention, attitude, insight, gut feeling, emotion, and identity. This is the reason I have characterised the extended body as an 'experienced' representation.

Because of the interactions between the many professionals engaged in supporting pupils at risk of exclusion from school, the pupil's extended body can become a site for conflict between professionals and between young people and professionals: 'contested space'. In Enway's Inclusion and Special Educational Needs Departments most people regularly commented that workers in different areas of Children's Services (addressing, for example, youth justice; mental health; social work; housing; or education) refused to emerge from their own organisational cultures - to 'come out of their silos'. I would imagine them, crouched sullenly like nuclear weapons, preparing to launch and defend their corner of policy; their way of working. Conflict did not always arise between professionals, of course, and on these occasions the actors have been seen to be colluding against the pupil,[3] or, ideally, collaborating for a positive outcome for the pupil.

Parents have their own extended bodies. In England, parents can be fined or even imprisoned for failing to uphold a parenting order to, for example, ensure their child attends school every day (Ward 2004). This situation represents a good example of the lengths to which the body can be extended and controlled. Their child, enacting the parent's behaviour (not sending her to school), could thus be seen to be a constituent of the parent's own extended body. They are then represented as 'a bad parent' and so the appropriate punishment for this labelled extended body is duly delivered. The punishment (for example, a fine for being a 'bad parent' who fails to send their child to school) constitutes the 'experiencing' of the 'representation'. Foucault (1977) describes the penetration of institutional power through children to their parents as it existed in Christian schools in 1760's France:

> [T]he ... school must not simply train docile children, it must also make it possible to supervise the parents ... [it] tends to ... penetrate even to the adults and exercise regular supervision over them: the bad behaviour of the child, or his absence, is a legitimate pretext ... for one to go and question the parent themselves ...

This was as apparent in Enway during the period of my research as it was in the Ecole Militaire in 1763.

Further instances of the contest for power between members of the Enway 'policy community' are described throughout the book. They illustrate my focus on those who do the representing as opposed to a focus on those who are represented- partially because I was a participant observer amongst workers, rather than service-users; and partially to avoid a stereotyping of the experiences of particular groups. It felt more congruent to describe the mechanisms of institutional racism, for example (in chapter seven), than to describe a constructed ethnicity-based group of pupils who were vulnerable to it.[4] In chapter five, which discusses issues around gender identity, *The story of Nama* explains how Nama expressed herself as 'angry' but that professionals described her behaviour as 'manipulative'. This label significantly delayed the implementation of the support she needed, with the result that she was excluded from school, and eventually, from her family. In chapter six, on social class, in the section headed *The cultural capital inherent in the language of exclusion,* I describe Jack, who was identified primarily as 'persistently disruptive' by his school teachers, but was thought to be suffering from a learning difficulty by his mother. So for Nama, the contest within her extended body was one focussed around the ways she would be treated dependent on which representation was accepted: 'manipulative' or 'an angry victim of family violence'. And Jack's mother was in conflict with a school which saw him as 'disruptive' and liable to exclusion, as opposed to 'learning disabled' and in need of support.

Excluding the transgressive extended body   The longer-lasting effects, described further in chapter five, of the (mis)representation of a pupil such as Nama as *transgressive* illustrates how the extended body can become fixed in its description.[5] Judith Butler (1999), building on Foucault's (1997) ideas, critiques 'the categories of identity that contemporary juridical structures engender, naturalize, and immobilize' (8).[6] Using Butler's (1999) language, we could say that, for example, Nama was 'naturalized' as 'manipulative' - a label which silenced and thus immobilised her. From a post-modern point of view, bodies are experienced/represented in a context-specific, ongoing, fluid, dynamic sense, and the propensity for institutions to 'fix' or 'immobilise' does not take account of this. Perhaps the government education policy of 'full inclusion' might have assumed an 'invented ideal' and fixed pupil body. In this model, where a pupil's behaviour (part of their extended body) is constructed as transgressive - as one which does not fit into the 'inclusion' model, it is 'permanently excluded': pushed outside. As Rose (1989: 6) in Slee (1995: 64) explains,

> [G]overnment is dependent on knowledge. On the one hand, to govern a population one needs to isolate it as a sector of reality, to identify certain characteristics and processes proper to it, to make its features notable, speakable, writeable, to account for them according to certain explanatory schemes. Government thus depends upon the production, circulation, organisation, and authorisation of truths that incarnate what is to be governed, which make it thinkable, calculable, and practicable.

So Nama's 'notable, speakable' feature – her ascribed quality of 'manipulativeness' – was produced and authorised to that she could be governed in a practicable way through permanent exclusion. To avoid this, Blackman and Venn (2010) point out, the body should be thought of as a process; not as a static representation. The extended body can be thought of as the space in which this process occurs.

How does 'an inclusive school' need to show itself to be inclusive? We must consider the idea that this might happen through the exclusion of the pupils it cannot include in a 'thinkable and practicable' (Rose 1989: 6 in Slee 1995:64) way if it is also to look like 'a good school' to OFSTED and in the league tables. The extended body, being in part an experienced representation, is vulnerable (as well as amenable) to construction. In order to validly exclude from an 'inclusive school', a student's extended body may be constructed as one that does not respect rules- for example, in the case of Jack, who was described as 'persistently disruptive' rather than as 'learning disabled'.

An Example of Representation as Exclusionary: the Concept of 'Need' as a Rationale for Exclusive Practices

Essentially, I am questioning whether school codes of behaviour management and discipline based on an idealised pupil model are appropriate for an existing (and sometimes un-ideal) population of pupils. In order to identify what kinds of pupils a school has – 'transgressive' or 'ideal', for example – a school code of behaviour management and discipline would require them to be subjected to a process of surveillance and description. Blackman (2001) directs our attention 'to the places in which aspects of our being become marked out for attention, and the ways in which these aspects of existence are made intelligible and amenable to particular kinds of intervention' (178). Rose (1999) and Slee (1995) have built on Foucault's (1977;

1989) work to chart the genealogy of this task in the field of 'special' educational needs through the implementation of the 'psy' disciplines. Slee (1995) explains,

> The nineteenth century witnessed a revolution in the 'psy' sciences for mapping the human terrain. Charted were the degrees, rates and pathologies of delinquency; typographies and causalities of feeble-mindedness; the concentration and spread of pauperism; and physiognomies and pathologies of madness.

(64–65)

'Need' based on, for example, disease or disorder (such as behavioural disorder) is often a feature of the constructed identity engendered (Butler 1999) or 'marked out for attention' (Blackman 2001) by professionals through these 'mapping' and 'charting' (Slee 1995: 64) psy techniques and projected inside the contested space of a pupil's extended body. Foucault (1989) explains that 'disease, with its structure of a picture, is articulated upon the thick, dense volume of the organism and becomes embodied within it' (9). Thus the medical gaze, adopted by the education community, creates a pathological representation of a young person, projecting and incorporating it into the extended body.

Discourses of 'need' (Thomas and Loxley 2001), when they are applied to young people at risk of permanent exclusion from school, render these pupils explicitly 'amenable to particular kinds of intervention' (Blackman 2001). Diagnoses of various kinds 'are promoted as representing the 'best interests' of the recipient of this attention' (Slee 1995: 64). Normington (1996), head teacher at a PRU,[7] demonstrates this approach in her description of her work with the pupils referred to her unit: 'The pupils' problems are usually behavioural but there are often associated learning difficulties. Pupils may be accepted for a maximum of six weeks for assessment, remediation and behaviour modification' (243).

But this process may be less about the pupil's needs and more about those of the excluding school. Slee (1995) explains that a main beneficiary of the removal of a student from school on the basis of their 'speakable, writeable' (Rose 1989: 6 in Slee 1995: 64) needs is '[t]he institution from which this person is extracted ... Diagnosis and therapeutic removal for treatment, pursuant to compliance, provide less disruption to the organizational tranquillity of the school' (68). As Osler and Vincent (2003) explain,

> [A]ccess to support is more likely to be triggered by a school's need to deal with an acute behaviour problem which is hindering the day-to-day business of the school and the teachers' work rather than a complex and rounded assessment of a student's social, emotional and learning needs.

(67)

This is rooted not merely in institutional pragmatism, but in the basis of juridical and authoritarian structures. It may go some way to explain why young people with diagnosed special educational needs are overrepresented in permanent exclusion figures at a rate of 8:1 (Wetz 2009). Many of the pupils I worked with at Enway were said in just this way to have 'needs' beyond what mainstream school staff felt able to provide, and this became a frequent justification for a disciplinary permanent exclusion - as in the case of the head teacher I interviewed (see chapter two), who felt that 'any mainstream school' was 'totally inappropriate' to meet a student's needs. And excluded pupils are seen concurrently to have 'needs' and to carry the responsibility for their behaviour. This would explain why some Enway teachers would consider permanent exclusion from school as a 'route to support' (see also Osler and Vincent 2003. As Rose (2007) explains, '(t)he attribution of responsibility... is a matter of the organisation of our modes of government, not a reflex of our knowledge of the brain' (236).

The ways in which a young person with stated 'needs' can be treated can illustrate the vulnerability of the extended body to an 'intervention' which actually entails exclusion. The kinds of 'assessment and support strategies' used in Enway in an attempt to control (or support the healthy development of) the 'extended body' of the pupil- such as his or her behaviour or attitude- exemplify this. The procedure has been incisively described by Thomas and Loxley (2001):

> [T]he metaphors and constructs which are used to generate understanding about ... difficult behaviour are often misleading, evoking as they do all kinds of quasi-scientific explanation ... a relatively recent concept, that of 'need', has come to reinforce ... concepts of deficit and disadvantage. Intended to be helpful, to place emphasis on a child's difficulties rather than simply naming a supposed category of problems, the notion of need has instead come to point as emphatically as before at the child. It has allowed to remain in place many of the exclusionary practices associated with special education.
>
> 46–47

The school-based support strategies discussed at pastoral support planning meetings were focused very much on 'therapeutic' 'extended body' factors as opposed to school or other institutional factors. Heads of year, for example, often referred young people designated 'at risk of permanent exclusion' to the school counsellor or learning mentor for cognitive behavioural therapy, 'anger management' activities, 'Circle of Friends' social skills groups and self-esteem training, or through the SENCO[8] to the educational psychologist for further analysis of their mental processes, such as short term memory function, or the congruence of their auditory-visual processing.

One of the impacts, then, of the threat or option of permanent exclusion can be the funnelling of pupils into these programmes. Of course, cognitive behavioural therapy and assessments of auditory-visual processing disorder can be extremely helpful to a young person. But they deal with individuals, not systems, and can come at a cost: heads of year are explicit about the fact that 'exclusion is often the trigger which allows an individual access to support' (Osler and Vincent 2003: 73).

Dealing as they do with what Foucault called 'the soul' (1977: 29), the kinds of 'psy' techniques employed in this work have been identified as key methods for the penetration of state power into individuals' lives and bodies (Foucault 1977; Rose 1999; Blackman 2001; Slee 1995). Rose (1999) calls this 'governing the soul'. As Blackman (2001) explains,

> The psychological sciences and the ways in which they frame and problematise human conduct and experience are important to analyse, because they claim the authority within the Western world to 'speak truthfully' about particular kinds of experience and understand them as signs of underlying mental pathology.

> (177)

In the field of school behaviour, the perceived link between this and mental illness was made clear as a basis for policy by the DfE and DOH[9] in 1994 (Circular 9/94 (7) in Booth 1996):

> Emotional and behavioural difficulties lie on the continuum between behaviour which challenges teachers but is within normal, albeit unacceptable, bounds and that which is indicative of serious mental illness. They are persistent (if not necessarily permanent) and constitute learning difficulties.

> (26)

Behaviour, then, is an aspect of the extended body particularly vulnerable to a form of control based on pathologising 'psy' discourses.

A pathologising intervention distracts attention from the institution 'Therapeutic' or pathologising descriptions/representations of children and young people, and the resultant interventions, whilst they may be able to ameliorate some issues, do not help to change the systemic conditions which may be contributing to problematic behaviour. They can also have the effect of directing attention to perceived deficits within that child as opposed to potential problems in the child's environment. Chris Searle pointed out in 1996, four years after the National Curriculum had been introduced, that it was

> forcing boredom and irrelevance into the heart of our schools despite the best efforts of conscientious teachers. Pupil rebellion and disruption becomes not only explicable but also, to its protagonists, justifiable and in the ballooning exclusion figures are to be found the true shape of its consequences.

> 45

So not only was a focus on within-child techniques of assessment distracting attention away from the institution - the institution could have been causing the very problem that had led to the pathologising of the student in the first place. As Sellman (2002) explains, 'Language is often used to pathologise individuals, with the effect of detracting attention from the possibility of institutional deficiencies'

(894). Foucault (1977) traces the genealogy of this set of strategies in authoritarian structures, including education, suggesting,

> [M]odern penality [involves] the problematisation of the criminal behind the crime, the concern with the punishment that is a correction, a therapy, a normalisation, the division of the act of judgment between various authorities that are supposed to measure, assess, diagnose, cure, transform individuals - all this betrays the penetration of the disciplinary examination into the judicial inquisition.
>
> 227

So, whilst promoting emotional awareness and resilience through interventions such as 'anger management' classes is a laudable goal, it is still an answer which focuses only on problematising the pupil. Thus '[d]isruption at school is typically reduced to the malevolent nature of the child, denying the culpability of other factors in the genesis of disruption' (Slee 1995: 75). This strategy serves to direct attention away from elements outside the extended body, such as the school environment and how sensitive it is to cultural congruence with pupils' home lives; a social worker's or learning mentor's input; the lighting and seating plan in the classroom; the teacher's abilities to build positive working relationships with children and young people; the school's behaviour management strategy and discipline policy; and the curriculum. This problem is at the root of my adoption of Nader's (1972) suggestion to develop a methodology capable of 'studying up' as well as 'studying down' (289).

BORDERLAND SPACES AND BORDERLAND PEOPLE: 'CONTESTED SPACE'

It is well-understood that school 'culture' might not always match or prioritise children's 'home culture', resulting in negative outcomes in terms of social and academic inclusion and attainment; that cultural congruence with pupils' home lives may well be absent in schools (Wright *et al.* 2000; Tatum Daniels 1999; Skeggs 1997; Phoenix 2009; Lloyd (Ed.) 2005; Lawrence-Lightfoot 2003; Gillborn 2009). Children, young people and staff wander around school buildings, which may or may not partially reflect or embody their own cultures, their multiple 'needs', appearances, cultures, ethnicities, economic statuses, and the assumptions of others about all these things, all contributing to the dynamics of their extended bodies. Anzaldua's (1987) conception of borderland spaces, introduced in the previous chapter, is useful here in understanding how these walking multiplicities exist as 'borderland people', and what this means.

Borderland people, in Anzaldua's framework, are those who experience some sense of tension between the different cultures through which they journey daily. A Texan/Mexican 'Mestiza' living on the US side of the border, Anzaldua described her own experiences of the stultifying pressures of being expected to function in a dominant culture:

"[A]lien" in the dominant culture, the woman of color does not feel safe … she can't respond, her face caught between *los intersticios*, the spaces between the different worlds she inhabits …

> We do not engage fully. We do not make full use of our faculties. We abnegate. And there in front of us is the … choice: to feel a victim where someone else is in control and to blame … or to feel … in control.

43

Given the powerful effects Anzaldua (1987) describes of being '"alien" in the dominant culture', whilst acknowledging that Enway in 2006–2008 and Southern Texas in the 1980s are culturally very different places, it became of concern to me during my fieldwork that young people were stepping into a borderland every time they left home and walked into school. This involved crossing borders of all kinds, including those relating to language, religion, and class.

There was a very stark illustration of the lines drawn between the dominant culture in which the school system had been developed and the multitude of cultures children brought to schools in Enway. This constituted the lack of local authority attention to the specific needs of young people who were members of ethnic minority groups, and is described in more detail in chapter seven as an example of institutional racism. Pomeroy (2000) addresses this concern when she considers the impact of 'borders' in school. She states that 'they act as barriers to achieving a positive experience of school' (131). Citing Phelan *et al.* (1993), Pomeroy identifies

> Several imposed borders that impact on … students … sociocultural, socio-economic, linguistic and gender. These borders exist when the knowledge and skill set of one group is valued over that of another … At schools this tends to mean that 'the culture' of the student is not recognised as valuable in school. The knowledge held by 'the school' and its agents is seen to be legitimate or 'right', while the knowledge that students bring from home and personal experience is disregarded.

131–132

Some students, of course, will be seen as more or less legitimate by the school, depending on how closely they match the culture and needs of the institution: this is becomes clear when we look at various kinds of institutional prejudice in chapters five, six and seven. But I want to give some brief examples in this area, below, to establish the importance of the idea of schools as 'borderlands'.

In Enway in 2006–2008 the attention given to what is termed 'Ethnic Minority Achievement' was seen to have succeeded in raising attainment to the point at which, in the quantitative data solicited from the local authority's own policy office, a group named 'white working-class boys' was seen to be in most 'need' of support. The Ethnic Minority Achievement Service was part of Enway Children's Services. They were a team of counsellors who conducted visits to home and school, connected newcomers with translation, housing, refugee and other support services, and supported access to universal services, such as schools. This team was cut from thirty officers in 2002 to just four in 2006. And following the 'white working-class' finding, the Chief Inspector for Ethnic Minority Achievement, a measured, academic man with years of experience and an innate knack of bringing a quiet, assured logic to policy planning and assessment, was subsequently made redundant, in order to make way for a single inspectorate manager charged with addressing all 'vulnerable children'.

Fundamentally, there was a problem with the fact that the 'white' data had at the time not been sifted for Traveller pupils; also the idea that pupils designated 'white' were not understood as having an ethnicity. But kaleidoscopically, through 2005–2008 Enway continued to change, its cultural borders shifting. As well-established populations settled in, new ones swelled. These included Somali, Eritrean, Iranian and Kurdish families and unaccompanied minors fleeing traumatic war violence. Cohorts of vulnerable Eastern European Roma girls were found to be not attending school, and described in a local paper as being prostituted in the main pedestrianised shopping street outside the council offices. Violence amongst young people in the city started to reach new heights, and yet another teenager was stabbed to death over the New Year of 2008. But the Ethnic Minority Achievement service had been starved into a skeleton crew, and school and children's services staff were slow to develop strategies to deal with what they named the 'gang violence'.

Nama's story, referred to above, also illustrates elements of the borderland experience rooted deep within what might be called 'institutional racism'. This can be defined within the context of this book as a series of normative (often inequitable) pressures on people in terms of aspects of their family, national, ethnic and cultural identity which is enacted through the policies, protocol, talk and culture of an institution (see chapter seven). Nama's family, Iraqi Kurds, had fled violence in Iraq. In England, Nama's father and uncle were unable to practise their professions in law and engineering, and had to live on welfare state support. However, it was difficult to find Enway staff who empathised with this situation. Nama was branded 'the most obnoxious little girl I have ever had the pleasure to meet' by the Head of Admissions, who had attended her exclusion hearing. Her raging behaviour was not understood as a reaction to a family experience signalling a marked cry for help. Anzaldua (1987) recognises the effects of feeling defensive rage in a system designed by and for the dominant culture:

> There are many defense strategies that the self uses to escape the agony of inadequacy and I have used all of them … I have used rage to drive others away and to insulate myself against exposure. I have reciprocated with contempt for those who have roused shame in me.

67

Anzaldua's understanding of the pressures on 'borderland' people continues to inform my analysis of instances of permanent exclusion. I have grown through applying her framework to understand some of the deeper implications of the conflict which may arise where a schooling system's rules and structures ('borders') do not align closely with a family's historical, geographical, political, cultural, religious and gendered experiences.

But how can the 'borderland' model help us to understand and perhaps ameliorate the causes and negative effects of permanent exclusion? Anzaldua (1987) is ostensibly looking at a different context. But the racism and violence generated by the cultural hierarchies she finds in the Mexican-American borderlands can also be found in our local borderland spaces: including our schools. She explains that

> The answer to the problem between the white race and the colored, between males and females, lies in healing the split that originates in ... our culture ... A massive uprooting of dualistic thinking in the individual and collective consciousness is the beginning of a long struggle, but one that could, in our best hopes, bring us to the end of rape, of violence, of war.

102

It might actually seem a bit dramatic to talk about violence and rape. But these issues existed in Enway during the time of my research. Gendered violence and racism erupted often in Enway, affecting major life-changing decisions made by local authority officers on behalf of their subjects: causing instances of permanent exclusion from school. The Enway Youth Offending Team worker once commented that a Traveller child should be 'tied to a tree'. There was an ongoing assumption amongst Enway's head teachers that Somali pupils would inexorably bring gang violence with them to school. And young men in Enway would often find themselves permanently excluded and on the sex offenders' register following yet another sexual assault on a girl in school. So Anzaldua's (1987) borderland concept offers a lucent model for the investigation of these issues.

SCHOOLS AS CRUCIBLES FOR THE REPRODCUTION OF SOCIAL HIERARCHIES

We have seen that as borderland places, schools will be subject to divisive, hierarchical 'dualistic thinking' (Anzaldua 1997: 102). 'Full inclusion' was seen by the New Labour government as somewhat of a panacea to deal with the 'problems' of what diversity, immigration policy, celebration of difference, or cosmopolitanism are perceived to have exacerbated around 'race' and gender (Sellman 2002). At one level, 'inclusion policy' seems to be aimed at designing a community of collaborative cosmopolitan citizens in every school. But there are tensions amid government mandates handed down to schools, such as between the policies of full inclusion, (regardless of ethnicity, ability, gender, class, and behaviour)- and the use of league tables, which measure schools according to attainment regardless of population (Osler and Vincent 2003; Cooper 2002; Rendall and Stuart 2005; Ball 2001). Does this mean that the 'education system', despite its ethical goals for inclusion, still inexorably reproduces or perpetuates social inequities?

Bourdieu and Passeron (1990) describe schooling as a process by which social selection is concealed 'under the guise of technical selection ... legitimating the reproduction of the social hierarchies by transmuting them into academic hierarchies' (153). They describe, for example, the ways in which young people who are already socio-economically disadvantaged tend to 'self-eliminate' (153) - which may involve behaving in such a way that a permanent exclusion follows - even before they have the chance to be subjected to examination at the end of each learning stage. Bourdieu's (1979) concept of 'cultural capital' is at the core of understanding the ways in which children can be 'valued' within an education system depending on the skills and advantages gained by them within their family situations, and is woven throughout this book, but developed particularly in relation to social class in chapter six. Fundamentally, it is important to note that

[e]very institutionalised education system owes ... its structure and functioning to the fact that ... it has to produce ... the institutional conditions ... necessary both to the exercise of its essential function of inculcation and to the fulfilment of its function of ... the reproduction of the relations between the groups or classes.

Bourdieu and Passeron
1990: 54

This idea, that schools are essentially designed to maintain existing social structures and inequities, is enmeshed with my Foucauldian (1977) understanding of the ways in which power works in a case of permanent exclusion. In other words, Bourdieu and Passeron (1990), in describing the class-normative work of schooling institutions, are explicating one of the ways in which Foucault's (1977) capillaries of power penetrate all aspects of people's lives. Governmental power, then, relies on normativity, including institutional racism and heteronormativity as well as class normativity, and this is addressed in chapters five, six and seven. In chapter eight, I discuss Zizek's (2008) related idea that social inequity is often produced by the very institutions tasked with challenging it, such as New Labour's schools. However, I challenge the inevitable quality of these paradigms through an alertness for chinks of vulnerability in the system it describes. In doing this, I am drawing on an approach of critical pedagogy (Freire 1996), culminating in the idea of the potential for a 'critical bureaucracy'.

THE PRACTICE OF RESISTANCE: CRITICAL ENUNCIATION AND CRITICAL BUREAUCRACY

Thus, in this book, I hope to consider whether, and how, policies, schools, professionals, and pupils might have the potential to counteract existing inequitable predictions about educational under-attainment and social exclusion as well as perpetuating or accelerating them. Implementing this might amount to a critical pedagogical practice. Perhaps, since I am including staff other than teachers, such as local authority officers, we might also accept the possibilities of a 'critical bureaucratic practice'. This has the potential to counteract inequity in the delivery of policy beyond that delivered through school-based teaching, and is discussed fully in chapter eight. To this end, I see the contested space of the extended body not just as a docile battleground between professionals, but a space for the potential exercise of the resistance-focussed agency of empathic professionals and young people. This contested space of the extended body is where people can project their own classed, 'raced', ability and gendered readings of someone- labels such as 'uncooperative', or 'girly', for example. But is also 'a space of critical enunciation' (Allen 2009) in which young people have the space to tell their own stories in all their complicated facets, demonstrating 'agency in resisting subjection into representations of themselves as innately incapable' (Phoenix 2009).

THE CAUSES OF PERMANENT EXCLUSION

Professionals Influenced by Institutional Prejudice

So, if schools are borderland spaces in which the transgressive extended bodies of pupils are constructed and sometimes excluded in order to maintain the reproduction of institutional hierarchies, should schools and professionals change their ways? It can be argued that every time a teacher or other professional involved in supporting vulnerable pupils describes or (mis)represents a young person, they are making a political judgement ascribing value to that young person; value which will affect how they are treated within the system of disciplinary practice, including disciplinary exclusion.

Instead of changing school practice to fit pupils at risk of permanent exclusion, it seemed in Enway that pupils were more likely to be passed on to 'specialists'. The political drive towards a reduction in the numbers of official 'Permanent Exclusions' in Enway during 2005–2008 promoted the purchase of increasing numbers of places at 'alternative education placements' offering reduced timetables and BTECs,[10] as opposed to GCSEs, in vocational subjects such as Construction, Hair and Beauty, Animal Care, and Physical Education (discussed further in chapters four, five and six). These placements do provide young people with potential employment skills and do not necessarily preclude progression to further or higher education, particularly in the UK. However, Bourdieu and Passeron (1990) have identified that

> [E]ven when it seems to be imposed by the strength of a 'vocation' or the discovery of inability, each individual act of choice by which a child ... resigns himself to relegation to a devalorised type of course takes account of the (relationship) ... between his social class and the educational system

155

'Choice' here might be viewed as much like the concept of 'need'- firstly, in the benign nature of the words themselves; and secondly, in their nefarious propensity to exert a subtle direction (Thomas and Loxley 2001) which can, perhaps, greatly exacerbate the negative effects of disciplinary exclusion from school. For example, if a pupil is at risk of permanent exclusion, a teacher may advise the family that she or he should take up a vocational qualification (often delivered in college or at a workplace as an apprenticeship for part of the week) rather than an academic one in order to keep them away from the school site.[11] I do not want here to ascribe a value (which would itself be class-related) to particular types of career choice. But the effects of such teacher advice might serve to limit the pupil's career options and to maintain the existing class hierarchy.

Freire and 'Horizontal Violence'; Zizek and 'Subjective Violence'

As I have begun to explain above, Paulo Freire (1996) built a philosophy of education based on the concept that choices in the way a system of education is implemented are inexorably political. His *Pedagogy of the Oppressed* explains the ways in which traditional education styles can perpetuate social inequities, and that there are alternative education strategies which can serve to liberate people through building respectful and mutually beneficial relationships between teacher and student. He describes those, who, '[c]hafing under the restrictions of [an oppressive system] … often manifest a type of horizontal violence, striking out at their own comrades for the pettiest of reasons' (44). Zizek (2008) draws a distinction between this kind of violence between individuals, calling it 'subjective' violence; and the 'objective' violence exerted on people through the workings of state and corporate machinery. I have drawn the two concepts together, and in chapters six and eight develop a concept of 'horizontal subjective violence' to describe the ways in which violence between pupils, which can lead to permanent exclusion, can be caused by the oppressive institutional prejudice woven though institutional protocols. I always had this concept at the back of my mind when I was considering the incidents for which pupils were excluded. Was the increasing number of sexual assaults I had to deal with in my work, by male pupils, on female pupils, one of the manifestations of disempowered young men's clumsy expression of a desire for self-value and belonging? If this is what led to some permanent exclusions from school, how had the sense of self-value and belonging been eroded? And how could a comprehensive and respectful theoretical approach provide suggestions to professionals, pupils and families in developing ways to collaborate in nurturing these essential qualities? In looking at the causes of permanent exclusion and the effects of its existence as a disciplinary option, I hope to answer these questions.

CONCLUSION

It is necessary to understand Foucault (1977) as explaining the technology of authoritarian and institutional power; with others extending this by explaining the construction of the subjects of this power on the basis of, for example, education (Bourdieu and Passeron 1977), gender (Butler 1999), ethnicity (Hall 1992), class (Skeggs 1997) or biopower (Rose 2007, Blackman 2010). Freire (1996) can then be employed to think about how to ameliorate these constructions through pedagogical changes. In chapter eight, the journey of institutional power will be mapped from government policy through to local interpretation and implementation. Here we trace the way power is expressed through government, local authority, and school, penetrating into the extended bodies of the subjects of this power: pupils, families and staff.

The approach is based on Foucault's (1977) theory on the historical development of a panoptic system of discipline delivered through an embedded surveillance of individuals within authoritarian organisations. Foucalt's focus on the expansion of the techniques of discipline to factors outside the physical body has led me to consider what happens when that 'extended body' becomes a contested space. This contest subsumes the 'real' needs of the individual young person (Thomas and Loxley 2001). It is a triumph of consequentialism over deontology, which will put institutional goals above individual needs. If, in being constructed as a distraction from these institutional problems, the 'extended body' of the student becomes so pathologised that it no longer belongs, it becomes a transgressive body (Butler, 1999), and is therefore excluded.

It is also important to be aware of the crystallising effects educational institutions can have as microcosms of society (Lawrence-Lightfoot 2003), potential implementation systems for the ideology of oppression or emancipation (Freire 1996), and organisational structures that reproduce existing societal inequities (Bourdieu and Passeron 1990).

The endeavour is to make visible the authoritarian power conditions described through a historical-genealogical approach by Foucault (1977), Butler (1999) and Rose (1999). These conditions are usefully understood here as a landscape. As Rose (1999) explains,

> The aim of such genealogies is a de-stabilisation or de-fatalisation of our present. In describing its contingency, in therefore opening the possibility that things could have been different, they try to make it easier to assess that present in order to make judgments about how to act upon it. If the history of our present is more accidental that we may like to believe, the future of our present is also more open than it sometimes appears.

xii

If the future of our present is open, I want to find some way, through understanding the ways in which people negotiate the authoritarian power flowing around experiences of permanent exclusion from school, to ameliorate its negative effects.

NOTES

[1] What one might call the physical body and its workings. For example, in chapter five, I discuss the case of a young woman whose diagnosis of PMS affected her experience and the development of appropriate support.

[2] Not an exhaustive list.

[3] Often on the basis of institutional prejudice: see chapters five, six and seven.

[4] It is important here to remember the caveat I introduced in the first chapter: professionals, of course, have their own extended bodies to contend with. The pressures exerted on a person experiencing their own representation of themselves as 'a special needs teacher' or 'a white middle-class female member of the school's senior management team' will be having their own effects on the ways in which professionals talk about and respond to children and young people. This is an illustration of the far reaching effects of Foucault's (1977) Panopticon: the 'guards' in a prison and the teachers in a school are just as much subject to its pervasive and penetrating surveillance and power as the ostensible subjects- prisoners and pupils. This book, however, focuses primarily on the extended bodies of children and young people.

[5] More of this is discussed in the chapter on policy (chapter eight), where Foucault's description of documentation as having the power to 'capture and fix' bodies (1977: 189) develops further ideas about how the subjects of permanent exclusion are created.

[6] Nader (1972) in her advocacy for 'studying up' (introduced and developed in chapters one and two) offers a methodological approach which can facilitate this task and which I am attempting to achieve in this book.

[7] Pupil Referral Unit: a school for young people and children who have or are in danger of being permanently excluded from school.

[8] Special Educational Needs Coordinator.

[9] Department of Health

[10] Business and Technical Education Council: a national body which validates vocational courses, generally Ordinary or Higher National Certificates.

[11] See chapter six for more detailed account of this kind of class-based institutional prejudice.

WORKING UNDER THE SHADOW OF PERMANENT EXCLUSION

An Introduction to Children's Services in Enway

INTRODUCTION

This chapter will establish the context in which the research was undertaken, introducing some key processes in the management of disciplinary exclusion in and around schools. It describes some of the procedures and meetings a young person at risk of permanent exclusion in Enway might go through, beginning with a general profile of the group of young people affected by permanent exclusion and discussed in this book. The chapter proceeds to discuss the 'prevention' strategies that were offered both within and out of schools to avert an official permanent exclusion, including pastoral support plans (PSPs), managed moves, and placement in the pupil referral unit (PRU). The local authority's multi-agency 'Hard to Place' Pupil Placement Panel, source of the cases I describe in this ethnography and central to the discussion in this book, will be described in terms of its protocol, positioning, gatekeeping strategies and rhetoric. A description of reintegration meetings introduces a sense of Enway schools' stress in relation to permanent exclusion underpinned by a general feeling that they were operating 'under siege', characterised by the interagency conflict I began discussing in previous chapters. The latter part of the chapter describes part of a PSP meeting and applies the 'extended body' theory to it: an introduction to its analytical application in general terms before the more specific material dealt with in subsequent chapters.

The Young People Described in this Book

During my fieldwork, as I explained in chapter one, I worked as a Pupil Support Officer (PSO) with secondary school girls and boys in Enway aged 11 to 16. Enway is a very diverse urban area with pockets of affluence and several deprived housing estates. The young people I worked with were described in their school paperwork as 'Turkish', 'Black British', 'Black Caribbean', 'Somali', 'Other African', 'Irish Traveller', 'White British', 'White European' and many other coded ethnicities.[1] The pupils with whom I worked were permanently excluded (or at risk of being permanently excluded) for issues ranging from kicking a teacher, sexual assault, or carrying a knife; to swearing, shouting, 'defiance', and 'persistent low-level disruptive behaviour'. As PSO I convened, attended and maintained records for several support planning meetings each week, at school and occasionally in people's homes, with families, pupils and professionals, and as I explained in chapters one and two, these meetings and the activities around them formed the basis of my field of research.

As the ethnography progressed, it became clear that permanent exclusion was just as significant when it was used as a threat, and that some pupils experienced what amounted to a permanent exclusion[2] without it being officially labelled as such. This has meant that in order to assess the impact of permanent exclusion, it became necessary to look at the multiple effects of its existence, and attempts to prevent it, as well as its official implementation (see also Macrae *et al.* 2003:92). I begin this task, below, with an overview of strategies implemented to prevent official instances of permanent exclusion from school in Enway.

'PREVENTION'STRATEGIES TO AVERT (THE COST OF) PERMANENT EXCLUSION: IN SCHOOL

Perhaps one of the most compelling reasons for schools to adopt prevention strategies designed to avert an incident of permanent exclusion was that removing a pupil involved a financial cost to the school. This represented one of the pressures brought to bear on the professionals who had to collaborate to plan for the support necessary to avoid this and the social cost of exclusion. It also offered an attractive financial reason for schools to choose an unofficial exclusion over an official one, and an official permanent exclusion over more expensive specialised alternative education placements. We might therefore suggest that one of the causes of permanent exclusion from school is linked strongly to a financial imperative.

This table details the financial implications of three of the choices open to a school dealing with a pupil described as experiencing 'challenging behaviours': a permanent exclusion, a managed move to another mainstream school for a 'fresh start', and a place at an alternative education placement.

Thus in Enway, if a pupil's behaviour was seen as problematic, schools had a financial imperative (as well as a legal and ethical mandate) to make recourse to a variety of in-school strategies before they resorted to permanent exclusion.

Spaces for Internal Support and Internal Exclusion

In-school behaviour support, pupil referral, and learning support units (BSUs, PRUs and LSUs) offered a space where pupils could go to receive more intensive one-to-one and small group teaching or therapeutic work. In Enway, these units often offered pupils at risk of exclusion a welcome break from the ire of their classroom teachers, and the benefits of one-to-one academic and emotional support. The teachers and support staff in these units were usually highly skilled and deeply caring, and demonstrated an ethic of social justice and care in their work. The work

Table 1. Comparison of Financial Cost to School Depending on Destination of Pupil at Risk of Permanent Exclusion in Enway in 2006

Placement type:	Managed move	Permanent Exclusion	Alternative Education
Explanation of placement:	Placement in another mainstream school for a 'fresh start' with support if available	Placement at PRU- smaller classes, therapeutic element	Privately run special education programmes 'bought in' by the local authority, often with smaller classes, a therapeutic element and detailed support for transition into work or further education
Explanation of costs:	Forfeit of AWPU (Age Weighted Pupil Unit)^3/52 (weeks) X number of weeks left to end of financial year	AWPU forfeit + a special Permanent Exclusion Deduction which varied depending on when the permanent exclusion was made	AWPU forfeit + market rate of private special education
Costs	In Key Stage 3 (Years 7, 8 and 9), AWPU was £2725	Autumn term permanent exclusion Deduction: £3640	Space for Me, available to Key Stages 3 and 4: £70/day or £13,300/year
Total sample cost to original school, based on a Year 9 pupil moving to a new placement in November (in 2006–2007):	£2725/52 X 20 weeks left of school year= AWPU **£1048**	AWPU £1048 + £3640 = **£4688**	Space for Me for 2.5 terms = £11,083 + AWPU £1048 = **£12,131**

would include academic and social-emotional support, including building positive relationships with parents and carers, and some pupils saw these spaces as a haven from the more difficult environment of the main school environment. Because they were relatively expensive to run in comparison to standard classrooms, they were often under-funded and oversubscribed, and consistently under pressure to take more pupils for longer periods of time. Pupils who had been managed-moved into a school for a 'fresh start' (discussed below) were often placed in these units. This practice raises questions about whether placements in LSUs, BSUs and PSUs perpetuated the 'weak' version of inclusion introduced in chapter one (Viet-Wilson in Macrae *et al.* 2003) which 'merely intends to include the excluded' (90), as opposed to changing the system under which the conditions leading to exclusion developed.

As Slee (1995) explains, 'units provide a regulatory mechanism for schools' inability to respond to, and value, diversity' (81).

Whilst LSUs, BSUs and PRUs were sometimes used for 'internal exclusion', if it was available, a separate 'seclusion room' represented a different type of setting. In some Enway schools these were used where a pupil had been disruptive in class, ostensibly either to give the teacher and the pupil a break from each other, or to ensure that the pupil was able to work free from the tantalising presence of people to distract. The seclusion rooms were also often used for what was known as 'internal exclusion', as an alternative to fixed term exclusion (what used to be called '*suspension*'). Children an young people placed in these rooms were often in them for several weeks. They started school earlier, finished later, and ate lunch separately from their usual classmates. The rooms were unadorned apart from notices requiring those confined to 'Work in total silence', and students worked isolated in carrels.

Internal spaces for students could thus offer a way to maintain a student's attendance at school despite being at risk of fixed term or permanent exclusion. There were situations in which this tactic worked to keep pupils from being excluded. For example, one-off 'offenders' placed there for behaviour which was out of character tended to see them as a deterrent. The head teacher at Church Forrest School in Enway had trialled a seclusion room as a deterrent to exclusion and had found that it did reduce 'low level disruptive behaviour'. However, she also found that on its own, it did nothing to reduce numbers of fixed term or permanent exclusions.[4] Staff-members in these rooms could identify specific students- usually those at risk of permanent exclusion- who had never managed a successful transition back into mainstream classes. These pupils were often referred to me for consideration on the 'Hard to Place' Pupil Placement Panel (discussed below).

So these internal units could be seen as providing a version of unofficial exclusion. Particularly in terms of the seclusion rooms, with their 'weak' model of inclusion (Viet-Wilson in Macrae *et al.* 2003), pupils were treated as 'docile bodies' (Foucault 1977) in a prison-like regime, and whilst there missed out on a rich range of social and academic learning experiences. This was a deterrent for pupils whose low-level behaviour meant that they were not at risk of exclusion, but did not appear to affect those who were already at risk.

A school discipline policy which involves a seclusion room might be thought to serve helpfully to identify children and young people who may be seen as needing extra support, and to provide them with a quiet space in which to work. But as Slee (1995) explains, '[a]lthough the diagnostic quest to redefine and separate children is advanced as serving the educational interests of the child, it may be better understood in Foucauldian vernacular of producing 'docile bodies' for the purpose of institutional equilibrium' (73). Because pupils who have been involved in disruptive incidents might need attention of some kind, the internal seclusion model does not align with the local and international imperative for educational inclusion discussed in chapter one. The silence of docile bodies is not conducive with the theories of Freire (1970), who sees dialogue as an essential component of effective learning, stating that 'without communication there can be no true education' (74). This can be applied to the learning of appropriate behaviour, as well as academic learning. Unless it is seen as valid that children and young people who are represented as displaying 'difficult behaviour' should be left out of the discussion when schools are implementing inclusion policy, I would argue that internal seclusion does not represent an equitable option.

Learning Mentors

Learning mentors worked in all the schools in Enway in order to support the government's inclusion agenda, and they engaged in activities designed to help pupils develop self control, organisation strategies, and self-esteem (DfES 2005). These examples of in-school strategies are cheaper to implement than a move to a new school, and notably, most include some element of working on a within-child basis (Rendall and Stuart 2005). Learning mentors were often attached to BSUs, LSUs and PSUs, and whilst their work was often deeply thoughtful and helpful for individual children, the justification for their choice of strategies was often a description of the child's behaviour as opposed to or divorced from a description of the classroom environment in which the behaviour had occurred.[5]

As I explained in chapter three, the measuring, describing and recording of the specifics of a pupil's behaviour serves to justify a focus on the child rather than on the environment or system within which the behaviour issues had developed (see also Macrae *et al.* 2003; Thomas and Loxley 2001). Enway learning mentors worked creatively and with great empathy to support the children and young people in their care. Their approach is much closer to Freire's dialogic, empowering pedagogical model than that of teachers. But whilst children have to leave the classroom to experience this, and the pedagogical, curricular and physical environment remains unchanged, it is perhaps unlikely that pupils will stop needing input from learning mentors.

Pastoral Support Plans (...and the Threat of Permanent Exclusion)

In order to develop the 'early intervention' strategies described above, Pastoral Support Plans (PSP's) were drawn up at school meetings in Enway.[6] These were specifically mandated by government to pre-empt permanent exclusions through the implementation of the Every Child Matters framework. PSPs incorporated behaviour targets, in-school provisions, and referrals to outside agencies, and could represent an opportunity to look at a student's situation more holistically. It was a large part of my role as PSO to facilitate these meetings. As described in chapter two, as part of my professional work, I was able to respond to some of the ideas developed through the ethnographic fieldwork, and this included changing the PSP form to include more space for the pupil's point of view (discussed further in chapter eight).

Pastoral support planning can be useful to help to keep a pupil focused and out of trouble at school. However, a permanent exclusion has to be mandated by a school's Governor's Disciplinary Committee hearing, and can then be challenged by parents in front of an appeals board at the Town Hall. So, in Enway, where a pupil was permanently excluded without proof that a school had done 'everything it could' to avoid an exclusion, and this was recorded in pastoral support planning documentation,[7] the pupil was likely to be reinstated. Consequently, PSP meetings were often set up in order to meet a less benificent agenda. As one head of year explained to me, 'We need to set up these PSP's because this pupil is going to be permanently excluded and we need to be seen to have crossed all the 'T's and dotted all the 'I's.' This cynicism was also encapsulated in another head of year's comment to me that PSPs were 'just a paper exercise'.

'PREVENTION' STRATEGIES TO AVERT PERMANENT EXCLUSION: OUT OF SCHOOL

Managed Moves: Fresh Start or Unofficial Exclusion?
(...and the Threat of Permanent Exclusion)

When PSP meetings continued over a number of months without a noticeable improvement in behaviour, they could sometimes lead to a decision that the pupil should leave his or her school to enrol in another through a process described as a *managed move*. Managed moves were promoted by the Enway local authority as another opportunity for 'early intervention' and to pre-empt permanent exclusion. It was one of the ways in which a pupil, whilst being merely threatened with permanent exclusion, might find her- or himself nevertheless attending a new school. Macrae *et al.* (2003) identifies this strategy as part of a range of 'tactics used by schools to conceal the true [exclusionary] situation' (92).

When considering the use of managed moves, it is worth noting (at Table 1 above) that when a school permanently excludes a pupil it is 'fined' a large sum of money. In addition, local authorities are scrutinised by government inspection bodies with regard to their efforts to reduce school exclusions. It was thus in the financial interests of the schools and the local authority to cut down on the numbers of permanent exclusions, and managed moves represented a significant proportion of pupil movement around the district. They were also cheaper than paying for a placement at an independent alternative education programme.

Slee (1995), discussing managed moves, found that '[d]espite referrals being described as voluntary, pressure was put upon students and their parents ... who were frequently unaware of their rights' (81). In Enway, parents were similarly often denied their right to refuse a managed move, and unlike in the case of a permanent exclusion, there was neither an automatic governor's hearing nor a clearly signposted right of appeal. Some managed moves may therefore be seen as unofficial permanent exclusions. One example of this practice was exemplified in a comment made to me by a Deputy Head Teacher at Enway College, 'it's a case of we had to say to the parent either you take this managed move or we'll have to permanently exclude him. Do you want to jump before you are pushed?' And an Enway parent advocacy worker told me, '[The school] advised [the pupil's] mum to find another school before he was permanently excluded'. This is an example of 'weak' inclusion (Viet-Wilson in Macrae *et al.* 2003), failing to deliver the right to a fair hearing enshrined in Article 12 of the UN Convention on the Rights of the Child 1989 (de Pear and Garner 1996).

Managed moves can, therefore, imply two different narratives. They are often 'sold' to parents as 'a fresh start', without the stain of a permanent exclusion on the school records. But a managed move can also be understood as an unofficial, cost-effective 'permanent exclusion', with no right of appeal. Worse, they could lead in any case to an official permanent exclusion. The Enway protocol for managed moves was that a student should try another school for a period of six weeks. If their placement was unsuccessful, they would be returned to their original school and were often immediately permanently excluded. This was referred to by head teachers and Enway Inclusion staff as a 'sale or return' policy.

THE PUPIL REFERRAL UNIT

Some of the money obtained from a school following a permanent exclusion was collected centrally and was intended to fund the provision of a Pupil Referral Unit (a 'PRU') in the local authority area. The Enway PRU looked after some young people who were at risk of exclusion, but, in another building, constituted the first offer of an education placement when a pupil was at serious risk of permanent exclusion and was deemed not able to attend a mainstream school. It was also the place to which pupils were sent once they had been officially permanently excluded. A PRU placement could be seen as a 'benefit' of an official permanent exclusion, as it offered smaller class sizes and a focus on behaviour management; and was cheaper than an alternative education placement in an independent school (see Table 1 above). Students achieved their GCSEs at the Enway PRU, and the art teaching in particular was particularly successful. The Enway PRU received an 'Outstanding' grade from OFSTED in 2007–2008. Because of this it was the reason permanent exclusion in Enway was sometimes described by several professionals (in hushed tones), as 'a road to support'.

The Enway PRU could be a difficult place for some young people, though. Girls, in particular, could be vulnerable as they constituted a very small minority, and physical bullying was relatively common there. The PRU had a separate section dedicated to supporting children who had the potential to reintegrate into mainstream school, and the unit sent staff-members into mainstream school to aid in transition. This did occasionally work. However, PRU transition staff, like those supporting young people subject to managed moves, often discussed the unwelcoming attitude shown to their students, with mainstream and new schools predicting a negative outcome for them and often behaving as though it had already come to pass.

'Gate-Keeping' and the Rhetoric of 'Need'

Despite the availability of more cost-effective support options, such as the PRU, managed moves and in-school support strategies described above, the number of secondary school pupils subject to an official permanent exclusion in the Enway district had risen from 31 in the academic year 2001–2002 to 89 in 2004–2005.[8] In 2005–2006 Enway was facing the prospect of finding mainstream school places for a growing number of pupils who had either been permanently excluded and whose parents had turned down the offer of the PRU, or who were at risk of permanent exclusion and were seeking a managed move. These pupils had a history of being described in terms of their behaviour management issues and were looking for a mainstream school placement. In response to new government initiatives, a Pupil Placement Panel[9] was developed in March 2006 for the 'gate-keeping'[10] of what was termed in the local authority's protocol as these 'Hard to Place' pupils.

Before the Pupil Placement Panel was instituted, heads of year at undersubscribed schools had often expressed concern at their schools being used as 'a dumping ground' for difficult pupils. It was hoped that this would fade away once the Panel started to distribute pupils in need of placements more fairly across the Enway district, but it continued. The phrase had the effect of ascribing a narrative of deprivation and hopelessness onto the pupils who were placed at their schools by the Panel. One of the ways in which this situation was negotiated was through the gate-keeping narrative described in chapter three and known as the 'threshold of need' (Thomas and Loxley 2001). Discussions around a pupil's needs often did lead to helpful support planning. However, the 'need' paradigm was also used in order to avoid or postpone making a difficult decision (Thomas and Loxley, 2001).

For example, one day in the September-December academic term of 2007, the Panel members read in their paperwork that Billy, a Year 9[11] pupil living in a neighbouring local authority district, had attended a 'Secure Unit' for 'violence towards a family member'. Because of this official history, the Panel felt very nervous about placing him in a mainstream school. Billy had been written up as a child who could be violent towards his family, and as Foucault explains, documents have the power to 'capture and fix' (1977: 189). The parents had exercised their legal right to request a mainstream placement at a school which had spaces - and had chosen a school in Enway. The head of the Enway School Admissions Department managed to postpone the decision for another six weeks by suggesting that Billy should be placed in his school of choice only once he had successfully completed a suitable number of weeks at a PRU in his home district. She explained: 'We take into account what he wants to do but we have to take his needs into account ... once we feel his needs are taken into account we can take his preferences into account.' Billy may have benefited from more time at the PRU. But this was contrary to the advice of his social worker, Youth Offending Team worker and the staff at the secure unit he had attended.

By generating a discourse of 'need' in pursuit of a longer PRU placement, the head of Admissions circumvented Billy's parents' right to choose, providing a gate-keeping service both to the Enway district and to the school the family had requested. 'Need' became an oblique, shapeless category, observed as valid perhaps only because of the powerful bureaucratic position of the person invoking it, and not even requiring recourse to any of the 'psy' technical language often relied upon to make a diagnosis (Slee 1995; Thomas and Loxley 2001). Perhaps 'need' was a form of 'psy' diagnosis in itself.

The Pupil Placement Panel: a Culture of Stress

The Pupil Placement Panel represented an attempt to tackle complex issues using a multi-professional approach. A range of professionals came from their own organisational cultures (described in chapters three and six), and the conversation around Billy's school placement, discussed above, caused a certain amount of tension among the Panel members. The subject-matter was often quite distressing. Billy's case, for example, addressed issues of his mother's heroin addiction and domestic violence. Sources of stress such as these were not uncommon, and perhaps in order to cope, the Panel had, since its inception in March 2005, developed its own particular cultural identity and habits and co-opted its own space. These cultural traits really demonstrated the level of financial and emotional stress and inter-professional and intra-institutional tussles for power under which the Panel operated. It was often within this environment that children's extended bodies were described, discussed and (mis)represented.

The Panel meeting was held around four large school desks pushed together in an old classroom on the top floor at one of Enway's special educational needs schools. A stained, scratchy brown local authority carpet soaked small tea-spills as the Panel participants, laden heavily with paper, carried their institutional vintage green cups and saucers from the tea urn at the side of the room to their cramped seats at the desks. Early arrivals spread out their papers, claiming their space, and quickly surveyed the snack situation, often taking two chocolate biscuits and putting one in their handbag or briefcase for later. Extra sugar was poured into the cups of tea in order to sustain the participants through what everyone knew would be a long, harrowing meeting.

The Panel meeting was chaired by the very patient and pragmatic Head of Inclusion (Behaviour), who arrived early, sitting next to me opposite the door on the longer side of the table so that she could watch the other members arrive and maintain a democratic and placating position within the circle of attendees. The meetings always included three head teachers who took it in turns to attend the Panel meetings, speaking on behalf of their colleagues. They were strong characters, each with their own interpretation of the importance of inclusion as an ethic. The broad range of professionals attending the Panel reflected the DfES's drive for 'joined-up' support planning. So, usually in attendance were the Head of School Admissions; the Exclusions Officer, who attended all permanent exclusion hearings; the head teacher at the PRU; an educational psychologist; a Safeguarding and Social Care manager;[12] a Special Educational Needs (SEN) officer; a Youth Offending Team officer;[13] a representative from the Attendance Advisory Service;[14] the chief executive at an independent alternative education unit, the services of which were bought in by the local authority area (see Table 1 above); and the Pupil Support Officer (myself), who carried out many of the decisions made by the Panel. Professionals from CAMHS[15] were invited, but never attended. I habitually sat next to the Chair so that I could watch the door and also discreetly pass on additional information to her as the other members thrashed out the merits of each case. Occasionally someone working more closely with the family, such as a Traveller Education advisor[16] or social worker, may also have attended to present their own or the family's narrative of events.

Conflicting Professional Agendas

When Billy's case came up on the Panel's agenda, his social worker and Youth Offending Team (YOT) worker attended the Panel meeting to lobby for a mainstream school in Enway. They told the Panel that 'it's the family's choice. Initially they were offered the local school but turned it down due to its reputation. The family feel that he's had his shock ... he sees the PRU as a punishment.' These two professionals were subjected to loud, censorious questioning, and after leaving the room, were mildly derided as unrealistic chancers by the permanent Panel members. However, during an informal discussion amongst Panel members after the meeting had finished, it was conceded that they were really stuck between the preferences and rights of the parents and the need for the Enway Panel to protect their secondary schools from the risk of potential violence. Whilst Billy's paperwork only referred to one incident of violence, focussed on his difficult home life, the Panel's gate-keeping narrative fell within what James and Freeze (2006) refer to as 'the admirable goals of reducing violence within schools and producing a safer learning environment' (585). It constituted what was frequently described by Panel members, particularly head teachers, as 'a duty of care to the majority'.

In addition to considering the relative safety of their existing pupils, head teachers joined the Panel decision-making process with an overview of their schools finances, and a keen focus on the government's requirements for school-wide proficiency in the areas of attendance and academic attainment. Head teachers attending the Panel thus frequently offered places to pupils with high SAT[17] scores, regardless of their behaviour record, as these were viewed as a predictor of good GCSEs, and these pupils were viewed as likely to help raise the school's position in the government's finance-linked yearly league tables (Rendall and Stuart 2005). Conversely, if a pupil's attendance at school was an issue (usually below around 90%) the discussion almost always prompted a head teacher to protest their school's problematic attendance rate in opposition to the pupil being placed at their school.

However, each pupil had to be provided with a place where they could be educated, and on each Panel list, there were between fifteen and twenty-five pupils. These young people were described in their paperwork[18] as having low attendance and academic scores, and often had a documented history of what was viewed as their behaviour management issues, requiring expensive support mechanisms to be put in place at the new placement. Each Panel member was given a printed list of the numbers of placements available in each Enway school that week. Referrals came from parents through the Admissions department and from schools, mainly for pupils who were at risk of being or had already been excluded; were being bullied; or were vulnerable due to, for example, their refugee or foster care status. Of particular note was the number of young people referred from neighbouring local authority areas due to a 'lack of space' in local schools. Parents could ask for a mainstream school place rather than the PRU if their child had been excluded only once. However, the rules around parental choice and the requests of some 'over-referring' schools were often creatively side-stepped - for example, 'more desirable' students were sometimes brought to the top of the agenda and placed at certain schools, taking up the space before a 'less desirable'[19] pupil was discussed later in the meeting.

About a quarter of the pupils had their requests for a placement turned down and were sent back to their previous schools 'for more information' or for a multi-agency meeting to assess their 'needs' further. Both requests often used by the Panel as gate-keeping and delaying strategies. Where all else had failed, pupils were given placements at alternative education sites. However, about half of the pupils at each Panel were placed at another mainstream secondary school in Enway. The table below details the placements made by the Pupil Placement Panel from its inception in March 2005 to the end of its first year in May 2007:

Table 2. Pupil Placement Panel figures[20]

Total number of pupils seen by the Pupil Placement Panel	216
Number of these pupils who were from a neighbouring local authority district	136
Pupils placed in mainstream school	150
Pupils placed in an alternative education provision	14
Total placed by Pupil Placement Panel	164
Pupils not placed, but sent back to referring school for more information, multi-agency work or for school to fund alternative provision	49
Pupils not placed, but sent back to referring school and subsequently permanently excluded	3

Parental 'Choice'

The figure in *Table 2*, above, for 'pupils who are from a neighbouring local authority district', is significant because as well as reflecting local authority pressure to move certain children out of their own school system, it represents one of the effects of the government's policy providing for parental choice of school. Pupils thus often came through the Panel to be placed in Enway schools from its two closest neighbouring local authority areas. One of these areas, Brendantown, similar to Enway in its level of social deprivation, claimed to suffer from a limited number of spaces in its schools. In addition, its Pupil Referral Unit did not offer GCSEs. So the parents of permanently excluded pupils and those who may otherwise have been subjected to a 'managed move' (described above) were often advised by Brendantown Inclusion staff to apply to Enway schools. The other neighbouring area, Prosper, constituted a wealthier neighbourhood with a high number of private schools, and a range of selective grammar schools just across their border in the countryside. Its state-funded schools were all run by academies and foundations, and there was a dire shortage of state school places. It also had a 'no permanent exclusion policy' and provided no alternative education placements. Pupils from Prosper's schools who were seen as having challenging behaviours were rumoured at the Panel to be simply told to stay at home, then referred by their schools to the Enway Panel as a means to effectively exclude the pupil from Prosper's system without having to make an official exclusion. Whether this was wholly true or not was irrelevant to Billy, described above, who was from Prosper. This was just another factor which made the Panel more protective towards Enway's 'own' schools when discussing his case.

Reintegration Meetings

Once a pupil had been placed by the Pupil Placement Panel in a mainstream school, it was my job as a Pupil Support Officer to manage their transition and successful settling-in period. I would begin this by writing to the new school, asking them to set up a Reintegration Planning meeting.[21] This was very similar to a Pastoral Support Plan (PSP) meeting (described above) and should similarly have included the pupil, parents or carer, head of year, and if appropriate, other involved professionals such as the social worker or Youth Offending Team worker. It was thus another opportunity for the multi-agency approach to support planning promoted by the DfES/DCSF. However, as I have explained, conflicting professional approaches, high work volumes and financial agendas often made it difficult to hold a meeting involving all professionals and to broker a fully effective support agreement.

Working with inter-agency conflict As a Pupil Support Officer, in addressing the conflict described above, I attempted to implement a 'strong' version of social inclusion (Viet-Wilson in Macrae *et al.* 2003). This approach, described in chapter one, 'addresses the mechanisms through which powerful constituencies exercise their power to exclude' (91). The dissonance between the multiple agencies involved in supporting pupils at risk of exclusion could be seen to constitute a mechanism of social exclusion, and one needing to be addressed. For example, I experienced some difficulties in gaining consistent collaborative input from the Enway Attendance Advisory Service (AAS). Its officers had expressed their concern at the rising numbers of what they called 'difficult kids' placed in 'their' schools and 'jumping the queue' for Pupil Support Unit, learning mentor and counsellor waiting lists.

Schools Under Siege

I've had it up to here, you get to the point where that door goes, a kid comes in, and I'm like, 'GRRR! Get over it! Deal with it!'

Pastoral Support Assistant, working in a LSU

Field-notes, December 2007

Collaboration in the Enway Children's Services department could be difficult because school staff, and to some extent, Panel members, could sometimes feel as if they were under siege from wave after wave of 'Hard to Place' pupils and the parents and other professionals who referred them. The comments and responses of professionals involved with the Pupil Placement Panel often therefore appeared to be suffused with stress. One of the most common complaints I heard from heads of year was that they could not afford to take another permanently excluded pupil from the Panel because their year group was 'unbalanced'. Heads of year often said that their Panel pupils were 'wasting' or 'using up' all their resources.

Some of the problems with multi-professional 'collaboration' may stem from the fact that before the New Labour government's policy of inclusion prompted the local authority to close its specialised behaviour management units, and money was devolved to schools to enable them to set up their own inclusion and behaviour management programmes, financing was centralised and so schools felt that the local authority would take care of the issue for them. The money has now been devolved, but some of the sense of responsibility has remained with the central bureaucracy (Rendall and Stuart 2005:4). And despite their best efforts, the Panel-members were not always able to use gate-keeping or procrastination tactics (as with Billy, above). This meant that when a new pupil arrived at a certain school they had often been given a place on sufferance, and – together with the supporting professionals, who may have been engaged in empathic support - may not have been made to feel particularly welcome.

Not all the heads of year and deputy heads or school inclusion managers in Enway were hostile to new pupils. Good SAT scores and a fair attendance percentage helped school staff feel more welcoming. And occasionally, teachers who were sceptical about the narratives recorded in the paperwork from the previous school tended to be more optimistic and to prefer to rely on their own judgment when interviewing a new pupil. But more often than not, Panel pupils were not greeted with a positive attitude. Thus a school attendance officer, when asked to work with a 'new' pupil, told me, 'It's not my job...', and heads of year were often reluctant to refer new pupils to a learning mentor or LSU on the grounds that they were 'jumping the queue' at the expense of what they described as 'our pupils'. The conflict engendered by the placement of Panel pupils could make reintegration planning meetings very difficult and pre-empt a successful reintegration. Sometimes, for example, a fully supportive plan for mentoring and special needs support was drawn up at the meeting, and on my return for a review four weeks later, nothing had been put in place, and the pupil was, not surprisingly, struggling.

In Children's Services, we were required to work within the parameters of the government's 'Every Child Matters' agenda, a DfES approach which promoted a multi-professional, holistic view of the needs of each child (DfES 2005). Why were the agencies charged with the important task of re-engaging excluded children failing to overcome their conflicts, undermining the delivery of adequate support for vulnerable young people in the process? Was this conflict a cause of permanent exclusion from school?

APPLYING THE THEORY OF THE EXTENDED BODY

The next section of this chapter draws on the extended body theory to discover how inter-professional conflict is so intractable in its contribution to instances of permanent exclusion from school.

The extended body, as explained in chapter three, is in part an experienced representation of a person, combining embodied, projected, chosen and conflicting assumptions and identities. It includes a construction of 'the soul' (Foucault 1977; Rose 1999) which is capable of being corporeally disciplined: for example, physically excluded from the school site. Some of the constructions and representations projected into a young person's extended body are detailed in *Figure 1*, chapter three, and include 'mental state', 'behaviour', 'attitude', and 'intention'.

The Myth of Becky

A discussion held at a Pastoral Support Plan meeting (on 14.5.07) for Becky, a Year 9 pupil[22] exemplifies aspects of some of the elements in the 'extended body' diagram (*Figure 1*, chapter three) and some of the tropes used to create representations, such as the discourse of 'need' (Thomas and Loxley 2001; discussed in chapter three). It demonstrates a professional-cultural conflict between professionals. Becky was asked to attend a meeting planned to discuss her fate. Should she stay at her school? Or should she be manage-moved to another? In this table, professionals' comments have been linked to aspects of the extended body:

Table 3. Aspects of the 'Extended Body' Discussed in a Pastoral Support Plan Meeting

PSP participant	Comment	Aspect of the 'extended body'
Social Worker	Becky is still grieving over the loss of her father … rejected by her mother, who had chosen her boyfriend over her; she's not a tough cookie … vulnerable …	mental state
Head teacher	Clearly we have empathy but it's going to take a long time. To keep her in a school environment enables her to fuel the negative behaviour and make it worse. She thrives on the audience; on the confrontation; she gets a kick out of it!	behaviour attitude discourse of need
Assistant head teacher	I would describe her behaviour as 'wild'- she was screaming at me. I know that's the pressure of the Year 9 SAT exams.	behaviour mental state
Behaviour respite teacher	We took Becky back because a. she's in care and b. we like her as a person.	mental state attitude intention
Head teacher	She came from [a big mixed-sex school]. The issue involves boys. She comes in as 'The Big I Am' - I think she's at risk.	attitude intention discourse of need
Foster carer	Something is not right. She went out and got drunk … is always attracted to boys…	behaviour attitude mental state intention
Head teacher	She will be permanently excluded.	Behaviour
Behaviour respite teacher	It's a life changing experience when they [are permanently excluded]. She needs to value herself. Education has got to come second - it's escalating, it will turn into violence …	behaviour attitude mental state intention discourse of need

Becky was brought in right at the end of the meeting. She became shy, probably because she was in a meeting with the head teacher and four other professionals in the head teacher's office, and her only comments were that she was unhappy at Enway Valley Girls' School and that she wanted to be at a mixed-sex school. Becky's voice, in this important discussion about her fate, was barely heard. And even when she was actually present, her presence seemed to be a token gesture towards involving her in the decision making process. Her extended body, 'Becky' herself, had been constructed as a representation of a girl: the myth of Becky. There had been a brief nod to institutional causes- the 'school environment' and 'the pressure of the Year 9 SAT exams' were acknowledged. But the focus had been broadly on a pathologising idea of Becky herself. In the meeting, this girl was described as grieving, rejected, and vulnerable, displaying negative behaviour and thriving on the audience to each confrontation; someone who was 'wild' and 'screaming'; a 'Big I Am' at risk through her drunkenness and attraction to boys; someone who was going to be – in fact, *needed* to be - permanently excluded and would in all likelihood become violent. Because of her silence, her self-identification was absent from the construction. But decisions were being made on the basis of it and its potential. The construction of the extended body, through its quality of 'being experienced', emerged from myth to become a 'true' story which was fully expected to be played out to its inevitable conclusion in permanent exclusion from school.

I have constructed (in chapter three) the extended body as 'contested space', where young people could add their own self-representation. But what was causing the subjugation of Becky's voice?

The 'Extended Body': Contested Space?

My first goal at the PSP meeting had been to help Becky avoid permanent exclusion. This involved persuading the school to partially fund an alternative education provision. This would give Becky an education environment where she did not need to worry about being reprimanded for lower-level issues such as school uniform infringements or talking in class. The social worker at this meeting collaborated with me to promote empathy over Becky's difficult family circumstances. The head teacher and her deputy were troubled with a problematic combination of concerns: avoiding a permanent exclusion, trying to evade having to pay for an expensive alternative education placement, and maintaining an orderly school environment.

The behaviour respite teacher was trapped between the two ethics, and found herself oscillating uncomfortably between the factions. This teacher became involved with Becky when she entered a programme designed to support pupils aged 11 to 14 with their behaviour. To enter the programme pupils needed to be *not* at risk of permanent exclusion. Because Becky did not appear to be meeting this requirement (that is, she was at risk of permanent exclusion), the behaviour respite teacher's primary concerns thus included the incongruent concepts of empathy for Becky and her speedy exit, as an unsuitable candidate, from the behaviour respite programme. The meeting was an attempt to use a 'multi-agency' or 'interdisciplinary' approach, and is an illustration of the range of conflicting issues inherent in attempting to collaborate across skill sets, contexts and disciplines (also see Heath *et al.* 2006). Perhaps one of the most striking elements of this story is that the 'myth' of Becky might perpetuate the ideology of need and the linked apparatus of intervention-which in turn perpetuate the myth.

Thinking about Becky's Pastoral Support Plan meeting, the Pupil Placement Panels and other meetings were what led me to develop an idea of the pupil's 'extended body' as *contested space.* Thus conflict exists not only between the pupil and the school and/or parents and carers, as many studies have found (Cooper 2002; Rendall and Stuart 2005; Wright et al, 2000), but also between professionals (Heath *et al.* 2006), to the detriment of the pupil.

CONCLUSION

In this chapter, I have introduced some of the procedures in and outside schools which were concerned with the administration of disciplinary support, inclusion and, sometimes, permanent exclusion from school in Enway. Details of the Enway Pupil Placement Panel were described, together with its procedures and strategies, and some of the young people whose cases were discussed there. I have thus laid out the stressful environment within which the procedures around permanent exclusion from school were embedded. This environment was stressful partly because of students' distressing stories, and partly because of the conflicting nature of the issues which faced gatekeepers or decision makers. Professionals were forced to make decisions about pupils in the face of powerful competition between the politically unchallengeable concepts of empathy, inclusivity, and attainment. Also competing were discourses about needs and costs; a duty of care for the majority; parental choice; attendance data and league tables; a perception that schools were 'forced' to take 'Hard to Place' pupils by the local authority; the view of new pupils as 'not belonging'; and the fact that budgets for behaviour management had been devolved with an incomplete transfer of the attached culture of responsibility. These stress factors exacerbated inter-professional conflict, situated within and affecting representations of the pupil's extended body, and taking interactions between staff beyond the parameters of the assumed task of pupil support. Permanent exclusion from school, then, could be called 'a critical incident'; a crystallising moment during which all these issues collide.

So it could be suggested that part of the cause of permanent exclusion from school is inter-professional conflict derived from institutional stress. Some of the effects of the existence of permanent exclusion from school as an option involve the feeding of the student's extended body through a pastoral support planning process into a system of in-school support strategies. These, although often empathic and supportive, serve to maintain a pathologising within-child view of 'behaviour problems', leaving the institutional environment unchanged. This book will suggest that the implications for this are circular.

The unchanged schooling environment – unchanged, because the problem is constituted within the child, not the institution - will be seen in the following chapters to be maintained and controlled through a series of norming imperatives which are underpinned by the existence of permanent exclusion from school. These norming imperatives are framed around institutional prejudice- normative forces, delivered through what Foucault (1977) called 'capillaries of power'. These forces are characterised by practices of institutional racism, classism and sexism and supported and mandated by a framework of policy techniques. Within this environment, pupils' extended bodies are constructed and (mis)represented as 'needing' a within-child or excluding intervention. The institutional environment is unchanged, and the cycle continues. The next three chapters will address the experienced effects of representations of the extended body on the basis of gender, class and ethnicity respectively.

CHAPTER 4

NOTES

[1]   It was difficult to maintain the ethnicity information gathering system in Enway. Schools and central admissions staff often omitted this information from exclusion forms; a significant issue in a local authority area where a disproportionate 35% of permanently excluded pupils identified as other than 'White British' (Enway Director of Children's Services 2007).

[2]   Often through 'managed moves', described below.

[3]   A set amount paid to a school by the government through the local authority to educate each pupil.

[4]   The success factor in the seclusion room experiment appeared to be pupils' isolation from their friends at lunch time. They wanted to return to the main school schedule so that they could socialize again, and so it constituted a powerful deterrent. But numbers of permanent exclusions at Church Forrest School dramatically reduced when the head teacher decided on a policy of zero permanent exclusions.

[5]   These descriptions are discussed in more detail in terms of pupil Behaviour Logs in chapter eight.

[6]   And are used across England.

[7]   Where there was not a serious one-off 'offence' such as serious assault, theft, or carrying a knife or drugs- although this boundary varied between schools.

[8]   Enway Director of Children's Services (2007).

[9]   This is frequently referred to in this book as 'the Panel'. It has since been rebranded as the 'Fair Access Panel'.

[10] That is, the making of placement decisions.

[11] Aged 14.

[12] Formerly Social Services, and a senior social worker.

[13] These officers monitor and plan support for young people who have received a court judgment.

[14] Attendance Advisory Officers monitor school attendance. They have the power to refer parents to court for a fine or even prison if their children fail to attend school. In some areas they are known as 'Educational Welfare Officers'.

[15] Child and Adolescent Mental Health Services.

[16] This worker provides liaison and education support services to pupils from Gypsy Roma or Irish Traveller families.

[17] Standard assessment tasks

[18] See chapter eight for a discussion of how documents can 'capture and fix' people in a representative paradigm (Foucault 1970).

[19] The rest of the book will explain, with reference to extended body representation, why some students are more or less desirable (in addition to their SAT scores and attendance record).

[20] These figures were derived from the database I was required to maintain as part of my work as a Pupil Placement Officer.

[21] For some reason, while 'inclusion' replaced 'integration' as the new policy enabling almost all pupils to attend mainstream school, once a pupil has left a school they are still re-included through a process known as 'reintegration'. This implies the view that whilst schools should endeavour to change their practices to include all pupils, once a pupil has been excluded, it is now up to the pupil to make the effort to reintegrate. See chapter 1 for the political etymology of the terms 'integration' and 'inclusion'.

[22] Aged 14

CHAPTER 5

'BITCHY GIRLS AND SILLY BOYS' [1]

Heteronormativity and Sexual Violence

INTRODUCTION

How might people respond if a teacher called a boy 'bitchy'? Perhaps because of an assumed biological constructed 'irrefutability' concerning sex (Butler 1993; 1999), experienced representations of the extended body are particularly vulnerable to influence by 'heteronormativity': the pressure caused by stereotypical normative assumptions about how gender should represent itself in a person.

In considering some of the causes of permanent exclusion from school, this chapter aims to look at the effects of institutional prejudice on the basis of gender, including professionals' heteronormative assumptions about gender identity and sexuality on effective support planning for young people. Inter-professional conflict will be seen to be less of a concern in relation to gender. In fact, the collusion within young people's extended bodies in terms of normative pronouncements on gender is testament to the power of heteronormativity. The conflict in the case of gender was more likely to be between young person and professional.

The chapter will begin with further details of Nama's story[2] in order to introduce some of the complex gendered issues experienced by pupils at risk of or subject to a permanent exclusion from school. Following this, the section will proceed with an overview of some of the concerns about gender in exclusion from school which are discussed in the literature. I will then describe some of the broad accepted understandings about gender identity and sexualised behaviour in Enway. Comparing some of the assumptions and pressures around gender identity raised in Enway's mixed and single-sex schools will provide a crystallised illustration of some of these concerns.

The following sections will focus on some of the gender-related issues which contribute to the particular circumstances surrounding exclusion from school. These include gendered class reproduction through the choice of GCSEs in a new placement school; the (in)visibility of issues of sexuality and gender in the field of professional consideration for children and young people at risk of exclusion; 'horizontal violence' (Freire 1996) in schools manifested as sexual aggression, sometimes leading to exclusion; and some of the interactions between the institutional prejudices on the basis of gender, ethnicity and culture which emerge under the crystallising pressure of a school disciplinary framework. The conclusion will clarify some of the links between gender normativity and instances of threatened or actual permanent exclusion, finishing with an account of some of the work in Enway to develop support strategies designed to tackle these effects.

The Story of Nama

Nama, at fourteen years old, was already used to inclusion and exclusion procedures. She was one of the only pupils I worked with who made her own phone calls to ask what was happening with her school place. She had been permanently excluded, and was discussed for the second time at the Enway 'Hard to Place' Pupil Placement Panel at the beginning of January 2008. Following a reasonably settled start at her new school, slumped silently at her desk, Nama had suddenly gone from weeks of a consistent sulky disengagement to a single lightning explosion of swearing and screaming in class. The Panel's Safeguarding[3] representative, a senior social worker, updated the rest of us on what may have instigated the event: 'Her brother found her with two boys in her room- he beat her up. She was taken under police protection because of ongoing violence towards her; we accommodated her [with a foster carer]. She's scared of her family, but was still talking to them on the phone.'

'That's very manipulative', volunteered one of the senior administrators, helping herself complacently to a biscuit.

'She's now with her uncle back in Enway,' continued the social worker, 'we will follow up with an assessment of the uncle and family and do a core assessment to look at safety in her life.'

'She's a very, very manipulative girl,' added a behaviour management teacher who had previously worked with Nama, 'this is a person running the adults in great numbers.'

'And there is still an unevaluated and difficult-to-quantify risk to this child,' finished the social worker, adding that there had been talk of her being at risk of either a forced marriage[4] or an 'honour killing' (in punishment for the incident in her bedroom).

I waited for the excited cross-talk to recede, then added what Nama had asked me to tell the Panel: that she wanted to move to Ennon Grand Academy - what would be her third secondary school - and which her cousin attended, close to the home of the uncle with whom she was now living. Nama had resolutely told me that if she could not get a place at Ennon Grand then she was 'not going anywhere else'. This tenacity, along with the perceived change of heart exemplified through Nama's telephone calls to her family whilst still under police protection, added to the concern among the Panel delegates that she was trying to 'manipulate' the situation.

I spent some time after this Panel meeting wondering why Nama had been described as 'manipulative' by two people during the social worker's report of her ongoing situation. The concept of manipulation seemed to me to be strangely incongruous when applied to a young person who was both lacking in control over her life choices and living with such a high level of apparent risk from her own family.

The following morning, I received an urgent telephone call from the head of year at Nama's temporary placement school. He said that Nama was refusing to leave school, and was saying that she was scared to go back to her uncle's house. I informed the Panel social worker who had given the report on Nama the day before, and received a follow-up email from him in which he responded to the news by describing Nama as 'very manipulative'. At this point, I lost patience with the 'manipulative' discourse and sought telephone advice from a trusted colleague: a senior education psychologist and a thoughtful practitioner.

'What does this word 'manipulative' really mean in terms of Nama's actual needs and the delivery of the most appropriate support?' I asked him.

He replied, 'The 'manipulative' thing is a red herring', and explained that Nama's ambivalence was something everybody demonstrates at one time or another. He suggested that there was a possibility that Nama was seeing her family as both good and bad, dealing with this by imagining that there were two families- a friendly, nurturing family, and a persecuting family. When she was at the foster carer's, far from home, she had called her family, seeking nurture from the only place she was familiar with. Returning to her uncle's house, Nama had shown signs of beginning to feel persecuted again, raising a renewed sense of the need to run away. Regarding her refusal to 'not go anywhere' if she could not have a place at Ennon Grand Academy, the school of her choice, my colleague explained that it seemed as if Nama, in the throes of her anxiety, was resorting to immature ways of dealing with things.

'At the moment', he expanded, 'she can only deal with things the way she wants them to be. And her silence/sudden anger at school indicates her degree of desperation and the level of emotional need.' I agreed that Nama was living in 'survival mode'.

I was struck by the potential level of empathy that this kind of interagency collaboration could engender, and which was missing from the Panel, where delegates had colluded (within the space of Nama's extended body, and in conflict with an alternative view of her as 'vulnerable') to describe and represent her as 'manipulative'. Such a collaboration could also challenge the objectifying effects of a within-child 'psy' technique (Sellman 2002; Slee 1995; Foucault 1977; see also chapter three), utilising it instead as useful information with which to investigate and adjust the institutional response to Nama's situation.

Butler (1999) explains Wittig's conception of language as 'a set of acts, repeated over time, that produce reality-effects that are eventually misinterpreted as "facts"' (147). I had a sense that the 'manipulative' quality ascribed to Nama, originally invoked by the interjection of a senior administrator at the Panel, had been taken on as a 'fact' by the other professionals, and that this (as well as the reasons for the danger Nama was in with regard to her family) had something to do with the fact that she was a girl. One of my colleagues also suggested that the Panel would not have called Nama 'manipulative' if she had been a boy. If this was right, what effect could a gendered label of this kind have on a pupil's chances of being kept included, safe and emotionally supported? Could it be a cause of permanent exclusion?

LeBesco (2001) suggests that the 'power of language isn't purely abstract ... it enacts physical and material violence on our bodies' (76). The label 'manipulative' had the power to undermine the professionals' belief and understanding of the actual danger Nama was in to the point at which something terrible could happen to her. When I had visited the home some months before, her family had seated me on a big chair in their elaborately carpeted living room, her four sisters lined up on the sofa, neatly and conservatively dressed and with little makeup, some holding their babies, their small, old bent-over mother draped in black and smilingly serving me sweet tea in a glass. She did not speak English, so Nama's sisters conducted the meeting. Her two brothers stayed out of the way in the kitchen, talking loudly on mobile phones. Nama, in contrast to her sisters, had stamped angrily down the stairs wearing skinny jeans and with her long wavy hair stiff with gel, dark kohl makeup circling her eyes, her stiff, tense shoulders, tight lips and avoidant eye contact suggesting that she might be bubbling under with a quiet rage. She barely spoke, but her family told me that they were very worried about her and confused by her behaviour. I wondered whether understandings that Nama's family had about how she should comport herself as a (Muslim, Kurdish) girl were causing some kind of pressure that was affecting her success at school. In fact, and perhaps because she was represented as 'manipulative' rather than 'vulnerable', 'the power of language' did 'enact ... material violence' (LeBesco 2001: 76). Nama eventually disappeared amidst rumours that she had been married in Turkey, at the age of fifteen.

This chapter aims to discuss the pressure on young people that I argue is partially caused by normed understandings about gender identity (Osler and Vincent 2003), sexuality and 'aggressive behaviour'.

HABITUS, EMBODIMENT AND THE 'EXTENDED BODY'

Where do assumptions about gender come from? According to Hoy (1999), Bourdieu understands 'comportment as predominantly configured by the social structures (the "habitus") that individuals acquire through their upbringing in a particular culture or class' (4). Bourdieu's concept of 'habitus' can thus be employed to explain how a girl, for example, will have learned from her family and her culture from a very early age what the normed way of being a girl 'looks like'. In other words, in behaving 'like a girl' she may be demonstrating the 'internalization of the principles of a cultural arbitrary capable of perpetuating itself' (Bourdieu 1977: 31). In Nama's family, it seemed as if her conservatively-dressed older sisters demonstrated what I would call their 'gender-habitus' through their comportment.[5] Nama's aggression at school, her anger at home, and her non-conservative way of dressing were outside this norm. She was not embodying (a culturally influenced) 'gender-habitus' in the same way as her sisters. Csordas (1999) explains that '[e]mbodiment is an existential condition in which the body is the subjective source or intersubjective ground of experience' (143). So a person's 'comportment', whilst deriving from its habitus, can embody, or is made up of, the *experience* of that habitus. Blackman (2001) describes 'embodiment' as referring to 'the 'lived body'- the notion that the body and one's biological or even psychological processes are never lived by the individual in a pure and unmediated form' (210). In the development of an experienced, contested representative space, the extended body theory brings the concepts of the 'intersubjective ground of experience' (Csordas 1999) and the concept of the 'lived, mediated body' (Blackman 2001) together. Thus I would suggest that Nama's anger did not appear out of nowhere 'in a pure and unmediated form' (that is, it was not simply 'manipulative'), but was related to lived experiences involving her schooling, her personal thoughts about her own identity, her history, popular and family culture, and her gender.

In the context of thinking about schooling, I understand all this to mean that Nama had transgressed the expected, normed, and stereotyped way that teachers and other professionals expect a girl, for example, to embody 'girlness'. As Osler and Vincent (2003) explain, 'how we think about what it is to be male or female has a real impact ... on the ways in which we conceptualise and respond to 'problem behaviour' and identify those in need' (62). Nama may have been under-supported by the professionals because she was expected to behave like her sisters had when they attended the same school- conscientiously and without demanding attention.

There is a further link between the concept of embodiment and that of the 'extended body'. Assumptions about gender do not just affect the way people *talk about* children; they *act directly on the child*.[6] The relationship between 'embodiment' and the 'extended body', then, is that the 'extended body' describes the contested space within which the conflicting substance of arguments about 'appropriate' forms of embodiment - in other words, normed ways of being - are conducted. Nama's behaviour (lashing out in anger) embodied a way of being that did not align with the professionals' normed understanding of 'appropriate girl behaviour' that had been projected within Nama's extended body. Their representations of her and her own self-representations were in conflict. Because she was 'the excluded young person', the dominant discourse was privileged, and so Nama's self-representation became transgressive, causing her 'material violence'. Osler and Vincent (2003) have found that 'girls who ... suffer in silence and finally lash out may find themselves subject to disciplinary exclusion' (55). A contributing cause of permanent exclusion, then, could be seen to be professional and prejudiced assumptions about gender. And its effects here were the crystallising effects of that prejudice to the point at which a young girl's life was immeasurably changed for the worse.

I hope in this book to contribute to a discourse which aims to 'deflate the tendency to think that there can only be one set ... of normal, socially-normed ways to exist ...' (Hoy 1999:9; also see Butler 1999; Hall 1992). The extended body is where pronouncements on embodiment occur, and are contested, and gender, with its 'biological obviousness', is a particularly focussed lens through which to investigate this. The next section places the extended body theory within a current literature context in order to further explain how it builds on related concepts.

CURRENT UNDERSTANDINGS ON GENDER AND HETERONORMATIVITY IN SCHOOLS

The role of conceptions about gender in schools in England and Wales is broadly discussed in the literature. Boys are seen to be disadvantaged in a multitude of areas (for example, behaviour and attainment). Underpinning anxieties about the underperformance of boys, for example, the theory of 'the feminisation of education' is concerned with the idea that there are 'not enough' male teachers and that as a result, schools, curriculum and teaching and assessment styles are more appropriate to the learning styles of girls (Wright 2005). However, Osler and Vincent (2003) have said that 'the assertion that boys' 'underachievement' or poor behaviour is caused by the feminisation of teaching is not something which is supported by research' (23). In addition, as Lloyd (2005) explains, 'the behaviour of girls continues to be policed in ways that the behaviour of boys is not. They are ascribed labels such as 'deviant' and 'troublesome' by professionals ... sexuality is central to the definition of 'troublesome' in relation to girls' (5; see also Osler and Vincent 2003). These labels constitute pre-packaged tropes easily projected into the extended body.

The literature also addresses interactions between ethnicity and gender. The perception of 'troublesome girls' may be especially marked with regard to girls from some ethnic minority backgrounds; Wright (2005) has described 'teachers' construction of young black females as 'marginalised' and troublesome 'others'' (104) (see also Lloyd 2005; Francis 2005; Osler and Vincent 2003; George 2007). Boys, on the other hand, tend to 'dominate classroom space' (Francis 2005:10; see also Osler and Vincent 2003). However, boys in English education identified as African-Carribean/British were long the group least likely to acquire adequate GCSE grades (Gaine and George 1999; Wright 2005; Rendall and Stuart 2005).[7] More boys in England are excluded than girls, and a higher proportion of boys and girls from ethnic minority backgrounds are permanently excluded than British-born white pupils (Wright 2005; Timimi 2005; Wright et al 2000; Rendall and Stuart 2005). Wright (2005), writing on black femininities in school, explains that 'within educational contexts that are normatively gendered, classed and racialised, issues of embodiment can become problematic ...' (105). As George (2007) explains, citing hooks, 'black girls ... carry the dual yoke of sexism and racism' (134).

Socio-economic class also interacts with constructions of gendered behaviour (George 2007), with working-class girls, for example, often seen as 'over-sexualised and over-assertive, referred to variously by teachers as "little cows' and 'real bitches"' (Francis 2005:11). The 'cultural capital' which gives middle-class children an advantage in schooling (Bourdieu and Passeron 1977; see also chapter six) can be supplemented with the judicious delivery of resources, but gender normativity interrupts this process, too (discussed further in this chapter, below, and in chapter six). Osler and Vincent (2003) explain that professional assumptions about gender in school have a real impact 'on the ways in which service providers allocate resources' (62). They report that '[g]irls are neglected because boys are getting, or demanding, all the attention' (21).

Related to the concept of heteronormativity is that of compulsory heterosexuality. Epstein and Johnson (1998) look at the experiences of lesbian and gay people to try to 'understand sexualities more generally, encapsulating and focussing the ways in which they are played out ... within school situations' (7). They draw on Adrienne Rich's conception of compulsory heterosexuality and Judith Butler's ideas of gender performativity and 'the idea that gender is culturally understood through the notion of heterosexual attraction to those of the opposite gender/sex' (ibid: 4). They begin by suggesting that '... the idea of childhood sexual innocence inhibits attempts to alter ... the terrible and oppressive tangles which form part of child-adult relations in our culture' (ibid: 2), and that ' ... schools are important sites for the production and regulation of sexual identities both within the school and beyond' (ibid: 108). At the root of the discussion is an understanding that, as Sanders (2008) explains, 'our schools are profoundly institutionally heterosexist. All our schools assume everyone's heterosexual unless you put up your hand and wave' (4).

Whilst schools can be understood as heteronormative or heterosexist sites, it should be understood that '[s]chool-based identity production is never final, nor can it encompass the whole of (even sexual) life – but it can have lasting, ramifying consequences in individual lives none the less' (Epstein and Johnson 1998: 2). And within the Foucauldian theoretical framework of this book, it should be acknowledged that state regulation leaches into both schooling and sexuality (ibid: 5). For example, the state is evident in schools through the construction of the national curriculum; and in sexuality through the laws around civil partnership, rape, and abortion. In DePalma and Atkinson (2008), a transgendered woman 'illustrates the ways in which a key aspect of her identity (sex:boy) was established for her from birth through the simple act of filling out mandatory bureaucratic paperwork' (57). And descriptions of 'the school experiences of a gay boy ... and ... memories of failing to fit into sex/ gender norms poignantly illustrate what can happen when children find themselves in the process of developing pathologised identities' (33). These stories illuminate the embedding in governance of hegemonic, normative capillaries of power drawn through channels of heteronormativity, from policy-maker through bureaucrat to policy-implementation, penetrating into the extended bodies of teachers and pupils. Indeed, 'in schools ... the terms on which sexual identities are produced are heavily determined by power relations between teachers and taught, the dynamics of control and resistance' (ibid: 108).

In the ways in which power is manoeuvred, schools can be understood as a 'microcosm' of society (Lawrence-Lightfoot 2003: 216; also discussed below and in chapters two and six). Epstein and Johnson (1998) acknowledge that 'it is impossible to discuss sexuality ... out of the matrix of other social relations or to detach schools from other social structures' (109). Their references to state involvement in the intersections between schooling and sexualities go some way to illuminating the idea that heteronormativity functions as one of the capillaries of state power exercised on individuals in the school system. This book offers evidence that institutional prejudice is an expression of normative state power which can both be traced as underpinning instances of permanent exclusion and as being felt more keenly by excluded pupils. Epstein and Johnson (1998) also point out that state policy pressures 'bear most heavily on children who are oppressed in other aspects: as children with inclinations to same-sex desire, or as children disadvantaged in education already for reasons of class, ethnicity or race' (196).

The literature has identified schools as institutions that are prone to be run along lines that involve a normed and heteronormative version of what it means to behave 'like a girl' or 'like a 'boy' with specific variations according to perceived ethnicity and cultural/economic background. A focus on girls' disadvantages as well as on the heterosexist nature of schooling has been useful in revealing deep veins of institutional sexism and heteronormativity. It is important not to underestimate the effects a professional can have through their own expression of hegemonic heteronormativity. Epstein and Johnson (2008) explain that '[o]ne way of understanding the roles of those who work with young people as practitioners and knowledge producers is that they/we operate as another source of cultural narratives and identities for young people' (42).

This is not an impossible situation. School staff are capable of educating themselves about the needs of young people who challenge a heteronormative world view. Hinton (2008), for example, discusses a young transgender person who was identified as a girl at birth, subsequently diagnosed with gender identity disorder, and supported to enter secondary school as a boy, prompting special arrangements for uniform, toilets, and physical education. Hinton offers a blueprint for supporting young transgender people in schools at the end of her chapter (88). But this approach is not taken in Enway. In this chapter I would like to make a deeper investigation into the effects of heteronormativity on young people (identified as) boys and girls, and to consider its role in the causes and effects of permanent exclusion from school.

IN CONTEXT: THE REPRESENTATION AND EXPERIENCE OF GENDER IN ENWAY

The Extended Body's Vulnerability to Description at Points of Transition

Pupils at risk of or subject to a permanent exclusion can find themselves having to transition, often multiple times, between schools and/or alternative education placements. Sitting on plastic chairs in the office of a head of year or an inclusion manager, at the reintegration meeting - the initial interview where I often met pupils and parents for the first time, and which constituted *the moment of transition* into a new school - pupils and parents in Enway schools were asked to complete a stack of 'admission forms'. Balancing the forms uncomfortably on their knees whilst the inclusion manager often reclined behind the ubiquitous large battered desk (a symbol of his or her authority), parents and carers filled out the pupil's name and address, contact telephone numbers, birth date and assigned gender (the choices were limited to either 'male' or 'female'), ethnicity and home language. In a clearly hierarchised environment, then, the pupil was thus ascribed an institutional identity through this series of 'fixed' word-labels. Once again, young people were captured and fixed in documentation (Foucault 1977). At the same time, reinforcing the norming task of the institution, the interviewing teacher often described the pupil's new peers. For example, at a reintegration meeting for a new pupil at Knightsdown College, Enway's biggest mixed mainstream school, the head of year told the 'new boy', 'you know how it is - we have silly boys and bitchy girls here, like anywhere else. Just keep your head down and don't get in between friends.'

This kind of normative language about gender was evident in all the transitional stages I saw pupils travel through in Enway. It is problematic because it sets up a tension between 'who-he-should-be' (projected into the extended body) and 'who-he-considers-himself-to-be' (self-identified elements of the extended body). What if this boy did not want to be included in the category of 'silly boys'? And is he now going to assume all the girls in his tutor group are 'bitchy'? Even in this instance of 'friendly advice', the norming procedure was unremitting.

Enway's 'Hard to Place' Pupil Placement Panel represented another of the transition stages through which a pupil at risk of or subject to a permanent exclusion had to travel and at which she or he had to be described and identified in order to be placed at a new school. Names, year-groups and gender identity were reiterated here in the paperwork; but in the absence of the pupil and family, Panel members often also described behaviour (one of the elements of the 'extended body') without the social restraint that might be expected if the family members were present. And behaviour was often described in relation to normative ideas about the appropriate embodiment of gender.

For example, April, a Year 9[8] pupil at risk of permanent exclusion, had been attending Newhall School and had been experiencing some difficulties with managing her anger in class. Her mother had taken her to the doctor and she had been told that this anger was symptomatic evidence of an extreme form of pubescent pre-menstrual syndrome (PMS). At school, April had been told that she would have to accept a managed move or be permanently excluded.[9] 'She has not very supportive parents', announced one of the head teachers, 'and she is a person who puts herself in trouble. There is some sort of collusion that goes on between April and her mum.[10] She's a big abusive girl, I mean she's big!'

'She may have the right to choose [her school placement]', responded another head teacher who had never met April, 'but she will cause major problems at mainstream.'[11] April's behaviour record showed that she had lost her temper with teachers a few times, and had been in a couple of small fights with other girls. This is a good example of the normative expectations of girls' 'appropriate' behaviour often exhibited at the Enway Panel; boys referred for placement who were at risk of permanent exclusion always had more than a couple of fights and a bit of a temper tantrum on their behaviour logs. April was placed at a new school, Enway Valley, and I planned a reintegration meeting for her, wondering if I would meet a 'big abusive girl', as reported.

When I met April for the interview a few days later, I saw that she was actually quite average in size. She was not abusive in the meeting, either, but smiled shyly, hiding behind her blonde hair. She talked about the stress of being at her old school; I knew that the school was going into 'special measures' due to an unsatisfactory OFSTED report; teacher morale was low; staff were struggling to maintain control of the classes, and there had been many reports of bullying.

A few weeks later, April was asked to leave Enway Valley due to 'rudeness'. As a result of the failed managed move, following the established protocol, she was then permanently excluded from her original school, Newhall. However, she finally settled down at another school, and at the time of writing was still attending, with no exclusions or fights on her record.

April's story exemplifies the connection between the embodiment of gender identity, and the 'extended body', with its vulnerability to being represented through the imagined descriptions of others. Her angry behaviour at Newhall School and her 'rudeness' at Enway Valley were possibly in part a result of the chaotic environment at her previous school. However, whilst April's behaviour was being pathologised, attention was distracted from the institution's problems (Sellman 2002; Slee 1995; Foucault 1977; see also chapter three). April was represented and pathologised through her gendered diagnosis of PMS and her description as a 'big abusive girl' exhibiting transgressive (aggressive) behaviour.

As Crozier and Anstiss (1995 in Lloyd-Smith and Davies) explain, 'boys are described in terms of their behaviour and academic performance, while girls are described in terms of their appearance and sexuality' (36). Not actually 'big', and despite medical and contextual evidence providing the Panel with the choice to adopt a reasonable explanation, April had been seen to have transgressed acceptable parameters for a girl, and her physical body had then been described in terms of an instance of her behaviour - her extended (imagined, describable) body. April and her mum travelled through three transitions - two reintegration interviews and a permanent exclusion - challenging the projected representation of her as a 'big, abusive girl' before she was able to settle down at her final school.

The 'Trouble' with Girls...

Perhaps because of abiding understandings identified in the literature about 'the relationship between young women and sexuality and the ways in which this relationship may be constructed as 'trouble'' (Lloyd 2005:191; see also Osler and Vincent 2003), the Pupil Placement Panel delegates were particularly prone to adopting gendered narratives about pupils' extended bodies. This really became a concern when they were discussing instances of non-consensual sexual contact and sexual aggression between young people. In particular, as Osler and Vincent (2003) suggest, there is to be found a 'general 'boys will be boys' discourse among professionals working with young people' (26).

For example, a fourteen-year-old boy was discussed at the Panel following his permanent exclusion from a school in a neighbouring district for, as the brief paperwork described, 'touching a girl's bottom'. There was a hint of male sniggering at this, and one head teacher at the Panel asked whether this was *'just* that he touched a girl's bottom, or more?' By the word *'just'*, it could be argued, the boy's behaviour was normatively validated as acceptable. However, when a girl's behaviour later at the same Panel meeting was described by one of the delegates: 'She won't leave the boys alone, pulling their trousers down …'; a (female) head teacher querulously responded, 'we have evidence of inappropriate sexualised behaviour! What assessments are being made of her as not a victim, but a perpetrator? A psychiatric assessment [is needed] in Enway Mental Hospital School!' This pupil, Rachel, was discussed at the Panel several times, offering plenty of opportunities for the delegates to pronounce upon conceptions of her behaviour in relation to her gender identity and her sexuality. She was seen as *dangerous* in terms of her sexuality (and described as 'wild' by one of her teachers when discussing the pulling down of boys' trousers); *at great risk* in terms of the physical features of her gender identity (of rape as a gang initiation strategy) and as *vulnerable* in terms of her gender-role (as a carer for her mother and baby siblings). It is of course not acceptable for any pupil to non-consensually pull down the trousers of another. But the range of consequences available to such behaviour span from a simple verbal redirection or one hour detention to a fixed-term or permanent exclusion. I read the Pupil Placement Panel's acute reading of the case as framed by the 'fact' that Rachel was 'a girl'.

Osler and Vincent (2003) have noted that girls are often discussed in terms of their 'promiscuity', pointing out that 'it is uncommon to find references to boys' sexual activity in professional discourses relating to youth disaffection' (24). In projecting a pathologised version of sexuality into Rachel's extended body to explain her behaviour, the Panel directed attention away from any possible institutional causes as to her difficulties in school (see Sellman 2002; Slee 1995; Foucault 1977 in chapter three). Osler and Vincent (2003) state that there is a 'widespread tendency to judge girls' behaviour more harshly than that of boys when they are seen to move beyond what are regarded as acceptable feminine norms' (25). The gendered territory of young people's extended bodies was often imagined, described, judged, and represented in this way by school staff and Panel delegates.

One of the causes, then, of the permanent exclusion from school of girls such as Nama, April and Rachel, could be said to be a general demonisation of behaviour applied to those girls who are represented as transgressing the 'normal' embodiment of gender, and a set of higher standards of behaviour for girls within a frame of institutionalised heteronormativity.

Single and Mixed-Sex Schools

April was moved to a single sex school because it was felt by Panel delegates that she may have been able to concentrate more easily on her studies in that environment. Girls are said to need a special space in which they can learn, free from what has been identified as the distraction of and dominance by boys (Francis 2005:9; Osler and Vincent 2003: 21). In looking at this, and at the institutionalised treatment of gender in educational contexts, it is telling to pay closer attention to the differences between single- and mixed-sex schools. It is also important to note here that heteronormativity, and the disadvantages it affords to girls in a schooling environment, can also have the effect of disadvantaging boys.

Osler and Vincent (2003) have reported that 'research in a boys' school indicated that students saw a direct link between the relatively harsh discipline imposed by certain male teachers and the violent and anti-social school behaviour of significant numbers of students' (23). This was evident in Enway. At Forrest Boys, the only boys' school in the district, a senior member of staff told me that she had lived 'in a constant state of shock' when she had first started teaching there. She explained that she had worked in girls' or mixed schools before that and that her shock had been at the physical way in which the Forrest teachers treated the pupils. They would casually slap pupils on the back of the head as they went past in the corridor; were usually less than sympathetic if a pupil hurt himself; and if the head teacher found a pupil who was 'bustin' low',[12] he would shout his objection and then pick him up by the waistband and shake him down into his trousers. I would argue that the nature of unmistakeably being labelled 'a boy', with all the normed expectations of 'boyness' - for example, ability to withstand physical hardship - is an inexorable result of attending a boys' school. Because of the 'power of language' (LeBesco 2001:76), this sexual-difference label of 'boy' 'enacts physical and material violence on bodies' (ibid).

The 'toughness' ascribed to Forrest Boys' School was compounded by the fact that as the only boys' school in Enway it became a repository for those permanently excluded for sexual harassment or assault against girls in Enway's mixed schools. In essence, they had been 'banned' from the company of girls, or permanently excluded from the presence of girls because of some danger to do with their sexual difference: because they were boys. But only one of the boys in this situation was offered psychotherapy to help him learn self-management techniques. The rest of them had not been explicitly supported in addressing their interactions with girls, and were left free to roam the parks, cinemas and parties of Enway after school and at the weekends.

In contrast to the single boys' school, there were three girls' schools in Enway. Enway Valley School for Girls had taken several of the 'vulnerable' girls at risk of exclusion from the nearest mixed school. Because of gendered violence at these girls' original school (discussed later in the chapter), in existing as a single-sex environment, Enway Valley, a small mainstream school, found itself being expected to provide automatic succour for large numbers of 'troubled' girls.

Because the experiences of single-sex schools in Enway appear to have presented particular issues with regard to mopping up the 'gendered behaviour' that occurred in mixed schools, it is of interest to consider what was happening at the mixed schools. Gaine and George (1999) explain the history of the rationale behind the setting up of such schools, and this may illuminate the roots of some of the current issues raised here:

> [E]arly supporters of co-educational schooling (in the 1920s) saw this form of schooling in terms of the many advantages it held for boys: a reduction in homosexuality amongst the boys; boys' behaviour would be less rough because of the 'civilising influence' of girls; the replication of family-like relationships would contribute to bringing about healthier marriages.

131

By the 1970s, mixed schools were seen to be the most appropriate option in terms of gender equality, 'giving girls the benefits of the kind of education more often reserved for boys (as well as giving the boys the benefits of the girls' 'civilising influence') …'(ibid). But by 2005, in Enway, for reasons concerned with religion, safety (discussed below), and attainment, girls' parents were more likely to want them to attend a girls' school. Partly because of this, and compounding the disadvantages afforded girls in such environments, mixed school populations only constituted between one third and one quarter girls.

In Enway, and despite these hopes for girls' 'civilising influence', almost all of the mixed schools were, during the period of my fieldwork, the sites of incidents of sexual aggression against girls, occasionally resulting in the permanent exclusion of the (almost exclusively, but not always) boys responsible-[13] many of whom were placed at the mixed Pupil Referral Unit (PRU). The Panel was often reluctant to steer 'vulnerable' girls towards the PRU. New Start, the alternative education provision for those deemed 'too difficult' for the PRU, was also mixed, but mainly populated with boys. So girls who had experienced male sexual aggression and who were non-attenders or who displayed angry and /or aggressive behaviour themselves were often designated 'vulnerable in the presence of boys' and placed at the mainstream girls' schools. The problem with this was that in the two smaller mainstream girls' schools, girls were less likely to have access to learning mentors, as there was less funding available for such services. Being placed in a mainstream school, they also missed out on the chance of the 'smaller class sizes and positive relationships with teachers' (Pomeroy 2000: 119) offered at most alternative education provisions, which although exclusionary in terms of mainstream education and reductive in terms of GCSE choices, were useful if they were to gain the confidence necessary to offer a contention for power in the contested space of their own gendered extended bodies (see chapter four).

As I described in chapter three, Anzaldua (1987) conceives of borderland spaces as places 'wherever two or more cultures edge each other' (26). However, with a caveat on the risk of essentialising or dichotomising the 'group experiences' of 'girls' and 'boys', I think it is useful to understand mixed-gender schools, where fairly established groups of boys and girls intersect, as generating a similar 'borderland' experience. Anzaldua (1987) describes her experience of being a member of the non-dominant population as one of choosing to 'abnegate'- to stay quiet and suffer- or to make a choice to 'take control' (43). If this framework of existence is transposed onto the experience of girls (who are usually in the minority) within a mixed school, it is possible to see that those girls who are experiencing difficulties may be pushed into either abnegation- disengagement and truancy- or into a wobbly adolescent version of 'taking control'- which may result in behaviour which is seen as 'too aggressive' (transgressive) for a girl. Nama, described above, tried first one and then the other of these strategies, without success.

Whilst each has its own set of advantages and disadvantages, an overview of the effects of mixed and single-sex schooling in Enway illustrates some of the weaknesses in the 'inclusive education system' and some of the causes and effects of permanent exclusion from school. A single-sex boys' school, for example, can 'brutalise' boys through a normalisation of more aggressive discipline strategies (Osler and Vincent 2003), producing boys' behaviour more likely to result in exclusion. At the same time, it can become the local repository for all boys excluded due to sexual aggression in a mixed school, adding to its brutalising environment. A mixed school can disadvantage and exclude girls who are seen as transgressive if they raise their voices to try to be heard against the louder group of boys. And a single-sex girls' school, in which excluded girls might be placed for what the Panel represented as pathologically sexualised behaviour in a mixed school, may be less likely to provide them with the range of choices and supports they need to succeed. It is suggested that these problems are not inherently to do with the schools being designated as single- or mixed- sex, but to do with the ways in which staff responded according to their perceptions of gender in these environments.

Choosing GCSEs: The Gendered Reproduction of Class

One of the effects of permanent exclusion from school can be a vastly reduced set of GCSE and BTEC choices (discussed further in chapter six), and this is only exacerbated by institutionalised heteronormativity. Collins et al (2000) in Osler and Vincent (2003) suggest that a 'full understanding of gender justice in education requires a consideration of ... the value assigned by the labour market' (29) to the qualifications students take with them when they leave school. Thus Bourdieu's (1977) conception of the reproduction of class in education processes[14] can be applied to the gendered 'choices' girls and boys make with regard to the vocational and/or academic courses they take in Years 10 and 11. So in addition to a reduction in available support, the Enway pupils who found themselves inadvertently in single-sex schools (due to an exclusion or a managed move) were usually offered a reduced and gendered choice in terms of curriculum, with just one of the three girls' schools providing encouragement for girls to do engineering- or construction-related courses, and Forrest Boys' declining to offer its pupils 'Hair and Beauty' or any kind of training related to a care vocation.

Mixed schools also exerted a heteronormative pressure on excluded young people in terms of their GCSE choices. During reintegration meetings with pupils who were moving schools in the middle of Year 9 or during Year 10 - at the stage where they needed to choose their GCSEs - I noticed that the mixed schools tended to funnel their lower-achieving[15] girls into 'Animal Care', 'Hair and Beauty', and 'Social Care' vocational courses, whilst their lower-achieving boys tended to be directed towards 'Construction' and 'Public Service'[16] tracks. A girl who wanted to take a construction course would of course be verbally encouraged to do so, but as exemplified in an enormous 'Work Experience Week' display at one of the Enway schools, featuring photographs of girls blow-drying hair in pink tabards and boys laying bricks and wearing blue overalls, she would find herself transgressing normed boundaries, and the task of building the self-esteem and courage it would take to do this constitutes a barrier (or a 'border': Pomeroy 2000) in itself. In any case, as Francis (2005) has identified, 'tendencies in mixed-sex classrooms [include] ... the ways in which some boys monopolise physical and verbal space, and the ways in which girls tend to defer to boys' (9), so a girl taking a construction course would need to be able to challenge these difficulties as well. Similarly, I did not during my research come across a boy who voiced a desire to join the Hair and Beauty or Social Care cohorts- although some heads of year joked about this in reintegration interviews with their new male pupils, invoking a mocking chauvinist humour and ridiculing any boy's genuine desire to gain these skills.[17]

Reintegration meetings for pupils who came with a behaviour log full of transgressions were always focussed more on the behaviour (the past) than on GCSE choices (the future), and the 'hmm, so what classes can we squeeze you into?' part of the meeting was often rushed, crammed as it was into the last few minutes. I often struggled to interject on behalf of the pupil to promote their views on the choices. Young people's voices were conspicuous in their absence during these discussions.[18] During these meetings I would ask the student a question about their GCSE choices, they would open their mouth and take a breath before answering, and that small space of time the head of year or parent would regularly answer for them. Parents often agreed to their children taking courses which would lead them to a similar career as their own. Because of this, gendered curriculum 'choices' were more likely to be pushed through without the extensive weeks-long period of guided research, parents' meetings and career consultations afforded to most pupils who were making their Key Stage 4[19] decisions in Enway.

Thus through the effects of the transitional process undergone by pupils at risk of or subject to a permanent exclusion, young people who were already disadvantaged by these circumstances were directed even more firmly than their peers to reproduce their parents' economic experiences, usually in gendered terms- an aspect of their habitus. Being given a place in the family business can be a beneficial outcome.

But the GCSE choice procedure would be more useful for an already-disempowered pupil if it provided the opportunity to think through the options.

Compulsory Heterosexuality: Sexuality, Gender, and Identity

I partially ascribe the gendered pressures around GCSE 'choices' described in the section above to the effects of 'compulsory heterosexuality' (Francis 2005:14). This device of institutional norming refers to the ways in which young people are required to exist according to stereotyped gender expectations. It exerts its own specific pressures on those young people who find themselves transgressing the boundaries of what is expected of them in terms of their gender identity. When a young person in Enway who is permanently excluded, or is at risk of being excluded, has a less well-understood sexuality-identity profile (such as 'gay'),[20] the matter tends to be ignored, invisible, or pathologised (Osler and Vincent 2003). This is an example of one of the main ideas emerging from this book: that permanent exclusion from school can, through the crystallising pressure of its status as a critical incident, both exacerbate and be exacerbated by existing institutional prejudices.

During the years of my fieldwork, I came across just three cases where there was a sexuality-identity component to the case as well as a risk of permanent exclusion. This in itself is another of the 'gaps' and 'silences' (Blackman 2001:8) I thought it important to pay attention to, as it suggests a problem in terms of what young people feel safe to identify in themselves. With around four hundred case-files in my battered grey filing cabinet, I should statistically have met many more young people who identified as gay or transgendered. If we consider the extended body, where self-identified aspects compete with projected representations, this is of concern. However, the three cases I did see and which are described below do raise significant issues.

The Appledown 'Lesbians' Vicky transitioned into Year 7 at Appledown Estate Girls' School without coming to the immediate attention of her tutor or head of year. She probably should have done, as it was subsequently discovered that at primary school she had been barely able to tolerate the classroom environment, spending most of her time sitting in a corner of the main office, helping with small photocopying jobs. Vicky had been experiencing a lengthy conflict with her mother, who had become a lone parent at an early age, and had developed great difficulties in managing her anger. Her primary school had neglected to forge supportive secondary school transition links with the Appledown inclusion staff: best practice where a pupil is identified as needing such support. When she met a charismatic older girl from Year 8 at Appledown, Vicky was distracted from the tenuous quietude[21] she had developed as a coping strategy at the enormous new school. The pair would sometimes run up and down the corridors together, truanting from class and shrieking as they ran away from any teacher who tried to calm them. The final straw, for the school, came when the older girl pulled her trousers down and 'mooned' at one of the senior staff-members through the front window of the main entrance, then grabbed Vicky in a warm embrace, pushed her against a wall in the reception area and kissed her. 'We're lesbians', they shrieked, holding hands and running away down the corridor as the Head of Inclusion bore down on them.

The first thing that happened following this incident was that the girls were separated. The inclusion manager explained that this was imperative to avoid further 'harm' to Vicky, and that, being younger, she could not have been held responsible for the 'disturbing' behaviour exhibited by the two. The older girl was sent away to an alternative education provision, and Vicky was also sent to be educated off-site in a 'respite' programme for pupils on long fixed-term exclusions. An urgent referral was written for her to the 'At Risk Teens Intervention' (ARTI), an intensive mental health project usually reserved for aggressive and sexually violent young people at risk of re-offending and incarceration. Despite a history in Enway of chronic problems in the obtaining of such services, and demonstrating the sheer power of institutional heteronormativity, Vicky's referral was taken without delay. As mentioned in the introduction to this chapter, the frequency of interagency professional collusion on the basis of heteronormativity in the context of a usually conflicted environment is testament to its institutional power. I attended meetings with Vicky's ARTI case-worker, a family therapist, and discussed the case four times before, frustrated, I asked whether any work had been done on Vicky's initial foray into her self-identification as a lesbian. I had hoped that this would be mentioned without me having to raise it, worrying that perhaps my own (lesbian) sexuality would undermine my reputation in this case as a reasonable professional. The ARTI therapist looked flustered and then said that if I thought it was important, she would raise it.

I was not concerned with whether Vicky was 'actually' a lesbian or not. But I was concerned that her claim had been first described as 'disturbing' and then ignored by those in the best position to support her with it. Blundering into a young person's extended body and labelling the embodiment of sexuality to be found there 'disturbed' effectively renders that aspect of her identity 'invalid'. Normative lines had been drawn in the contested space of her extended body.

Bizarre, disturbed and weird Kate's social worker referred her to the Pupil Placement Panel at the beginning of the 2007–2008 school year, telling me that she was unsure whether mainstream school was appropriate. I asked why, and the social worker said that Kate's behaviour was 'bizarre; disturbed'.

I asked for more details, and the social worker haltingly said that this girl 'was saying she is a boy stuck in a girl's body; she looks really weird'. I asked why she was saying that Kate looked 'weird' and the social worker told me that she had shaved her head. I took a deep breath and asked whether the social worker had considered the idea that Kate might be exploring a transgender identity. She told me that this was something she had not thought about. I asked if there were any other issues to discuss, and the social worker told me as an afterthought that Kate had been deemed to be a threat to younger children as she had threatened to take her new baby brother to the canal and drown him.

By mentioning Kate's embodiment of a possibly transgendered identity first, it seemed to me that the social worker had seen this aspect of the case as more worthy of the 'bizarre' and 'disturbed' labels than the threat to drown the baby brother. Kate was placed in foster care in another district shortly after this, so I never had the chance to meet her/him. Seeking to investigate and challenge the apparent inexorability of sexual difference, this young person had transgressed the normed borders of 'acceptable behaviour'. Kate's mental state (distressed), intent, attitude, and behaviour (for example, the shaving of her/his head), being conducted as they were both on the physical body and inside the porous skin of the extended body's contested space, became vulnerable to representation and invalidation as 'bizarre'.

Over my dead body... Michael came through the Enway 'Hard to Place' Pupil Placement Panel twice. He was first placed at Cherry Tree School, and I heard many discussions about him before I met him. He did not do very well at Cherry Tree. He was engaged in a several weeks-long period of truancy when I was sucked into a brief corridor exchange in November 2007 with the head teacher (Mrs McMillan) and inclusion manager (Mr Stansfield) at Cherry Tree, while I was hustling from one reintegration meeting to another. I recorded the exchange in my field-notes book:

Buttonholed by Mrs McMillan.

Mrs McMillan: Michael Cornwell. Over my dead body is he coming back here.

Me: That's crystal clear.

Mr Stansfield: He was close to ... close to...

Mrs McMillan: he was close to being killed by one of us!

November 17th 2007

I remembered this conversation, and a few days later at the Panel I was able to inform the delegates that Michael was likely to be permanently excluded from Cherry Tree if he returned there from his spell of truancy. I had heard Mrs McMillan call Michael 'a thug' on several occasions. I was looking forward to meeting him.

Michael was given a place at Forrest Boys, and I sent the necessary papers through to arrange the reintegration meeting. I met Michael for the first time as he hastened with his mother through the sliding glass double doors into the Forrest Boys atrium. He was a heavy-set boy with a shaved head, much bigger than most boys of his age. In his paperwork he was described as 'Caribbean British'. He caught my eye and his face cracked into a broad and sweet smile, and I shook his plump, sweaty hand before leading the family down to the inclusion manager's office.

'She's really nice', I told them in my usual pre-meeting pep-talk. 'Just remember, this is kind of like an interview, so smile, use eye contact, say you want a fresh start, OK?' Part of my job was to help the family present themselves as a desirable package, to avoid an instant negative judgment. It helped to smooth the transition, giving pupils the best possible chance of a successful reintegration during the first tentative few weeks. We sat down and the inclusion manager asked Michael how he was. He smiled broadly, looked briefly at me, mentally rehearsing his answer, and then told her he was fine, and that he wanted a fresh start.

On hearing Michael speak for the first time, I caught my breath, adrenaline flushing my chest. Csordas (1999) explains that the body is 'now understood as a tool for research' (149), and that one can take a 'twinge in the gut as an indicator of inner accuracy of interpretation' (ibid). Blackman and Venn (2010) describe something similar as 'an ineffable quality that was felt rather than seen' (24). Using this methodological tool, I reflected on the idea that perhaps my 'gaydar'[22] had been alerted. Michael's voice was high and light and his hand-gestures were exaggerated, soft and fluttering, both unexpected and thrown into contrast by his stolid, squared body. They made him look and sound 'camp'.[23] I caught the eye of the inclusion manager. She did not appear to have noticed what I had noticed, although I considered her to be an open-minded and inclusive professional, and I knew he had charmed her with his smile.

After a troubled few weeks at Forrest Boys, Michael eventually moved to Fresh Start, an alternative education provision, because he was annoying his teachers, fidgeting and talking on his mobile phone in class. He could not seem to focus on his work. But his placement at Forrest Boys did not fail because he was dangerously disruptive. It was just felt that due to a lack of focus, the school was concerned that 'he was unable to access the curriculum'. Note that the school did not say 'we are unable to support Michael to access the curriculum', but chose the within-child narrative instead. His truancy habit also made the school's attendance records look bad.

I later asked several of the people in Enway who had previously worked with him if they knew whether or not he was 'working through identity issues'- local authority and education code for 'thinking about coming out as gay'. All looked at me with mild surprise, not seeming particularly interested in the idea. Michael subsequently came out as gay following a presentation at Fresh Start by an LGBT[24] youth service. Struggling with his sexuality/identity might explain some of what was behind his lack of focus, and could at least have warranted investigation before he 'failed' to integrate into two mainstream schools. Butler (1999:147) argues that heteronormativity, or 'compulsory heterosexuality', is so pervasive as to prevent observers- such as two (excellent) inclusion managers and a head teacher, in Michael's case - from seeing the possibility of someone (especially a black boy described as 'a thug', with all its masculine overtones) as being gay.

Osler and Vincent (2003) suggest that those 'whose identities do not include being heterosexual may experience ... isolation and stress within schools which fail to acknowledge other identities ... such experiences are likely to be exclusionary in outcome' (55). The stories of Vicky, Kate, and Michael, above, challenge school and other professionals' heteronormative comprehensions of sexuality. In all cases, the young people were displaying emotionally distressed behaviour that could have lead the professionals working with them to at least *offer* information and support on issues of sexuality and sexual/gendered identity. In all three cases, I could not find one other professional who seriously considered that these young people might be gay or transgendered- among them, a social worker, a family therapist, a head teacher, and two inclusion managers.

This section has addressed the effects of institutionalised gender prejudice and heteronormativity on the causes of permanent exclusion from school, and on the propensity for permanent exclusion to exacerbate the experience of prejudice. The next section looks at the interaction between this and the gendered violence between young people which can also lead to instances of permanent exclusion from school.

Sexualised Behaviour; Sexual Aggression and Violence

Behaviour represented as being 'sexualised' formed the basis of the discussion around several of the cases brought to the Pupil Placement Panel: the Appledown 'lesbians', for example, and Rachel, who was discussed earlier in this chapter as needing to go into the Enway Mental Hospital School for pulling down a boy's trousers. In November 2007, another pupil, Mahad, was permanently excluded for a serious sexual assault,[25] resulting in a court case and an eighteen month control order with the Youth Offending Team.

Further cases of sexual aggression and violence began to arise in Enway as 2007 turned into 2008. In March a 16 year old girl was discussed at the Pupil Placement Panel. She had been permanently excluded for using her mobile phone to video and subsequently post online footage of a sexual assault by a boy from her year group on a much younger girl. And during a discussion around whether another girl should go to a mixed school, one of the head teachers cautioned, 'we all know that some of the Enway Boyz[26] are heavily involved in rape as an initiation ... is she vulnerable ...?' At one of the other mixed schools, the head teacher had been forced to resign, the behaviour management situation becoming so bad that scores of girls were truanting following threats of rape by boys at the school. Several of the boys were finding themselves on the sex offenders register as a result. Most of these young people were either permanently excluded or at risk of being excluded. I and many of my colleagues felt that the situation was out of control; we felt out of our depth. We could not understand it. Why was all this happening in Enway?

Sexual and Domestic Violence: Horizontal Violence

The sexual violence I encountered in Enway schools during my work there seems to me to be a form of what Paulo Freire (1970) calls the 'horizontal violence' (44) (see chapter six) demonstrated by people living within an oppressed society. According to this theory, oppressed people tend to try to adjust their hierarchies and to assert their self-worth in struggles with each other, unable to strike out at those in power. I would suggest that sexual violence within the school context constitutes a version of this 'horizontal violence', its sexual nature instigated and exacerbated by gendered inequities.[27]

Examples of the inequities of horizontal gendered violence include the high proportion of socio-economically disadvantaged boys being excluded or moved; the invisibility of pupils' lesbian, gay and transgendered identity issues in professional discussions about support planning; the gender-stereotyped vocational course 'choices' available to excluded and managed-moved pupils; the poverty experienced by children living with unemployed parents or single mothers (Ridge 2005:24); and the great proliferation of domestic violence in Enway witnessed by the population of young people who were at risk of or subject to a permanent exclusion and discussed at the Pupil Placement Panel.

Almost all of the cases I worked on which involved an incident of permanent exclusion for violent behaviour featured domestic violence towards mothers by their male partners. One boy, Will, whose mother, Sandy, was in this situation, started at Knightsdown College, the largest mixed comprehensive school in Enway, after she was 'persuaded' to take him out of a school in the neighbouring district of Prosper because he was at risk of permanent exclusion for fighting. She had been through a very serious period of domestic violence, including several hospitalisations; Will's father was now in prison, but Sandy told me that she was still deeply affected by what she had been through. Like many of the other mothers I worked with in Enway who had been subjected to domestic violence, Sandy explained that she felt unable to rouse the strength she needed to draw firm boundaries at home, and told me that she felt very guilty about what she saw as failing to protect her children from witnessing the violence. For example, she was unable to insist that Will took his diabetes medication, and had a difficult time standing her ground around issues such as homework and getting the children up and ready in time to get the bus to school.

One of the causes of permanent exclusion from school, then, might be seen to be gendered violence that emerges under pressure of societal inequity and is then reproduced in schools. Often already disadvantaged through domestic violence, some young people, through being excluded, then feel the exacerbated pressure of institutional heteronormativity. Schools can thus be seen to 'in vivid microcosm ... mirror societal priorities, values, and conflicts [and] ... magnify and intensify them' (Lawrence-Lightfoot 2003: 216; also discussed in chapters two and six).

INTERACTIONS BETWEEN GENDER, ETHNICITY AND CULTURE

Having considered gendered violence as 'horizontal violence' (Freire 1970: 44) on the basis that the men and women involved existed within the same class, it is necessary to also consider it as non-horizontal violence.

The wide prevalence of domestic violence towards women in Enway permanent exclusion cases points to a general state of disempowerment amongst mothers in these families. Anzaldua (1987) discusses these issues, describing the difficulties of existing as a woman across worlds: a 'borderland' person, a *mestiza* blend of

Texan, Mexican, and indigenous. She graphically explains the compounding effects of being both of a minority less privileged ethnicity and of a less empowered gender. She writes,

> Internal strife results in insecurity and indecisiveness ... the *mestiza* faces the dilemma of the mixed breed: which collectivity does the daughter of a darkskinned mother listen to? ... But it is not enough to shout ... questions, challenging patriarchal, white conventions. A counterstance locks one into a duel of oppressor and oppressed; locked in mortal combat ... both are reduced to a common denominator of violence.

100

Anzaldua's (1987) description of the 'internal strife' experienced by the *mestiza* explains a possible source of some girls' aggressive behaviour at school. It approximates to my understanding of the struggle within the extended body experienced by some girls described as 'minority ethnic'. This struggle, I would suggest, results from conflicting normative institutional understandings about the girls' ethnicity and their gender identity (further addressed in chapter seven). And in concert with Anzaldua's concern over 'which collectivity does the daughter of a darkskinned mother listen to?' (ibid), Wright (2005) explains that

> [e]xploring gender differentiation in the context of discourses of 'race', in specific relation to black female experiences of schooling, produces a paradox whereby gendering the experiences of schooling of black females serves both to detract from essentialising conceptions of blackness, while simultaneously reifying more complex forms in which blackness can be further scrutinised as 'other'.

105

Thus I do not want here to essentialise a common 'othered' experience of 'Caribbean-British girls' or 'Somali boys', or of any other person, but to describe the effects of the institutionalised essentialising that occurs wherever a pupil's educational career is condensed into the discussions surrounding instances of actual or threatened permanent exclusion. Osler and Vincent (2003) state that '[i]n the case of black girls the forms of exclusion may be further complicated by elements of racial harassment and by differential responses from teachers, operating within racial frames of reference' (55; see also Blair 2001). Evidence from the field and the literature (for example, Francis 2005:11) suggests that young Muslim women in schools who exhibit anger or aggression may attract more negative attention from teachers and other professionals because of assumptions about the normed behaviour of Muslim girls. Nama, the Iraqi Kurdish girl described as 'manipulative' and discussed above, whose experience of schooling, gendered expectations and cultural/ethnic background could be seen as having intersected with devastating results, was initially permanently excluded from school after she explosively lost her temper in the classroom. Her behaviour had been seen as simply not fitting within the expected framework- she transgressed the institutionally normed view of 'girl' and of 'Muslim girl' and was thus outside the accepted framework for inclusion, rendering her into 'the domain of abject beings' (Butler 1993:3; Weiss 1999:50): permanently excluded.

Mahad

The story of Mahad illustrates further gender/culture interactions affecting permanently excluded pupils, specifically related to the experiences first and second generation immigrant families often undergo in their bid to maintain links with their home culture and relatives. Mahad's mother had gone to visit her family in Turkey when he was only five years old. He stayed with his mother's boyfriend while she was away and at the weekends went to visit his father. She had been away for several weeks when one day she called his father's house down a crackling phone-line.

'Are you sitting down?' she asked Mahad's father. 'I have something to tell you.' Mahad's father cried as she explained that for the past few weeks she had not been visiting family at home, but was in prison in the North of England having been caught by customs officials bringing opium into the country. She was short of money and had been pressed to carry the drug in return for the paying off of some of her debts. It had been difficult to refuse her male relatives. In a demonstration of the rift between school and other professional services, whoever was responsible for the social and family issues raised by the imprisonment of Mahad's mother had failed to alert his primary school to the situation. Without support, his school behaviour declined markedly following her 'disappearance'. And seven years later, when she came out of prison and tried to resume her place in his life, Mahad, now in secondary school, began to behave with a new lack of respect towards female class-mates and women teachers. Without the support and empathy to discover Mahad's own version of events, the situation escalated slowly over the next two years, culminating in his permanent exclusion for sexual assault. Mahad's father told me that he was 'so ashamed'- not of Mahad, but of having to attend school meetings to discuss all of these things. He had felt it unnecessary to ask for help with his son. The fact that his wife had led the family into what he saw as a shameful situation immobilised him. And the motherless Mahad's own needs were subsumed under a headlong rush towards a permanent exclusion exacerbated by teachers' assumptions about the inexorability of the disrespect Turkish boys are expected to have for (white) female teachers. This is perhaps a result of what Wright et al. (2000) describe as 'how different racial masculinities and femininities are produced[28] in relation to the racial and gendered background of teachers' (13). Mahad's teachers had not appeared to have looked any deeper than the fact that he was a Turkish boy and therefore his behaviour was seen as inevitable. His voice was completely absent from his permanent exclusion paperwork. Because of this, he had not received an assessment of his needs or support to develop the strategies necessary to cope with and stay included at school.

Questions of agency might be raised here: Mahad himself did commit sexual assault. But his identity, expressed and defined within his extended body, was subject to pressures from outside himself. So, in Mahad's case, some of the causes of permanent exclusion could be said to be a lack of privilege given to his version of events; institutional prejudice - here, institutional sexism and racism; and a failure in interagency professional collaboration when his mother was jailed. The effect on Mahad of the critical-incident permanent exclusion was to further crystallise and focus the impacts these problems on him.

Mahad's case demonstrates the effects of misrepresentation: his voice and needs were subsumed in an extended body infected with assumptions about 'Turkish boys'. The next section looks more generally at the effects of professional assumptions about Somali and Turkish students in Enway as a case study of the interaction between gender and ethnicity and its relationship with permanent exclusion.

Gendered Conceptions of the Somali and Turkish Communities in Enway

Francis (2005) explains that 'Asian' girls are often positioned by their (usually white, middle-class and female) teachers as 'ruthlessly oppressed', and that those 'who break the stereotype by being outspoken and disruptive in class are likely to be penalised particularly harshly by teachers. Meanwhile African-Caribbean girls tend to be stereotyped as loud and 'unladylike" (11). Somali pupils, then, the girls wearing Muslim hijab head coverings (often read as a sign of being 'ruthlessly oppressed') and with their African/Middle Eastern cultural connections, are important to discuss here because schools' understanding of them appears to fall between that of these two named groups- ('Asian' and 'African-Caribbean') -in borderland space (Anzaldua 1987).

Despite the Chair's constant efforts to refocus the conversation, the Pupil Placement Panel in Enway developed the habit of narrating all Somali pupils as probably involved in some kind of gender-specific 'gang' activity. Somali boys were often rejected by attending head teachers as potential placements as 'probably involved with the Enway Boyz',[29] whilst Somali girls who had screamed, shouted, sworn or spat at teachers and pupils were usually assumed to have been sexually initiated into the Enway Boyz. The Panel, having developed over the few years it had been in existence to deal efficiently with twenty-five or so at-crisis young people in two hours every two weeks, had become accustomed to tapping into this swift narrative by asking, 'is he/she Somali?' The Panel Chair did her best to re-direct the discussion to specific issues related to the young person's needs, but the state of 'being a Somali boy' or 'being a Somali girl' brought with it a powerful set of assumptions. This included a conception that the pupil would likely be physically violent, especially if male, and violent, sexually active, vulnerable/or aggressive, especially if female.

Somali and Turkish mothers in Enway were often perceived by school staff to be ineffective when it came to garnering their support to reinforce school rules- for example, to attend school 'in correct uniform', 'every day' and 'on time'. This is assumed to be because in absence of the father (which was frequent), the boys were thought to become 'the man of the house' when they were thirteen or fourteen. As with Mahad, any negative behaviour towards women teachers was often framed within this context. In other words, the heads of year and inclusion managers I spoke to tended to assume that Somali and Turkish boys were 'difficult' because of some defect in the way their families were organised in relation to their gendered ethnic and cultural background. Pastoral staff tended to frame the problem in terms of the relationship between Somali and Turkish boys and women teachers. Whilst student/teacher conflict did exist, I did not hear the same gendered ethnicity/culture explanation of the behaviour of the white working-class boys in Enway (many of whom also lived in single-parent, female-headed households) who threatened girls with sexual violence or were rude to teachers. These cases were more likely to be explained in terms of 'bad parenting'; a 'lack of boundaries' at home. However, despite the prevalence of professionals' gender-normed responses described above and discussed elsewhere (for example, Cooper 2002), in none of these cases was the problem acknowledged as one which might be partially rooted in or affected by the gender-normed institution and its staff. All explanations were within-child or within-family: in other words, all within the extended body, distracting attention from the institution (Sellman 2002; Slee 1995; Foucault 1977; see also chapter three). This mechanism could be seen as both a cause and an effect of permanent exclusion from school. A focus on the child or young person leads to the exclusion of the perceived 'source of the problem'. And having taken the action of excluding a pupil, the institution is seen to have 'dealt with the problem'.

CONCLUSION

This chapter has offered a range of evidence which develops the idea that some permanent exclusions from school happen because of assumptions about pupils, most of which are projected and negotiated within the contested space of pupils' experienced extended bodies. Gender is a useful prism through which to investigate this problem because its inexorable 'biological' reputation stretches the limits of stereotype deconstruction. Normed, fixed and essentialised understandings about gender and its interaction with class, ethnicity and sexuality/identity have a profound and complex effect on judgements made about pupils at risk of or subject to a permanent exclusion. In addition, many of the incidents leading to permanent exclusions and managed moves involve a component of gendered violence, which may for the purposes of analysis be read as 'horizontal violence' (Freire 1977) in one sense and non-horizontal in another. Because of this, the contested space of an excluded pupil's extended body becomes even more likely to be populated with normative pronouncements about pupils' genders and gendered behaviours.

CHAPTER 5

Gender and the Extended Body

Along with behaviour, intention, attitude, and mental state, gender is an aspect of the categories of things which make up the extended body, vulnerable to imagination, stereotype, and description precisely because its perceived biological elements make it so easily accepted as a norm. What Csordas (1999) calls the 'imaginal constitution of intersubjectivity' can be applied to the power of assumptions about gender. For example, the normed response on meeting a girl is that one 'knows' she is a girl and 'should' behave like a girl because she *looks* like a girl. Behaviour in schools is constantly predicted and categorised according to gender-identity- hence a head of year's sanguine description, discussed above, of 'bitchy girls and silly boys'.

When the behaviour, intention, attitude, and mental state of the extended body of a permanently excluded pupil (or a pupil at risk of permanent exclusion) is considered with reference to gender, the contested space of that extended body can become contested *because* of its gender. Thus the struggle to invoke an appropriate level of empathy and practical support for Nama in the face of her being labelled 'manipulative' and over-aggressive was conducted within the contested space of her 'femaleness'. The perceived 'fact' of her gender-identity (and the interactions between this and her ethnicity and cultural background) was a normed state- one *expected to be* embodied in a certain way- against which criticisms could be made on the basis of relativity, undermining appropriate assessment and support planning procedures.

Professional Agency and the 'Plasticity' of Habitus

Professionals' understandings about gender could be said to derive from an inevitable habitus (Bourdieu 1997). I do not think that most of the teachers and other professionals who were involved with inclusion and exclusion at schools in Enway *reflexively* made negative judgements about pupils on the basis of their gender identities. However, as Hoy (1999) states, the 'all-pervasive' quality of habitus means that '[w]e tend to prefer the familiar that we have already coped with and we build up non conscious, unwilled strategies for avoiding the perceptions of other possibilities...' [15]. Teacher fatigue in the face of multiple administrative, financial and emotional pressures (Osler and Vincent 2003: 50) must play a part in the development of this habit of avoidance. But the blind acceptance of institutional norms is not an inevitable state of being (Pomeroy 2000; Slee 1995). Perhaps there is a space for the exertion of professional agency, even in a panoptic (Foucault 1970) environment, in the idea that habitus does have 'a degree of plasticity' (Hoy 1999: 14; discussed further in chapter eight). This points to the value of making space for education, discussion, philosophising, reflexivity, criticality, and questioning in the professional lives of teachers and other staff involved with vulnerable children.

In fact, some Enway Children's Services and school staff *were* reflective and responsive about the problems experienced by young people, at risk of or already permanently excluded, with regard to assumptions made about their gender identities. Hence a sign on the wall of the breezeblock stairway up to the Enway Appraisal Unit advertised a Boys' Group, promoting the discussion of 'self-awareness, self-development, personal hygiene, socially acceptable behaviour, body image, sexuality, role models, social skills, basic skills, life skills, friendships, life-choices, careers, learning and enjoyment.' Admittedly, some of these factors, depending on the degree to which they were sensitively delivered by the convenor of the Boys' Group, had the potential to undermine the potential for boys' empowerment and resilience through self-identity. For example, the plan to promote role models involves the risk that they may all be 'normed male' role models; social skills have the potential to be taught in a stereotypically gendered way. However, the fact that this discursive space had been opened up at all provided the opportunity to learn and teach in a way that was sensitive to stereotypes made about gender.

The Norming Procedure

It seems that permanent exclusion can act to exacerbate existing gender inequities, barely hidden under a fascia of political correctness which tears like tissue paper where the norms are transgressed by a young person. If schools are understood to be as institutions which reproduce the social order (Bourdieu 1977; Freire 1996; Lawrence-Lightfoot 2003), then they must be understood as institutions which are bent towards reproducing the 'normed' gendered aspects of this. And, I would argue, part of the expression of administrative power through this normalising process requires recourse to 'performative exclusions that mark the threshold of the abject' (Weiss 1999:50).[30] The next chapter addresses the workings of this administrative power through inequitable assumptions made on the basis of social class.

NOTES

[1] Field-notes: said by head of Year 8 at Enway 's largest mixed comprehensive school
[2] The Iraqi Kurdish girl introduced in chapter three.
[3] Originally known as Social Services.
[4] A forced marriage, which is characterized by an absence of consent, is not the same thing as an arranged marriage, which involves mutual consent.
[5] Nama's sisters will have their own extended bodies and I am aware that as an ethnographer I am participating in a construction of these here.
[6] The Panel delegates' naming of Nama as 'manipulative', for example, opens her up to the risk of further violence against her, such as forced marriage.
[7] Although in Enway white British working-class boys are now the group least likely to achieve 5 GCSEs at grades A* to C
[8] Fourteen years old.
[9] A common pressure, as described in chapter four.
[10] Parents who demonstrated empathy towards their children were often called 'unsupportive' or 'collusive'. Those who did not were often called 'neglectful'. Those who were supportive towards the school were conversely often labeled 'manipulative' or 'interfering'.
[11] That is, in a mainstream school, implying she would do better at an alternative education placement

[12] Wearing his trousers pulled down so the waistband goes across the buttocks in a trend popularised in part by American hip-hop and rap music videos.

[13] See below under the sub heading 'Sexualised behaviour; sexual aggression and violence' for a more detailed discussion of this phenomenon.

[14] See Theoretical Framework, chapter three.

[15] As in most schools in England and Wales, 'achievement' was measured in Enway schools by academic level.

[16] Army, police, fire service, etc.

[17] Although barbering qualifications are among the more popular to be achieved by young men in prisons.

[18] One of the significant 'gaps' and 'silences' (Blackman 2001:8) I discussed in chapters one and two.

[19] Years 10 and 11, when students are aged 14–16 and when then majority of GCSE and BTEC learning and teaching is undertaken.

[20] My use of the words 'gay' and 'lesbian' as opposed to 'homosexual' in this section was a conscious choice because I dislike the pathologising implications of that word.

[21] An example of Anzaldua's 'abnegation' (1987: 43), mentioned earlier in the chapter.

[22] 'Gaydar' is a cross between 'gay' and 'radar', described by Nicholas (2004: 60) as a 'folk concept used within the gay community to name the recognition of verbal and non-verbal behavior associated with gay identity'. I acknowledge 'gaydar' as a cultural construction and a feature of my positioning.

[23] I am using the term 'camp' here as a term often understood as stereotypically 'gay-acting'. Susan Sontag (1966) identifies 'Camp' with 'naïve', 'flamboyant mannerisms', 'resting on innocence'. Here I use this word specifically from a positive and non-heterocentric point of view. Of course, Michael may also be a 'camp' heterosexual boy.

[24] Lesbian, Gay, Bisexual, Transgender; now sometimes including Q and I for 'queer' or 'questioning' and 'intersex'.

[25] The details of this assault cannot be discussed here for reasons of confidentiality.

[26] A local 'gang', some of whose members attended the school under discussion.

[27] It should be said here that I am utilising the concept loosely and with the concession that horizontality might be contested on the basis of gendered power relations. Gendered violence is thus also discussed below as 'non-horizontal' violence.

[28] Which I understand to mean described within and thus represented by the extended body.

[29] A suspected 'gang'.

[30] See also Kristeva (1982) and chapter three of this book.

CHAPTER 6

'GET OUT OF MY CLASS!'

The Reproduction of Socio-Economic Hierarchy

Just as permanent exclusion can act to exacerbate existing gender inequities, there is evidence in this chapter which suggests that another of its effects, albeit entangled with gender and 'race' (discussed in detail in chapters five and seven respectively), is to exacerbate inequity on the basis of socio-economic class. If, as examined in the previous chapter, schools are understood to be institutions which reproduce the social order (Bourdieu 1977; Freire 1996; Lawrence-Lightfoot 2003), then they must be understood as institutions which are bent towards reproducing 'normed' class-related aspects of this.

This chapter will begin with an overview of some of the literature around class and school exclusion before defining the terms implemented to discuss the issues. In particular, it is established that it is important not to essentialise class experience. Class will then be described in terms of its place within the vulnerable, imagined, describable and experienced contested space of the 'extended body'.

The chapter will move from theory to context to discuss the interaction between class-based assumptions and permanent exclusion from school. Professionals' talk about class will be described as oblique and hidden, and so the following sections are an attempt to decode interactions between professionals and families and to look for references and assumptions about class within them. The status of schooling as an economic enterprise will begin this discussion in order to contextualise it. Decoding will be attempted through the scrutiny of ethnographic examples of the uses of language, accents, and classed 'authorising narratives' (Skeggs 1997). Using this information I will consider professional assumptions about class and their role in the causes and effects of permanent exclusion from school.

In the subsequent discussion, school will be reconfirmed as reflecting the wider social hierarchy, generated through professional actions based on assumptions about 'family background' and the 'classed' hierarchy of local authority areas, schools and related support services. Engaging in the contested space of the extended body through multi-agency working will be theorised as class conflict. Finally, looking more broadly at the context within which Enway exists, the chapter will discuss the connections between prejudices on the basis of class, 'race' and gender in exclusion from school.

A CULTURAL THEORY OF CLASS IN EDUCATION

As I have explained in chapter three and below, Bourdieu (1986) posited a theory of class which went beyond the economic, addressing its formation within and across a number of social fields, and based on levels of a range of types of capital in addition to economic capital: particularly social, linguistic and cultural. This raises ethnicity and gender as important factors in discussions around identity and experience in terms of class. Thus Archer and Francis (2007) 'assert the importance and relevance of social class for the study of social identities and inequalities ... ' but state that 'care must be taken when extending these notions to minority ethnic communities' (34).

Addressing a set of stories emerging from the intersection between gender and class, Arnot (2003) discusses Paul Willis's (1977) *Learning to Labour*, a seminal text addressing how working class boys left school to do working class jobs. She reports on how his 'theory of class resistance through youth cultural forms' (102) underpinned much subsequent study into youth, masculinity and class. Arnot also suggests that Willis places 'the study of gender well within the analysis of working-class cultures in education, at the interface between schooling and shop-floor culture, and within the study of anti-school cultures' (103). She aligns Willis's analysis with that of Bourdieu (1977), proposing a model of working class masculinity that rejects bourgeois educational aspirations as emasculating and conformist.

Arnot (2003) also draws on McRobbie's (1980) and Skeggs' (1992) analysis of Willis's work, pointing out that he omitted to report on a gender dichotomy which placed young working class men in positions of relative power over young working class women. This tension is discussed further in the previous chapter, where I theorised sexual assault and other kinds of gendered violence as both a form of 'horizontal violence' (Freire 1970) and as non-horizontal violence. Looking in closer detail at the relationships between the experience of 'class', gender and the recent governmental discourses of meritocracy, neoliberalism, and increased class mobility or classlessness, Walkerdine *et al.* (2001) identify the pain involved in class change and the classed pressures that still exert themselves powerfully on young people's lives and educational experiences. In this schema, '[y]oung women watch their mothers struggle and do not want to have to combine work and family, but know very well that is precisely the future they face...they may also have to cope with men who are feeling intensely the loss of previous modes of masculinity' (216).

Current concerns about the drop in boys' school achievement against a rise in that of girls often fail to recognise that it is middle-class girls that tend to do well educationally, and that middle-class men have recourse to work in financial services, whilst manual labour jobs for working-class men have almost disappeared (Walkerdine *et al.* 2001:212). They also suggest that 'it is social class that massively divides girls and young women in terms of educational attainment and life trajectories' (4). Similarly seeking to look at the effects of class inequity on women in terms of the interactions between families, social class, and school, Reay

(1998) brings Bourdieu's (1977) cultural capital into a feminist context, arguing that 'inequalities of gender, 'race' and social class are embedded in the home-school relationship', and relating 'the crucial part mothers play in social-class reproduction' (167) through their interactions with their children's schools. Reay (1998) points out that middle-class mothers have access to more resources of cultural capital than working-class mothers, and so whilst both groups interact industriously with their children's schools - to a large extent, without the useful support of fathers in either case – working-class mothers' work with schools is less effective in generating success in their children's educational career (Reay 1998; see also Walkerdine *et al.* 2001).

It is important to look at class, gender and ethnicity together, as concerns about achievement in terms of gender alone, for example, can preclude attention to issues of disadvantage related to class or ethnicity. But this is not without its problems. Maguire *et al.* (2006) raise a concern that the statistics on the higher level of exclusion experienced by 'black' boys 'might work to alert teachers to the 'fact' that children, boys especially, from particular groups, are more prone to challenging behaviour' (93). This could also potentially 'sideline the evidence that shows it is mainly working-class children and children designated as having 'special educational needs' who are disproportionately excluded' (93). This is not to say, of course, that inequity on the basis of ethnicity and gender should be ignored in favour of attention to class inequity. However, I want to acknowledge here that it is essential that in using a cultural theory of class to look at education, intertextual relationships between class, gender and ethnicity should be problematized as well as taken into account.

Class and Permanent Exclusion from School

In Reay's (1998) study of working-class and middle-class mothers, she recounts stories of two of the working-class mothers who had themselves been excluded from school. Both mothers blamed themselves, but it is clear that they had been attending schools which were violent and difficult places to be - and that because of socio-economic disadvantage and inequality, there was no sense of choice in terms of where they could have gone to school. Reay (1998) suggests that 'it seems unlikely that the damage inflicted on these women by their own educational experiences will make it an easy task to remedy any damage they may perceive in their own schooling' (53). In addition to their legacy of problematic school experiences, Reay (1998) also found that working-class mothers were disempowered in their interactions with school, especially around discussions about their children's behaviour. They were held to account for their children's behaviour in school, and less able to advocate for their children in discussions about behaviour incidents than were middle-class parents (see also Walkerdine *et al.* 2001).

Rendall and Stuart (2005) identify 'special educational needs and socio-economic deprivation ... as common circumstances that surround pupils who have been excluded from school' (10). Similarly, Maguire *et al.* (2006) have said that '[o]verwhelmingly, excluded children come from families who are under stress, who are less likely to have employment and who are experiencing multiple disadvantage' (29). And Skeggs (1997), in her ethnographic study of white working-class young women in the North West of England, felt that 'the most fundamental marker of class was exclusion … from positions in the labour market, the education system, (and) from forms of cultural capital' (162). Wright *et al.* (2000) similarly see that '[i]t is possible to regard exclusion as one of the ways in which schools choose pupils … for schools, the marketability and desirability of pupils operates through social class, race and gender' (121).

The data discussed in the chapter below shows that children and young people are more likely to be excluded from what can be read as 'middle-class' schools if they are 'working-class', and that because of this, 'working-class' schools are more often expected to use their resources to support incoming young people who have experienced or are at risk of experiencing an exclusion.[1] Gerwitz *et al.* (1995) explain that this classed division between schools has been exacerbated by the increased marketisation of schooling. Thus offering parents a 'choice' of schools means that they need to draw on their economic, cultural and social capital in order to access more 'desirable' schools – and through their cultural capital, contribute to maintain them as 'more desirable' (24). It is acknowledged that house prices around 'good' schools can shape the class identity of their intake. Ostensibly, admissions rules are designed to avoid the overt selection of pupils. However, exclusion can be read as a form of selection, and schools, in their drive to attract socio-economically privileged families, respond through a series of 'quick fixes' (157) in order to manage their 'representation to the outside world' (156). Among these 'quick fixes' is the permanent exclusion and less-official 'constructive exclusion' (Gerwitz *et al.* 1995: 158)[2] of children who challenge the school's place in the league tables, or its image as discipline-focussed. Maguire *et al.* (2006) also report that head teachers in urban primary schools in disadvantaged areas could sometimes exclude children where 'they wanted the local community to know they meant business'; and that they used exclusion in such a way that it 'massaged their intake … excluding the most difficult children who had to go elsewhere' (63). Social class disadvantage is evident in this picture: one Education Welfare Officer interviewed by Gerwitz *et al.* (1998) describes a clear disadvantage on the part of working-class families (and the interlinked issues around ethnicity and gender) in this situation, invoking a meeting about a child's behaviour attended by 'a Black, working-class, single-parent mum, who's called to the school and … faced with a whole little row of people … who have got suits on who are White men who know it all' (158).

It can be seen, then, that young people's likelihood of being excluded and their experiences once inside the exclusion process can clearly be linked to their class, in multiple, embedded and complex ways. In this chapter I will be further investigating the interaction between 'socio-economic class' and exclusion from school, beginning with the theoretical framework for the discussion and moving on to apply this to details from the ethnographic context.

A NOTE ON TERMS

Below, I take, along with an economic job/salary index, two of the indices of 'class' defined by Bourdieu (1979, 1991)- style/distinction and language- in order to make an attempt to define the 'class' into which certain groups of people fall within Enway schools.[3] In this paradigm, teachers, especially those in management positions, are generally seen as middle-class. Of the two hundred or so cases of pupils at risk of or subject to a permanent exclusion from school seen in Enway each year, I only understood two or three to be middle-class. So, generally speaking, in a meeting held as a result of a threatened or actual permanent exclusion, the family was understood by all attending as 'working-class' and the professionals as 'middle-class'.

So at the risk of essentialising, but to maintain the task of 'studying up', (Nader 1972; see also chapter two) I will be using the term 'middle-class' to describe the sector of Enway professionals who are in positions of authority, who tend to be living in relative affluence, and who appear to be making judgements on the basis of class. The term 'working-class' will be applied mainly to the low income families I encountered as part of my work in Enway state schools. However, this needs to be problematized. The terms 'middle-class' and 'working-class' are unsatisfactory, partially because they are inexact. They are used flexibly to describe a population ranged across a detailed class spectrum and which is capable of transitioning between classes. They also risk essentialising the experiences of those so labelled. The term 'working-class' is sometimes used to cover all those who are not perceived as middle-class by those who identify as middle-class. In this sense the language functions to maintain the boundaries of the middle-class. As Skeggs (1997) explains:

> Class is a discursive, historically specific construction, a product of middle-class political consolidation, which includes elements of fantasy and projection. The historical generation of classed categorizations provide discursive frameworks which enable, legitimate and map onto material inequalities.

> 5

The term 'working-class' is thus relative depending on who is using it and about whom it is used. But it will be useful to utilise Bourdieu's (1977) definition of the effects of belonging to a more advantaged sector of society as 'cultural capital'. It is from this theoretical standpoint that I will be assessing the impact of class, and in order to do so it will be necessary to group people into class categories. So in this chapter, in order to look at the effects of institutional class prejudice, I am using 'working-class' to describe families who are living on a low income without the cultural capital to choose to do so.

CULTURAL CAPITAL IN A MERITOCRATIC SYSTEM

It is generally agreed that schools under New Labour and the previous Conservative government were (and almost certainly continue to be under the new coalition government elected in 2010) run on the basis of a meritocracy which ignores the inequitable factor of cultural capital (Reay 2008) and is hugely exacerbated through the privilege given to league table results uncoupled from their socio-economic contexts (Ball 2001; Ball 2008; Mehan 2008; Reay *et al.* 2008; Skeggs 1997). For example, 'value-added' results, which look at school attainment within its socio-economic context, are not used to help OFSTED decide whether a school should be put into special measures and taken over by a centrally appointed head teacher. As Radnor *et al.* (2007) suggest, '[g]overnment policy ignores class and emphasises the individual. It concentrates on developing an education system that operates on the assumption that the school student as an individual has equal access to education' (296). But those who are successful within a meritocratic institution such as a school may have been supported by the effects of 'cultural capital' (Bourdieu 1977). To apply this theory to the issue of exclusion from school, I suggest that those with cultural capital are likely to bring what is perceived as 'added value' to a school and are thus less likely to be excluded (see also Wright et al 2000).

THE 'EXTENDED BODY': SPACE TO DESCRIBE AND RESIST

In this book, then, allowing both the use of Bourdieu's (1977) 'cultural capital' theory and Skeggs's (1997) conception of 'working-class' as partially a middle-class 'fantasy', class is considered in terms of its place within the imagined, describable and experienced contested space of the 'extended body'. In other words, it represents something that can be identified by the self; claimed; experienced; embodied; and/ or described or ascribed by others; projected into the extended body to be accepted or contested.

In her research, Skeggs (1997) describes a process which I would align with the effect the extended body might experience in relation to class. She frames a group of young white working-class women's class self-identification around a concept of '(Dis)identification' (74). This implies an effort to re-narrativise the self in terms of what one is not, rather than in terms of what one is:

> Class was central to the young women's subjectivities. It was not spoken of in the traditional sense of recognition- I am working-class- but rather, was displayed in their multitudinous efforts *not to be* recognised as working-class. They disidentified and they dissimulated. Theirs was a refusal of recognition rather than a claim for the right to be recognised ... A denial of the representations of their positioning ... the label working-class when applied to women has been used to signify all that is dirty, dangerous and without value.

> 1997:74, original emphasis

The space of the 'extended body' is where 'the representations of their positioning' are projected and experienced. The extended body might thus to some extent provide what Skeggs (1997) appeals for in these circumstances:

We ... need concepts that ... can encapsulate experiences otherwise unnamed ... (which) ... can create what Cole (1995) identifies as rhetorical space, so that experiences cannot be dismissed as illegitimate just because they are not known by those who have the power to effect judgements on others. This leads to a more responsible knowledge and representations.

1997:166

The formulation of the 'extended body' as a space vulnerable to experienced description also offers a location for the *responsible* use of its representative and experienced space. Skeggs's (1997) research found that white working-class women 'are located (that is, more than others) in temporal processes of subjective construction' (162). The contested-space, flexible and kaleidoscopic nature of the 'extended body' can cope with the issue of temporality. It also offers a field in which although '[t]here are limitations on how they can be', we can consider the process which Skeggs's interviewees experience as they 'deploy many constructive and creative strategies to generate a sense of themselves with value' (ibid).

It is the very vulnerability of the 'extended body' to description by those with authoritarian power that also offers the possibility that the young people, families and professionals who are involved with permanent exclusion from school can collude to 'deploy ... constructive and creative strategies' (Skeggs 1997:62) in a bid for equity and social justice in education. It represents that elusive agency-potential that is rendered less likely but not impossible by Foucault's (1977) theories of 'docile bodies'[4] (discussed in chapter three). The task of self-actualisation in the face of powerful institutions requires knowledge of those institutions. This chapter 'studies up' (Nader 1972) on the institutional uses of class distinction.

HORIZONTAL VIOLENCE: SPACE TO DESCRIBE AND RESIST

One of the difficulties inherent in asserting self-actualisation within a panoptic system such as a school is that other disadvantaged people are also engaged in trying to assert their own. In this chapter, I understand the root of some of the 'horizontal violence' (Friere 1996:44, discussed in chapter three) for which pupils are permanently excluded (directly against another, such as fighting and name-calling) as related to Zizek's concept of 'subjective violence' (Zizek 2000:10).[5] The oppressive or pressurised conditions imposed by the authoritarian institutions governing a hierarchical society amount to what Zizek (2008) calls 'objective violence' (10), often administered in a nefarious circularity in response to 'subjective violence' (between citizens). Taking Freire (1996) and Zizek (2000) together, then, 'horizontal subjective violence' could describe what we might call the 'jostling for position' that occurs between peers oppressed within the less advantaged levels of a hierarchical society. Thus in this chapter I am reading instances of exclusion from school partially as an example of 'objective violence' (Zizek 2008) - in other words, of the reproduced social hierarchy Bourdieu and Passeron (1977) identified as the project of state education. The concept of 'objective violence' has the potential to challenge institutions for answers to what have been posited as individual pupils' 'behavioural' issues, distracting attention from the institution's own behavioural issues (Sellman *et al.,* Foucault 1977; Slee 1995; Thomas and Loxley 2001; discussed in chapters three and four).

CONTEXT: THE INTERACTION BETWEEN CLASS ASSUMPTION AND
PERMANENT EXCLUSION FROM SCHOOL IN ENWAY

If institutions are to be challenged on the subject of objective violence, it is necessary to 'study up' (Nader 1972; see chapter two); to find out if they are aware of its existence and the extent to which it is expressed. This section will look at the class-context of schooling in terms of a marketised meritocracy (Wright *et al.* 2000), and then apply the theoretical analysis laid out above to some of the themes arising in the ethnography.

Just as professional negative and normative assumptions about gender were seen in chapter five to both cause permanent exclusions and to become exacerbated by permanent exclusions, it is suggested here that assumptions about class can have the same effects. In order to try to match up the 'objective violence' (Zizek 2008:10) of a permanent exclusion from school with assumptions made about pupils' social class, I have tried to investigate the ways in which professionals identify and talk about class. Class in Enway children's services was to some extent 'the elephant in the room'- not politically correct, perhaps, to discuss openly, and therefore hidden in a variety of coded words, phrases and policy discourses.

Professionals' Opaque Talk About Class

In thinking about the links between exclusion from school and social class, I soon realised that in the discourses of Enway professionals the link was opaque. This is reflected in government policy: in discussing the 2005 White Paper on education, Tomlinson (2006) explains that 'parents are treated as a homogenous group with no recognition of social class' (52). The relative absence of a class discourse appears to contribute to the maintenance of the 'meritocratic' discourse (Tomlinson 2006; Radnor *et al.* 2007) of the current education system started by the Tory government and maintained by New Labour- and which largely ignored the concept of cultural capital (Bourdieu 1977). Where policies did acknowledge class inequality (Aim Higher and Gifted and Talented funding, for example), they tended to apply to a very small number of students and were largely constructed to appeal to middle class parents (Tomlinson 2006). Or in cases such as value added scoring (where schools were measured according to how far pupils had moved from their own academic baselines), the policy addressed a measure of class inequality, but failed to link the measure to any funding implications. In this way, education policies underpinning an ethic of meritocracy enable the state to 'declare that they are promoting equal opportunities while they maintain practices that hide class structured economic inequalities within the education system within a meritocratic veneer' (Radnor *et al.* 2007: 297). And a perceived meritocracy is a key component of the neo-liberal marketisation of schooling.

Schooling as an Economic Enterprise

The entanglements between socio-economic status and permanent exclusion may be exacerbated by the fact that schooling in England is also now seen as a primarily economic enterprise. Ball (2008) explains that the project of education has become a project guided by economic ideas. Wright *et al.* (2000) suggest that 'it is possible to identify the processes by which pupils are constructed as 'marketable' or otherwise and which could have an effect upon their educational careers' (5). And Tomlinson (2006) also feels that education has gone from an expression of the welfare state to being a central plank of global capitalism. This is borne out in Enway's professionals' understandings of the purpose of education. As I have explained in chapter three, Foucault (1977) suggests that the project of schooling is to produce economically viable citizens so that the capitalist state can continue to replicate itself. Shayne's case, below, demonstrates how this worked at the Pupil Placement Panel.

At a Panel meeting in May 2008, we viewed a set of school paperwork describing a pupil who was seeking to move schools because he was at risk of permanent exclusion. In the paperwork, the head of year had written, 'Shayne must decide how he wishes to conduct his life. I have seen the cooperative Shayne as well as the other character, so I know that he is intelligent and should use this gift to set himself up for a great earning potential.' The Head of Year had conflated 'intelligent' with 'cooperative'. He had identified Shayne's own behaviour as what needed to change, pathologising his 'problems' and deflecting attention from potentially beneficial changes which could have been made in the institutional framework in which he was educated (Thomas and Loxley 2001; Foucault 1977; Slee 1995; also see chapter three). But significantly, and illustrating Tomlinson's point (2006, discussed above) about the shift from welfare to economics, the head of year had finished his referral with an economic imperative, rather than a social-emotional goal. So the discussion in this chapter should perhaps be understood in the context of an education system which targets economic goals as important. Because cultural capital leads to enhanced economic outcomes, social class might therefore be seen to have some importance within such a system. But, perhaps because I was in this research dealing with a meritocracy, professional talk about class was not entirely visible. I intend here to illuminate the presence of Enway professionals' consciousness about class, and then to consider the effects of class prejudice in permanent exclusion from school. An investigation into the effects of 'classed' language will be the first clue.

Wielding the Power of Language: 'Social and Economic Deprivation'[6]

Vuillamy and Webb (2000) refer to something I heard many Enway education professionals cite as a reason behind the kinds of behaviours which lead to permanent exclusion: the 'I blame the parents' narrative. They explain, '(t)here is usually a cause of severe pupil misbehaviour and this cause lies either in particular family circumstances or in problems of home-school interaction or in the manner in which teachers respond to children from such backgrounds' (1). Vuillamy and Webb (2000) do acknowledge the problems associated with home-school interaction also identified in other studies of permanent exclusion from school (Rendall and Stuart 2005; Cooper 2002). However, they cannot resist using delicate oblique references to a family's ascribed/embodied class identity: 'particular family circumstances'; 'children from such backgrounds', and later, 'social and economic deprivation' (10).

What exactly is meant by 'social deprivation'? I understand it to describe some of the negative effects of Bourdieu's (1977) 'cultural capital'. But I prefer Bourdieu's formulation of the problem because it situates the issue within the broader hierarchised context, less as a 'deprivation'- which invites pity and an acceptance of its inevitability - and more as 'in the place currently assigned to it by those in authority' - which describes it in terms of relativity and provides the possibility of change through political resistance.

Disengaged? Re-engage through Vocational Qualifications

The language of 'social deprivation' in its decoupling of impoverished communities from wealthy ones is used to de-problematise the concept of an inevitable state of unsuccessful or troubled existence. Another policy-discourse[7] which reveals systemic class prejudice in the machinery of school discipline is that of 'engagement'. Young people 'at risk' of permanent exclusion are often described as 'dis-engaged' and identified as needing to be 're-engaged'. However, I rarely heard an Enway professional proposing to 're-engage' a young person with the standard academic GCSE curriculum, either by thinking about making it more interesting (that is, addressing the institution rather than pathologising the child) or by trying to support access to it through tutored support.

How, then, were Enway pupils re-engaged? One of my colleagues reported at our monthly 'Enway Inclusion Team' meeting that she had been to a seminar called 'Re-engaging youth and reducing exclusions'. 'Torbay's local authority engaged with the voluntary sector and have links with employers,' she reported, 'we need to do that if we're going to engage 14–19s.' The team then discussed the fact that in the next academic year pupils would for the first time be expected to stay on at school until the age of seventeen. 'But we haven't got a curriculum!', worried another of my colleagues.

But there is 'a curriculum'. In addition to the new 14–19 Diplomas[8] and BTECs, 'AS' levels were and still are available for sixth form students to achieve half an

'A' level before perhaps dropping one of four subjects and finishing the remaining three with a view to going on to university. Why were AS levels not even mentioned as an option for these seventeen year old pupils who will be staying on for the first time? For Skeggs (1997), 'class' in the education system operates to allocate working-class students into the 'unequal division of labour' (161). Perhaps this is why 'A' levels were not even remembered as an option for 'disengaged students' at the Enway professionals' meeting. One of the effects of permanent exclusion from school as an option, then, could be seen to be the reproduction of socio-economic hierarchies through the placement of 'disengaged' students in alternative education environments that remove the option of studying the academic subjects needed to apply for university. Bourdieu (1991) states that

[p]rofessionals ... objectively invested with the monopoly of the legitimate language ... produce for their own use a special language predisposed to fulfil ... a social function of distinction in the relations between classes and in the struggles they wage on the terrain of language.

52

So the language that is used in discussing pupils at risk of exclusion from school (such as 're-engagement') could be seen to enfold the mechanisms necessary to maintain class hierarchies. 'Re-engagement' through the use of vocational qualifications is a version of the use of the discourse of 'need' (Thomas and Loxley 2001) as a gatekeeping strategy (discussed in chapter four).

Professional 'middle-class' language can thus be seen to perpetuate class hierarchy and inequity by being inexact about its causes (as in the case of 'social and economic deprivation') or by subsuming class replication under a language of aspiration in response to 'need' (as in the case of 're-engagement' through vocational qualifications).

Accents

Whilst the class hierarchy was maintained through their own 'special language' (Bourdieu 1991), professionals made prejudiced assumptions on the basis of the local Enway accents, marking people out as 'of a different class' to the middle-class professionals working with them.

I met Jack at an Enway 'At Risk Teens Intervention' (ARTI)[9] support planning meeting in May 2008. The meeting had been convened to discuss support planning for him. Jack was a bouncy, articulate Year 7[10] boy with a keen grin, freckles, and a problem with truancy, climbing scaffolding, annoying dangerously volatile older pupils, and fighting with his mother. Jack's school was very close to permanently excluding him.

In contrast with the middle-class professionals' speech, Jack and his mother and aunt had Enway working-class accents. In the meeting room, although we were all, professionals and family, sitting in a nice non-threatening and non-hierarchical circle, and everyone was given an equal chance to speak, the division between the two groups (which we might call 'professional' and 'family') was made more obvious by the clear difference in the accents common to each group. Bourdieu (1991) has explained that 'there exists, in the area of pronunciation, diction and ... grammar, a whole set of differences significantly associated with social differences' (54). So both the 'special language' (ibid: 52) and the accents of the 'professionals' served to delineate their social difference (and therefore their social power). How this power was expressed is illustrated below.

Who is Allowed to Talk About What? 'Authorising Narratives'

As well as having a special language and a differentiating accent, there was a difference in what each of the two groups ('professional' and 'family') were 'allowed' to validly discuss. Skeggs (1997) has suggested that 'the only authorising narrative [the working-class women she researched] have to explain their identities is pathology' (167).[11] In Jack's case this was something his mother did try to use. What happened when she attempted this illustrates another of the undermining effects one's ascribed 'class' can have within processes designed ostensibly to support pupils at risk of or subject to a permanent exclusion. Thus, in the ARTI meeting, Jack's mum suggested, 'I want him tested for AHD'.

The two clinical psychologists, the social worker and the deputy head of year looked sidelong at each other, smirking. I suspected that they all felt that Jack's mum was hoping to find a pathologised 'authorising narrative' (Skeggs 1997: 167) explanation for his behaviour in a possible diagnosis of Attention-Deficit Hyperactivity Disorder.

'Do you mean 'ADHD'?' asked one of the clinical psychologists, imperiously, adding, 'Jack, do you know what ADHD is?' Jack smiled confidently, and answered, 'yeah it's like me, it's when you want attention from your mates!' The psychologist frowned at him and one of the other psychologists giggled. Later she shook her head at me. 'He hasn't got ADHD', she told me.

As Skeggs (1997) found, 'pathology' *can* sometimes be available as an 'authorising narrative', as with April, who I discussed in chapter five and whose anger had been interpreted as a symptom of PMS. As I identified in chapter four, although an unsatisfying route, this is often the quickest way to access the fund of 'psy' techniques (Rose 1999) on offer as a range of support strategies in the face of an institutional framework reluctant to turn its powers of critical surveillance on itself. However, it is often unavailable to those deemed 'not allowed' to talk about such lofty 'scientific' ideas. As Bourdieu (1991) explains,

> The competence adequate to produce sentences that are likely to be understood
> may be quite inadequate to produce sentences that are likely to be listened
> to ... speakers lacking the legitimate competence are de facto excluded from

the social domains in which this competence is required, or are condemned to silence.

55

I often confronted this situation in my work as a pupil support officer in Enway.

Professionals Using Assumptions About Class to Make Decisions

As well as excluding families from 'authorising narratives' on the basis of their class, Enway professionals also described pupils (albeit obliquely) in 'classed' terms and used these to make placement decisions. At the Pupil Placement Panel at the beginning of May 2008, two colleagues, Jacques and Mia, described a pupil called Alfie (Year 8):[12]

> Mia: He's receiving services from the Youth Offending Team. His siblings are very tough, really macho, very 'fight with your fists', they're really proud of him if he comes back with a scalp. He's trying very hard to go on his mum's side; dad's been in prison ... they are nice kids. They've got the right intentions. Alfie could become one of the statistics, if we don't do something with him. He could follow his dad ... he told me, 'good weight, copper. Shouldn't nick lead off church roofs, though'. It was nice to know he had a moral line. He's a rogue!

> Jacques: He's very keen to learn, except for exams ... he has aspirations to join the armed forces.

The Panel placed Alfie in a mainstream school. I think this placement was won due to the fact that he had been cast as 'a working-class boy' who through his open and honest discussion of the relative merits of copper and church-roof lead 'knew his place': an honourable thief who would tidily take himself off to be a soldier once he turned seventeen years old. 'Knowing one's place', Bourdieu (1991) explains, 'implies a tacit acceptance of one's position, a sense of limits' (see also Skeggs 1997). Alfie 'knew his place'; won the hearts of the Panel members, and was rewarded by being given the chance to prove himself at mainstream school. He was only allowed to do so, I suspect, because he had already mapped out for himself a working-class future (and I am making an assumption here that this was as a rank and file member of the armed forces) which did not threaten the class hierarchy.

The discussions, above, concerning professionals' uses of class, evidence a seam of class prejudice running through the multi-agency system that swings into action when a young person is at risk of or subject to permanent exclusion from school. Institutional prejudice, here on the basis of social class, can perhaps be seen to be exacerbated when young people are subject to the crystallising effects of a permanent exclusion from school.

School as a Reflection of Social Hierarchy

As I explained in chapter two, schools can be considered to be places which 'in vivid microcosm ... mirror societal priorities, values, and conflicts (and) ... magnify and intensify them' (Lawrence-Lightfoot 2003:216). Similarly, Bourdieu and Passeron (1977) view schools as places which function to reproduce existing social hierarchies. Anzaldua's (1987) description, discussed in chapter five, of the stresses attached to existing within 'borderland' spaces, can also be applied to class divisions between the staff and students in Enway schools.

Professionals' Assumptions About 'Family Background'

I have discussed, above, the idea that class is a relative concept which in part serves the middle-class in defining its boundaries by being able to say 'what it is not' (Skeggs 1997). Perhaps as a result of the perceived class distinction between those who are being permanently excluded and those who are doing the excluding, Enway professionals often appeared to assume that there was some deficiency in the pupil's family background that created the circumstances leading up to the exclusion. This link between class and various conceptions of 'deficiency' is a common theoretical paradigm across the literature. An account from the field of education history reports that

> [I]t was 'part of the [1870s] teacher's work to turn uncouth boys and girls, grimy and inarticulate, into decent members of society, with some small measure of grace of speech and charm of manner'. The school was seen as a place where 'proper' values were taught, compensating the child for the unsatisfactory values learnt in the family.

> Williams in Aldrich 2004:122

A study on permanent exclusion from school published in 2005 in the field of educational psychology states that 'family stress, special educational needs and socio-economic deprivation [are] common circumstances that surround pupils who have been excluded from school' (Rendall and Stuart 2005:10). And a report on a government study of exclusion from school identifies the prevalence of pupils who are not from middle-class families as a financial burden on schools which are 'faced with having to support disproportionate numbers of socially and educationally vulnerable children without the resources necessary to do so properly' (Vuillamy and Webb 2000:5).

Whether accusatory or empathic, these accounts from across a range of disciplines seem to assume that it is something about the pupils' families' 'class-based behaviours' that cause the kinds of behaviour that lead to permanent exclusion. Perhaps it is the 'critical incident' nature of permanent exclusion that exacerbated this meritocratic, prejudiced understanding often demonstrated by Enway professionals. The next section suggests that this was exacerbated under the pressure of a hierarchy amongst neighbouring local authority areas.

The 'Classed' Hierarchy of Neighbouring Local Authority Areas

Just as it is difficult not to render a person static and two dimensional by ascribing them a social class label, it is difficult to do justice to local authority areas by labelling them as predominantly working or middle-class. But given this, in naming things which are usually kept unnamed, we can sometimes reveal the source of their power, and that is my goal in this chapter. So this section addresses some of the causes and effects of permanent exclusion from school in terms of the 'class identities' of Enway and its surrounding local authority areas. Middle-class local authorities (that is, those based in areas benefitting from features such as relative affluence and low street crime) tended to permanently exclude children who were resident in working-class areas, and excluded students tended to be placed in schools in working-class areas. Working-class local authorities tended to exclude children to each other. A middle-class area did not tend to take a child excluded from a working-class area.

As mentioned earlier, middle-class families who lived in Enway tended to send their children to school either in the grammar-school system of neighbouring middle-class Prosper, if they passed the 11+ entrance exams, or to an independent (private) school. This left Enway a town with sought-after homes and pretty tourist-attracting parks and architecture, and an ethnically mixed population of working-class families living in run-down estates whose children attended a set of schools that had been rejected by middle-class parents as too low down the league tables and not properly socially comprehensive. There were very few middle-class families in Enway schools. So whilst the district had some middle-class features, the schooling system in Enway could be characterised as working-class. On the other side of Enway lay Brendantown, a working-class town with a mainly black Caribbean population.

The 'Belonging Regulations'[13] on residence and school attendance provide that if a pupil lives in one local authority area and attends school in another, if she or he is permanently excluded, the local authority area in which she or he lives must take responsibility for the education provision. In 2008, due to a local drive to reduce permanent exclusions, the Enway Pupil Referral Unit (PRU) should have been empty and ready to take some 'early intervention' cases instead. But because of exclusions from neighbouring local authorities, it was full. So whilst the Enway PRU was empty of pupils excluded from Enway schools, it had now filled up with pupils who were Enway residents but who had been permanently excluded from Brendantown schools. Communications between Enway and Brendantown local authorities were not well-established, so there were only rumours around the Panel. But these rumours stated that Brendantown head teachers were being advised by their own local authority officers to exclude non-resident children rather than trying to find alternative arrangements or support to stay at school. This meant that a child or young person was more likely to be excluded if he or she was living in one borough and attending school in another.

Up until the December of 2007, following an ethic of responsibility for its own school pupils, the Enway Pupil Placement Panel was dutifully finding new mainstream school places for pupils who happened to live in Brendantown but who were at risk of exclusion from Enway schools. However, since the PRU had filled up with Brendantown pupils, any non-Enway residents at risk of exclusion now became likely to be permanently excluded to be looked after in the Brendantown education system. Compounding this situation, whilst the Enway PRU offered its pupils the chance to take around five GCSEs, the Brendantown equivalent did not even offer the option.[14]

So the local authority area in which a pupil lives may have a direct effect not only on whether she or he is permanently excluded, but also whether she or he will have a chance to take GCSEs- ostensibly an opportunity to become 'upwardly mobile' within a meritocratic education system.

The tussle between local authority areas affected a wide range of cases heard at the Enway Panel. At a Pupil Placement Panel in late Spring, the Panel discussed Ahmed, a Year 9[15] boy who was a Brendantown resident. Ahmed was on roll at Enway's Newhall School, but had been stopped from attending by his father when he had been assaulted. Ahmed had had his nose broken in a scuffle on the wide curving staircase that flowed from the upper deck of the school down towards the large sliding glass doors leading to the reception area. But on the paperwork, the Newhall Inclusion Manager had written that Ahmed would not be welcomed back as he was suspected of bringing cannabis onto the school site. There was, however, no proof; nor had there been an exclusion or an investigation about the allegation.

'This is a backdoor exclusion, either they take him back or it's an exclusion,' suggested one of the head teachers attending the Panel, indignantly. Despite this, the Panel agreed that the pupil probably would not return to Newhall due to the assault, and I recorded in my notes: 'Brendantown resident: School Admissions to advise parent to seek place in Brendantown school'. Ahmed had not been permanently excluded, but an allegation had been made against him and recorded in official paperwork, and the fact that he had been assaulted was barely acknowledged. Because he lived in Brendantown - despite the requirement for schools to ensure that on-roll pupils are educated appropriately - this pupil, assaulted at school, isolated at home, and blamed for an unfounded drugs offence - was told that there was nothing that could be done to help him in Enway.

Brendantown and Enway, then, with their school populations of working-class families, were engaged in horizontal violence (Bourdieu 1977) against each other- horizontal because their school populations were both generally working-class- and objective violence (Zizek 2008) against each other's pupil populations, competing to resist responsibility for the education of young people at risk of exclusion. Ahmed's extended body, vulnerable to description, had to take on the qualities of 'one who is suspected of bringing cannabis to school' and 'a Brendantown resident'. Because of the privilege given to professionals' voices, Ahmed's real needs following his assault withered away, infected by the assumptions injected under the skin of his extended body.

A Hierarchy of Local Authorities

Whilst Brendantown was to the North, Silvertown lay South of Enway, and to the West of Prosper. Like Prosper, Silvertown's state-school population was more 'middle-class' than that of Enway, and it maintained a grammar school system, with those pupils with 'cultural capital' (Bourdieu 1977) passing the '11+' entrance exams. The smaller population of working-class students were shunted into deprived 'secondary modern' schools, many of which had in the preceding two years fallen into 'special measures': failing to pass OFSTED inspections and having been given 'notices to improve'. Two or three of Silvertown's beleaguered 'secondary moderns' had in 2007–08 permanently excluded large groups of pupils in an effort to improve their broader behaviour management situations. Parents have a right to request a mainstream school within one and a half hour's travel from home if their child has been permanently excluded only once, and some of these excluded pupils' paperwork had come across the district boundary to the Enway Pupil Placement Panel with a parental request to be placed in an Enway school. As one of my colleagues announced at an Inclusion Network meeting in May, 'we've taken seven permanently excluded youngsters from Silvertown ... and yet we're doing better than Silvertown in the league table of exclusions'. Because of this, the Enway Pupil Placement Panel had also become reluctant to support Silvertown pupils at risk of exclusion from Enway schools.

For example, at one of the Panels, a discussion was held on a girl in Year 8 (aged thirteen), who lived in Silvertown, and who was at risk of exclusion from an Enway school.

'Permanently exclude back to Silvertown, we've already tried to get Silvertown involved', said an Admissions Officer. I protested at the levels of gratuitous permanent exclusion of out-of-Enway residents. The Chair of the meeting agreed with me, albeit pragmatically: 'I'd only want to permanently exclude if we had a better outcome', she said, asking me to put together a multi-agency meeting to try and arrange 'an alternative'. She meant that I should try to talk my Silvertown counterpart into funding an alternative education provision or finding a mainstream school place for the pupil without the need to permanently exclude her. I knew she was not keen on the inter-authority issues which had led to this situation, having said at a previous Inclusion Managers' Meeting, 'we can't just permanently exclude because they're not ours.' But this is exactly what had been happening. I was particularly interested in the perception that non-Enway residents - despite being Enway pupils - were seen as 'not ours'.

What effect did this have, this propensity for local authorities (like Silvertown) with large middle-class pupil populations to shift pupils at risk of or subject to exclusions onto schools in local authority areas serving mainly working-class families? Often the parents of Enway-resident pupils who were threatened with permanent exclusion from Silvertown and Prosper schools told me that their schools actively advised them to look in Enway and explained where spaces would be available. Vuillamy and Webb (2000) found a similar situation between schools in their research, suggesting that

> Over-subscribed schools concerned to preserve their image and good position in league tables may resort to threatening children with exclusion ... this results in undersubscribed schools being faced with having to support disproportionate numbers of socially and educationally vulnerable children.

5

I would suggest that this applies to local authorities as well as to schools, and that league-table pressure can have a 'classed' homogenising effect on local authority school populations.

Because of the corporate images promoted by local authority areas, perceptions of each of them may not be accurate. One locally-resident academic, on reading the context study which became chapter four of this book, assumed that Enway was affluent, because of its well-known venerable architecture and historical tourist attractions. Similarly, at a boxing club for children in Silvertown, a promotional video of their project showed shots of young people in deprived-looking areas resplendent with graffiti, boys looking wistfully over a dirty wall across the high-rise flats to Enway, saying 'the community's not dealing with us. On the other side they're trying to make it all look posh. They got more things to do over there.' This may be part of the reason that Silvertown education officers did not balk at permanently excluding Enway-residing pupils from their schools. But if they had walked across to have a look, they would have seen that behind the organic cafes and craft fairs of the historical district and the cosmetically 'regenerated' areas of 'luxury flats', aging and dilapidated grey concrete housing estates were still packed in behind the 'improved' shopping district at the centre of Enway.

Because of the competition generated by education league tables and the funding arrangements attached to inclusion strategies and exclusion protocol, Enway children's services were forced to see their residents as 'ours' and those from other local authorities as 'not ours'. Through the effects of being sandwiched between a local authority area still using a grammar school system and another equally 'socially deprived' neighbourhood, this 'othering' effect was exacerbated in Enway by perceived differences in social class, and this became a cause of some permanent exclusions.

The 'Classed' Hierarchy of Enway Schools

Just as Enway had fallen into a 'classed' hierarchy of local authority areas, Enway's schools were widely treated as if they constituted a 'classed' hierarchy of their own.

And as Vuillamy and Webb (2000) have identified, 'the policy of open enrolment can lead to a status pecking order of schools whereby (oversubscribed) schools can refuse to admit pupils whom they believe are likely to be a problem whereas other schools are forced to take them'(10).

The place of each of Enway's schools within the 'pecking order' appeared to be partially affected by long-standing reputation; partially by placement in the league-tables; and partially by perceptions of each school's markers of 'social class'. Bourdieu (1979) has identified what I understand to be the 'classed' and somewhat overlapping differences between these sets of 'markers' as 'distinction', demonstrated by roughly correlated sets of, for example, 'taste', 'ascetic disposition', and economic practices. In *Language and Symbolic Power* (1991) he extends this to the use of language (as evidenced in Jack's story, above).

I will attempt to demonstrate the effects of this 'school class distinction' on the flow of children and young people caught up in the disciplinary process in Enway. The stories of Lakeisha, Aisha, Helen and Joelle, below, give some examples of professionals' and families' understandings of the distinctions between the perceived 'low-income disadvantaged working-class' status of Newhall and Church Forest schools, the 'respectable working-class' and 'lower middle-class' Knightsdown College and Enway Valley School for Girls, and the 'middle-class' Pope John Paul Catholic School, set amongst ancient oak trees within the more affluent sector of the white enclave at the South end of Ennon Heath.

Lakeisha   Lakeisha, in Year 10, had been attending Enway Valley School for Girls. Her case had been heard at the Pupil Placement Panel; she was at risk of permanent exclusion for 'persistent disruptive', 'rude' behaviour, and had been placed at Church Forest School for a six week trial on a 'managed move'.[16] Enway Valley teachers and reception staff spoke softly in what I considered were middle-class accents and wore matching skirt-suits, and the uniforms there were feminine blouses with rounded collars in pastel colours. At Church Forest, many of the pupils were from Traveller backgrounds, and they wore their choice of black trousers with a green sweatshirt over a white polo shirt. The Church Forest interview was conducted by a genial loud-voiced PE teacher in a tracksuit with a strong Bradford accent. Lakeisha walked shyly into the room with her mother and aunt. She was identified as Caribbean-British (as her mother recorded on the ethnicity monitoring form), tall and solidly built - as the PE teacher suggested, she 'would be very good at the shot put and should try for the 2012 Olympics'- with a timid but broadening beautiful smile and large thick gold earrings. Her equally sparkling mother and aunt were similarly built; her mother was wearing a tight Lycra leopard-skin wrap-around top and had a gold front tooth. Both had strong Enway accents and grammar. Once Lakeisha realised that the PE teacher was friendly and was going to give her 'a fresh start' she visibly relaxed.

When asked what had gone wrong at Enway Valley, she shrugged and said, 'I don't know … but the teachers there are snobby.' She and her mother were relieved to be at Church Forest, and surprised that the uniform was only going to cost them £3.

CHAPTER 6

Aisha At the Pupil Placement Panel, Aisha, a pupil in Year 8,[17] was said by one of the admissions officers to have 'parents not perhaps as helpful as Enway Valley would like', and was placed at Newhall School because she already had friends there. There was a general sense at the Panel that she would be better off 'with her kind', Newhall being seen as the kind of school that a girl with 'unhelpful parents' would fit into. There had recently been a steady flow of pupils out of the drastically struggling Newhall School. These pupils were from aspiring working-class and lower middle-class families, and were moving to other schools generally because their parents were very unhappy with the quality of the education offered at Newhall. Newhall was thus becoming a school of those whose parents had not chosen or known to seek better for their children, and the spaces opening up there were filling up rapidly with pupils at risk of or subject to a permanent exclusion from Knightsdown and the similarly aspirational Enway Valley School for Girls.

Helen Just after Christmas, there was an incident at Pope John Paul, a mixed Catholic school set in a leafy stand of oak trees. The initial rumour around the local authority offices was that there had been a 'drugs scandal'. The thought of a drugs scandal amongst Pope John's pupils, the girls in their long dark green plaid kilts, and the boys with their mandatory short hair and smart blazers, all of whom were required to address women teachers as 'Madam', was quite surprising to many of my colleagues. But it was subsequently found that a girl had brought in some Paracetamol, pretended that it was the illegal drug 'ecstasy', and then taken a dose together with two friends. The three had spent the afternoon giggling and falling about in the learning support unit, and were subsequently 'managed-moved' out to other schools under threat of permanent exclusion.

The head teacher of the other Catholic school in Enway, Mary Magdalene Convent, was appealed to at the Pupil Placement Panel to take Helen, one of the pupils. However, she responded angrily, retorting in her strong Scottish accent, 'They are all spoilt middle-class girls; I'm not taking them!' I later contacted the family, and far from the privileged life that had been assumed for Helen, it transpired that the family was living on welfare benefits, and that her mother was a carer for her father who had been debilitated by a stroke two years before. She was also caring for Helen's grandfather, who was suffering a terminal illness in hospital in a neighbouring town.

Helen was subsequently moved to Enway Valley School for Girls. At her four week review meeting, I was concerned to see that she had lost weight, had very pale skin, was missing school due to tiredness and headaches, and had a row of lumpy yellowed sties under her eyelids. Her head of year assumed that these symptoms were due to 'the shock' of going from the solidly middle-class Pope John's to the working-class/ aspiring middle-class Enway Valley. I asked Helen what she was missing about Pope John's.

She told me, 'the people are snobbier at Pope John's, but I used to have 'common friends' when I was there. Not in school; out of school.' I did not quite understand whether or not Helen was saying that she missed Pope John's. Then I realised that she saw the 'snobbiness' of her Pope John classmates as a positive attribute, and meant that she could manage peer relations at Enway Valley because she had already been used to spending time with what she had described as 'common friends'. I looked at her mother, who was nodding sagely in agreement with her daughter, although she did look slightly concerned at Helen's assertion that she had already had 'common friends' when she was attending Pope John's. The head of year similarly appeared to understand what Helen was saying.

Helen's language reflected perhaps the experience of a family that had worked hard to achieve a place in the aspiring middle-classes. But this was by no means clear. Bourdieu (1979) explains the confusion: that 'we can speak of a class fraction although it is nowhere possible to draw a demarcation line such that we can find no one on either side who possesses all the properties most frequent on one side and none of the properties most frequent on the other' (259). Social class is fluid, complicated and entangled, and somewhat of a blunt analytic tool.

However, no matter how inexact such an attempt at a description of 'classed' hierarchies is, it is possible to say that Helen's move from Pope John's was precipitated by an act (the Paracetamol incident) which would probably have been roundly ignored at, for example, Church Forest, a school characterised by its population of working-class families. Further, Helen's worrying physical symptoms embodied class conflict: they were agreed by the head of year and her mother to be a result of a move to a school 'below' Pope John's in the social hierarchy of Enway schools. And finally, Helen herself had identified a difference between what she called her 'snobby' Pope John friends and her new 'common' friends at Enway Valley.

Joelle   A meeting was held at Newhall School to discuss Joelle, who had moved from Knightsdown Academy after she had been threatened with permanent exclusion for fighting, truanting and persistent disruptive behaviour. Her mother, Hannah, had had enough of arguing with Joelle, and was saying that she wanted her to go and live with her father. The family was struggling to function on a very deprived housing estate where the children were threatened by other young people on a daily basis at the bus stop outside their house.

Before the family was invited into the multi-agency meeting room, the head teacher of the Catholic primary school the children had attended, who had been invited to provide a background history of work with Joelle and Bradley, had told us, 'they're an unusual family for us. Usually they just go straight across to Pope Johnny's'.[18] I understood the familiar 'Johnny's' to denote an assumed automatic relationship. The head teacher continued, in amazement, 'there is a claim that she's a midwife!'

'I wouldn't want her delivering my baby,' joked the school's Attendance Officer. The head teacher laughed at this, continuing, 'she has this incredible control over men, I've seen it at work, she crashed the car outside school and called some man who just dropped everything … I don't know how it works'.

In other words, the Catholic primary school's 'usual' families automatically chose to attend the middle-class Pope John Paul's - and did not require any kind of support with socio-economic issues, such as asking a friend to help with a car crash as opposed to calling up the RAC. And the fact that the family was struggling with housing and behavioural issues placed them in a classed category that precluded Hannah from being allowed to have validly achieved a professional midwifery qualification. Further, the fact that she was a well-dressed and attractive woman, and yet appeared to the head teacher to be from a place in the social hierarchy 'below' that assumed of the 'usual' families attending the Catholic primary school, precluded her from being innocently allowed to have male friends who could assist her if necessary.

The stories of Helen, Lakeisha, Aisha and Joelle suggest that a classed 'social hierarchy' of schools existed in Enway and could perhaps have caused or exacerbated incidents of threatened or actual permanent exclusion. The incidents described above suggest that those Enway pupils who found themselves in a school which may not have matched their family's place in the 'social hierarchy' might have found themselves being over-reacted to, like Lakeisha; misunderstood and invisible, like Joelle; or, like Helen, pathologised as 'ill'. Table 1, below, shows a comparative view of the Enway schools and pupils I have discussed in this section, together with some of the marks of 'social class' I have mentioned and the relationships these may have with permanent exclusion. These include GCSE grades, uniform, location and linguistic features.

Whilst there will always be exceptions, this table suggests that in general for this small sample, the more expensive the uniform, the higher the GCSE results; there is also a correlation between the GCSE results, the social class suggested by some of the 'marks of distinction', and the level of severity of the acts for which pupils may be threatened with permanent exclusion. Osler and Vincent (2003) found a similar effect, particularly with reference to GCSE grades, suggesting that '[s]ince school exclusion is subject to market forces … [t]he only vacant places may be at schools where attainment levels are well below the national average and where the staff are already struggling to meet the needs of the students' (42). It can be seen that the movements of the pupils with whom I worked - that is, those at risk of permanent exclusion - tended to be in a downwards direction through the social class hierarchy, demonstrating the homogenising tendencies described by Vuillamy and Webb (2000).

Stephen Ball (2008), who has written extensively on social hierarchies in education, has suggested that classed hierarchies in education have not changed over the centuries. He draws some parallels between 'contemporary education policy issues and those in play at the beginning of education policy in the mid-19th century and some of the generic themes, continuities, recurrences, patterns and trends in education policy' (8). Classed assumptions, labels, and narratives had been imposed into Lakeisha's, Helen's, Joelle's and Aisha's extended bodies, via observations made about their parents, in some cases, rendering them transgressive and incompatible in terms of social class with their original schools. The contested space element of the pupils' extended bodies were here the site of contests between professionals from different schools.

Table 1.

School	Attainment (% of pupils who achived 5 A*-C grades at GCSE including maths and English in 2007)[19]	Pupils discussed above, with direction of movement from original school (▼) to destina-tion school (■)	Marks of school's class distinction (Bourdieu 1979)	Pupils (including those described above) have been at risk of or subjected to a permanent exclusion from this school for:	Suggested 'social class' of school:
Pope John Paul Catholic School	61%	Helen ▼ Joelle ▼	Uniform: £30 blazers; long kilts and blazers Pupils described as 'snobbier' Addressing women teachers as 'Madam' Leafy suburban location Catholic school	Bringing Paracetamol to school; pretending it was 'ecstasy' Causing death to a living creature (child with Tourettes Syndrome threw a frog across a room)	Middle-class
Enway Valley School for Girls	41%	Lakeisha ▼ Aisha ▼ Helen ■	Uniform: £15 pastel blouses Pupils described as 'common' Teachers' middle-class accents Long history as a respectable girls' school demonstrated in mini-museum in reception area	Persistent disruptive behaviour Swearing Not following instructions	Working-class/ aspiring middle-class
Newhall School	19%	Aisha ■ Joelle ■	£3 uniform (polo shirt) Chaotic behaviour: text books thrown out of windows; multiple sexual assaults in school; pupils escaping over fences Rubbish-strewn grounds	One for disruptive behaviour One for head-butting a teacher None for several instances of sexual assault- no clear framework	Low income disadvantaged/ working-class
Church Forest School	15%	Lakeisha ■	£3 uniform (polo shirt) Many Traveller families Accent and casual dress of interviewing teacher	Just one in two years- for lighting a firework in an upstairs corridor- head teacher did not agree with permanent exclusions	Low income disadvantaged/ working-class

Engaging in the Contested Space of the Extended Body Through Multi-Agency Working: Class Conflict?

Just as local authority areas and schools might be seen to have their own 'class hierarchy', I have attempted to unpack inter-professional conflict by considering some of the various 'support' agencies in similar terms.

The 'psy' techniques identified by Rose (1999) and discussed in chapter four as disciplinary mechanisms used to maintain support and attention on a within-child basis, were sometimes delivered in Enway through family and individual therapy sessions and forensic psychological assessments by the local Child and Adult Mental Health Services (CAMHS). These were required to be delivered as part of a cohesive plan of support in partnership with the other agencies working with a young person. As the government of the time explained,

> Because services that contribute towards the mental health and psychological wellbeing of children are provided by so many agencies, including universal services, the effective commissioning of CAMHS is inescapably a multi-agency activity … There should be full participation and ownership of the process by health, social services and education, and other key partners such as youth justice.

> DCSF: 2003

However, this 'full participation and ownership' process proved to be difficult in Enway. One of my Inclusion Team colleagues, on return from a planning meeting for a school conference on CAMHS therapeutic techniques, told me that she had advised the organisers to 'speak a language schools can understand if they are going to invite them'. The Enway CAMHS workers I came across tended to have middle-class accents and were very articulate. This sometimes had the effect of belittling other professionals, especially those who did not use the same kinds of technical vocabulary.

Other services also established classed boundaries between professions. For example, Jacques, an education officer colleague within the Youth Offending Service (YOS)[20] told me that he was not being called 'an officer' but had been:

> given a label as a specialist 'worker' … they've already sidelined me. Then you have the massive animals in there. YOS stick together and YISP (Youth Inclusion and Support Project) stick together and YOS see YISP as glorified youth workers … they don't really know.

> Field-notes December 2008

In his mind, my colleague explained, 'a glorified youth worker' commanded a lower salary, and correspondingly, less professional respect. So when a young person had, for instance, a YISP worker, a senior teacher, and a forensic psychologist from CAMHS, all working together, class-based power struggles between the professionals may sometimes have distracted attention from the young person's wants or needs.

This power-struggle was in evidence when a referral was made to YISP, asking them to engage Jack, described above, in some out-of-school activities to help keep him focussed. But because CAMHS were involved, the YISP worker kept telling me that she was anxious not to 'overload' Jack with services. It was not until after a multi-agency meeting where I expressly asked the CAMHS forensic psychologist and the social work manager to detail what it was that the YISP worker should be doing to help Jack that I was able to persuade her to start her work with him. The time between referral and agreement was around four weeks. In the meantime, with nothing else to do after school, Jack continued to roam the streets, annoying dangerous older peers, climbing scaffolding, and taunting the police. It may be that if the YISP worker had felt that she was on an equal level with the CAMHS staff and social work manager, she may have been able to suggest a programme of activities, instead of waiting to be told what to do.

Another example of the effects of the 'classed' hierarchies between services involved Vicky, the Appledown pupil I discussed in chapter five. Following a long period of adjustment during which time she had worked extensively in a small therapeutic unit on her self-esteem and social confidence, Vicky had been given a placement at Knightsdown College. Knightsdown was a very large school - one of the biggest in Enway - but it was also one of the best organised. It benefited from a large cohort of professionals able to use 'psy' techniques to support her: learning mentors, counsellors, transition workers, and behaviour support assistants. There was also an immediately available space in the year group, and Peter, the educational psychologist, and I made a home visit to explain that it was the fastest and most supportive option available. However, we had a long struggle on our hands. Without having consulted with those of us who worked within education services, Vicky's mother had been told by a CAMHS family therapist that Knightsdown was 'too big' for Vicky and that she should try to get a place at Ennon Castle School. Peter and I were perturbed at this: Ennon Castle was admittedly not as big at Knightsdown, but it was much more chaotic; given Vicky's experiences at Appledown and the length of time she had spent cocooned in a small unit, I was not happy about the idea that she might have to cope with institutionalised disorganisation. I knew, also, that there was a significant bullying problem at Ennon Castle, and that some girls had been subjected to sexual assault. With some difficulty, we managed to persuade the family that Knightsdown was the better choice. Was our CAMHS colleague's propensity to give education advice without consulting education specialists a result of the elevated social status of her organisation? As an education worker, I would never have presumed to have done the opposite and given Vicky a mental health diagnosis.

So it can be seen that stepping into the borderlands (Anzaldua 1987) of class difference and class prejudice between schools, local authorities, and professionals can have the effect of disadvantaging young people who are within range of a permanent exclusion.

CLASS, 'RACE' AND GENDER IN EXCLUSION FROM SCHOOL

Entangled with class struggles between local authorities, schools, and professionals, and between professionals and families, were assumptions made about gender and 'race' or ethnicity. As I described in chapter five, because of their gender, many of the girls in Enway who had had to move because of the threat of permanent exclusion had to accept places on vocational courses focussed on 'care' professions - whether animal, child, or beauty - rather than the more academic GCSEs. And in terms of perceptions about cultural heritage, 'race' and ethnicity (discussed in detail in chapter seven), Nama, the Iraqi Kurdish pupil at risk of a forced marriage introduced in chapter five, was disadvantaged partly because of the loss of social standing experienced by her father and uncle on their arrival in England. In the push to raise the family's social standing, their sense of hope for her educational attainment had served to push aside all other concerns about her mental and emotional health. When she began at Ennon Castle school, for example, Nama's father was anxious that she be placed in the 'top' class for science, and did not mention that she had stopped eating and taking the insulin injections she needed to survive her serious diabetes condition. He was worried that Ennon Castle might not want to take her in if they knew about her medical needs. Staff at Appledown, Nama's previous school, had known that she was diabetic, and she had had regular appointments with the school nurse. But on being permanently excluded from Appledown, Nama had to attend a school that did not know this about her. And the complex dissociation from his social class and professional identity that her father experienced as a result of having to flee, a refugee, to England, had prompted him to place his daughter's career potential above her health.

There is a risk of thinking about class ethnocentrically. Taking into account the wide variety of cultural backgrounds within Enway school populations, it is important to acknowledge the idea that social class may look different depending on the dominant cultures. Bourdieu (1979) has himself warned against 'the dangers of a facile search for partial equivalences which cannot stand in for a methodological comparison between systems' (xii). In Enway schools, social class was often ascribed or assumed by reference to parental work status, and this precluded the possibility that class may cut across families more often in some cultures than in others. However, Bourdieu (1979) also suggests that 'there is nothing more universal than the project of objectifying the mental structures associated with the particularity of a social structure' (xiv). With a reflexive approach to the normalising pressure to think ethnocentrically, the complex class-'race'-gender interactions revealed by stories like Nama's, above, can still benefit from a partial analysis through the concept of class.

CONCLUSION

This chapter has illuminated some of the coded class prejudice which might be seen to exist within and between schools, local authorities and professionals in and around Enway. In carrying out this survey, I have investigated the effects of this class prejudice on children and young people at risk of or subject to an incident of permanent exclusion from school.

Education can be seen more as an economic enterprise designed to produce workers for a socially hierarchised economy than a means to foster a love of learning and develop self-esteem and resilience (McCarthy *et al.* 2005; Ball 2001; Tomlinson 2006). This has focussed the effects of a pupil's own socio-economic status even more keenly on his or her schooling experience, including his or her experience of disciplinary frameworks.

It is apparent that the schools are aware of the inequities reproduced through the education system, because 'the motivation to massage (quantitative performance data) arises not only from schools wishing to present themselves in the best possible light but also to counteract simplistic inter-school comparisons arising from the lack of a level playing field' (Vuillamy and Webb 2000:10). Schools are usually run by educated professionals who tend to be middle-class. And even whilst many schools acknowledge and try to ameliorate disadvantage, they may be distracted by the 'weak' version of inclusion (Viet-Wilson 1998 in Macrae *et al.* 2003: 90; introduced in chapter one), failing then to effect systemic change in what this book suggests to be a systemic problem. And as I suggested in chapter one, it may be the case that governments are more concerned with listening to middle-class conceptions of 'what needs to change' in education, looking on working-class families who do not have a choice about living on a low income as constituting 'a social problem'. In fact New Labour's education policies have been described as 'based on a notion of the 'ideal' parent ... one with middle-class resources, dispositions and values' (Reay 2008: 643).

And whilst middle-class parents and professionals have something to gain from their socio-economic position, it is difficult to understand how change will be made. Perhaps this is why the framing of 'social deprivation' and the corresponding focus on parenting skills as a cause for educational failure uses social class hierarchy to distract attention from institutional failures. These circumstances conspire to make it more difficult to challenge existing inequities in the administration of permanent exclusion from school.

NOTES

[1] How a school may be defined as 'working-class' or 'middle-class' is defined with regard to Bourdieu's (1977) theories of social, cultural and linguistic capital, below.
[2] 'Constructive exclusion' here could as well be applied to the processes of 'managed moves' I have described in chapter four.
[3] Although I acknowledge the risk of essentialising on the basis of a class label.
[4] This possibility for the position of expressions of agency in the extended body is developed further in other chapters, notably chapter eight.
[5] Horizontal violence is often subjective, but subjective violence is not always horizontal.
[6] *Vuillamy and Webb (2000: 10).*
[7] See chapter eight for a detailed explanation of the origins and effects of policy narratives.

8   At the time of writing, the future of 14–19 Diplomas are in doubt, and the four 'academic' Diplomas, due to go on-stream in September 2010, were cancelled by the incoming Conservative-Liberal democrat coalition government in June 2010.

9   ARTI was an intensive multi-agency project intended to support young people at risk of violent or sexual offending, permanent exclusion from school, and/or going into foster care; first mentioned in chapter five.

10   Aged eleven to twelve years old.

11   The effect of a discourse of pathology has been seen throughout the previous chapters to distract attention away from institutional failings, so perhaps this is one of the reasons it is so readily available.

12   Twelve to thirteen years old.

13   Education (areas to which pupils and students belong) Regulations 1996

14   The implications of vocational education have been discussed here and in chapters four and five.

15   Aged 13–14 years old

16   Managed moves are explained in chapter four.

17   Aged 12–13 years old.

18   Pope John Paul's Catholic Comprehensive School- widely acknowledged in Enway as at the top of the hierarchy of schools.

19   www.DCSF.gov.uk

20   Introduced in the previous chapter.

INSTITUTIONAL RACISM AND THE SOCIAL BOUNDARIES BETWEEN PEOPLE

The research laid out in chapter six suggests that social class was opaque in professionals' conversation, but class prejudice was readily detectable under the surface. The discourse on 'race' and ethnicity is similarly understood in this chapter to be layered thickly under a 'colour-blind' surface. Professional discourses about particular cultural groups in Enway worked to distract attention from institutional failures. And as in the cases of gender and social class, institutional racism in this chapter will be explained as both a cause of some permanent exclusions from school, and as an exacerbated feature in the experiences of children and young people who are excluded or at risk of being excluded. As Gillborn and Youdell (2000) explain, 'the colour-blind nature' of New Labour's education policy belied 'the racialised reality of life in contemporary Britain' and threatened 'racist consequences' (29). These consequences emerged throughout my fieldwork. For example, I wrote in my field-notes:

A Youth Offending Team education officer made a joke at the last Panel about how the most appropriate education placement for a Traveller pupil would be 'tied to a tree'. There was much laughter. At this week's Panel, in an attempt to redraw the ground rules, the Chair reminded the Panel members that 'in Enway we treat all members of society with respect'. Her comment was met with much groaning, giggling and rolling of eyes. It was as if the statement was 'political correctness gone mad' and that racist jokes about Traveller children should be acceptable. Later on, a long conversation about whether a young person's mother was capable of educating her at home[1] was only halted when it was pointed out that there was no evidence that she could not, and that the only information we had about this pupil was her name, which 'sounded Indian'. There was an embarrassed lull as Panel members acknowledged that they had been making assumptions based on the girl's name. But it's difficult to keep pointing these things out; it seems that around three such comments at each Panel is all that can be tolerated before people start 'tutting' and muttering about getting on with the job at hand.

February 2008

This chapter thus attempts to approach an entangled subject which benefits greatly from the use of ethnography, with its requirement for attention to syncretic detail. It requires what Back (2008) has called 'training a serious attentiveness' onto a subject thick with misconceptions and assumptions.

INTRODUCTION

This chapter begins with an overview of some of the research around exclusion and ethnicity. In order to try to avoid misconceptions in discussing this subject, the chapter proceeds with a clarification of the importance of not essentialising experience on the basis of someone's ascribed 'race', defining ethnicity as 'relational and processual' (Eriksen 1995: 254). A definition of 'institutional racism' in administrative practices of representation follows, drawing in the complicating issue of self-representation. The interaction between professionals' assumptions on the basis of 'race', gender and class is then described. The chapter moves on to look at the policy context of the discussion, addressing policy discourses on multiculturalism, including the invisibility and inaudibility of ethnicity in both policy discourse and professional talk.

The ethnographic section of this chapter focuses on a range of issues, each illustrating the idea that institutional racism may be, like classism and sexism, a cause of some permanent exclusions and an exacerbating and exacerbated effect of school disciplinary frameworks (see chapters five and six). It addresses an ignored series of racist conflicts in one of Enway's schools; the way in which the Traveller community was treated; language issues, particularly around translation services; and the effects at the Pupil Placement Panel of age assessments carried out on young immigrants by border control officers. The section ends with an illustration of institutional prejudice through the Panel's response to a white boy's claim of racism; and issues around cultural attitudes towards mental health services. One family in Enway tried to address institutional racism directly, naming and challenging it, and the chapter concludes with a discussion of what the consequences to this approach may have meant.

ETHNICITY AND EXCLUSION

Inequity in Attainment and Exclusion

Inequities in the education system on the basis of ethnicity are a long-standing feature of research into exclusion. As Christian (2005) explains, 'Black underachievement and exclusion has been a mainstay in the British education system for decades' (328). He suggests that this problem emerged against a landscape where 'Black British presence was viewed as largely problematic and a threat to the "British way of life"' (328). A resultant pathologisation of children and young people who are perceived as 'not white' is thought to be partially at the basis of the educational circumstances and teacher attitudes underpinning 'black' underachievement and exclusion. As Christian (2005) explains, 'Black male children ... have been ... pathologised as being aggressive ... White teachers' expectations are low and any sign of a child's dissent ... leads to a labelling and stigmatization process that follows him ... through each stage of schooling' (340). These labels are further embedded through stereotypes perpetrated in the media (Blair 2001).

Parsons (2008) reports on a continued disproportionately low level of achievement and high level of exclusion amongst 'black' and other minority ethnic young people in England, including gypsy Roma and Irish Traveller children (see also Christian 2005). For example, an overview of national data for the years 1998 to 2006 reveals the fact that 'Black Caribbean pupils are 2.6 times as likely to be permanently excluded compared with the average' (408). He partially attributes this to 'a neo-liberal cultural and political stance which upholds a competitive individualistic educational environment' (402). As Parsons (2008) identifies, this political stance also 'disregards enduring group under-achievement and remains passive in the face of evidence of racial inequalities' (402), and this is borne out in the ethnographic evidence, below, of Enway schools failing to recognise or even speak of 'race'-based inequity, either institutional or between pupils.

Disaffection

A theme running through conceptualisations of particularly black underachievement and exclusion is the notion of disaffection (Graham and Robinson 2004; Christian 2005; Izekor 2007). As Izekor (2007) states, 'the descriptors vary but not much, 'low-achievers, socially excluded, hard to reach, at risk of offending, not participating, difficult to engage''(65). Compare these labels with the name given to those young people who are discussed at the Enway Panel: 'Hard to Place'. These are labels, pathologising the child. What has led to these labels, so easily applied, and which lend themselves to a pathologising stance? Izekor (2007) asks, 'how is it that many young black boys appear to become increasingly 'disruptive' as they progress from primary to secondary school?' (65). Graham and Robinson (2004) explain that

> Schools are ... racialized places where deeply held beliefs and expectations are an integral part of the school process and practices. Black children enter these contested public spheres where issues of race and gender are inextricably tied to education, achievement, and success.
>
> 655–656

It is this institutional context – similar to Anzaldua's (1980) description of borderland space (see chapter three) - which can perhaps lead to a child's abnegation. Blair (2001), in her interviews with black young people, demonstrates some of the evidence which might lead to a young person looking 'disaffected'. She has reported them to be 'demoralised'; to feel 'a great deal of rage and confusion about their schooling' (73) She attributes this to a system which 'denies them recognition through the curriculum, undermines their sense of self, appears indifferent to their needs, makes learning meaningless and is so ... controlling ... that they find little to distinguish between schools and detention centres' (73). Izekor (2007) explains that 'the young men themselves ... respond to their perceived socio-enemies by seemingly fulfilling the stereotypes and finding new ways of hitting back at a society that seems determined to see them as problems to be solved'(66).

Institutional Racism and Institutional Silence

The pathologisation of 'black' children in education has also meant that 'Black families have been the main locus of debate and discussion about the educational "problems" of their children' (Graham and Robinson 2004: 654). This representation of the parents of 'black' children as problematic is often exacerbated by parents' defensiveness in the face of school inequities. School staff often respond by arranging meetings with several colleagues designed to outnumber the parents – who often have negative memories of school themselves (Izekor (2007). The discussion of Thomas and Loxley (2001) in chapter three explains how the pathologisation of individual students directs attention away from an institution. In this case, it could be directing attention away from institutional racism. Parsons (2008) points out that '(t)he differences in attainment of some minority ethnic groups, especially black Caribbean pupils ... and the different characteristics of black pupils excluded from school call for closer investigation of the possible operation of institutional racism' (415). Christian (2005) agrees, suggesting that the high proportion of 'black' students permanently excluded from school indicates that 'Britain is a racially prejudiced nation in that its major institutions have negatively perceived and reacted to the presence of people of color' (328). Many theorists see a manifestation of this institutional prejudice in a set of 'race relations' policies which fail to incorporate context, and focus on an assimilationist model which fails to account for and provide adequate frameworks for ameliorating inequity (Parsons 2008; Christian 2005; Graham and Robinson 2004). This amounts to a silencing in terms of institutional discourses about racism. In fact, Graham and Robinson (2004) speak of a 'continuing denial of race and racism in British educational policy' (656) and a directly related failure on the part of most schools and local authorities to address educational inequity on the basis of ethnicity.

Why are schools seemingly so reluctant to name and deal with issues of institutional racism? This could partly be as a result of the issue of motive. Blair (2001) acknowledges this as 'a sticking point' around possibilities for addressing racism in schools. She explains that '(b)ecause a teacher's intentions are not malicious, it is often assumed that the fault lies with the 'chip on the shoulder' of the person who experiences a particular interaction as racist' (9). This, exacerbated or constructed by the legal construction of prejudice (that is, it is the perception of the recipient of the prejudice that is taken into account: Race Relations Act 1976) leads to a silencing effect on any claim of racism. As Gordon (2001) explains, silence of this nature is 'a social construct, critical to maintaining the societal taboo around racism in ... British society' (319 in Graham and Robinson 2004: 655). The evidence of institutional racism surrounding cases of permanent exclusion from school, and the silence around racism in schools, is a central finding of this chapter.

ON NOT ESSENTIALISING 'RACE'

Against the backdrop of these reports of inequity, the problem with trying to talk about 'race', ethnicity, national identity, or culture, is that as with an essentialised conception of gender (Butler 1999 and chapter five), and of class (discussed in chapter six), it is difficult to categorise people without doing them the disfavour of essentialising their alleged experience (Hall 1992; Gilroy 1998; Ball *et al.* 2002; Archer and Francis 2007; also see chapter one). As Izekor (2007) explains of the most common short-hand 'ethnicity' label in education policy and schools in England – 'BME' (black and minority ethnic): it is

> an incredibly wide grouping that means all things and nothing all at once ... [in an] attempt to wrap up the needs, desires and challenges of young men from north, south, west, east and Central Africa, the many islands of the Caribbean, most of eastern Europe, Asian, Muslim, Christian, Sikh, gypsy, Irish and any other minority community in England at any given time.

68

In a time when places and people can be described as 'multicultural', 'multiracialised', or 'culturally entangled' (Archer and Yamishita 2005: 120), any essentialising description based on 'race' or ethnicity constitutes a clear intrusion into the extended body - vulnerable to an imagined representation because of its porous boundaries and with all the attendant 'validity' of the biological discourse (discussed in relation to gender in chapter five). Gilroy (1987) describes a group of writers who have 'made 'race' into a synonym for ethnicity and a sign for the sense of separateness which endows groups with an exclusive, collective identity ... for these writers, blacks live not in the castle of their skin but behind the sturdy walls of discrete ethnic identities' (3). The extended body, with its double porous rings, reflects the body's vulnerability to being represented within this kind of framework (and therefore it becoming part of one's experience), the inner circle corresponding to 'the castle of their skin'; the outer ring being 'the sturdy walls of discrete ethnic identities'.

Further complicating the issue, because of social and professional linguistic filters (known sometimes derogatively as 'political correctness'), people working in the children's services department and schools of Enway were sometimes not verbally direct about the judgements they were making on the basis of a person's perceived 'ethnic identity'.[2] Because of this, I am taking the approach in this chapter that whilst "cultural traits' do not entail ethnicity ... the focus of research ought to be the social boundaries between groups rather than the 'cultural stuff' they contain ... ethnicity must therefore be seen as an aspect of a relationship, not as a property of a person or a group' (Eriksen 1995:251). Gilroy (1987) describes 'the cultural not as an intrinsic property of ethnic particularity but as a mediating space between agents and structures in which their reciprocal dependency is created and secured' (3). In other words, 'race' and ethnicity are relative concepts (Eriksen 1995; Gilroy 1987), and as with 'class' (see chapter six) and gender (see chapter five), assumptions based on 'ethnicity' have at least as much to reveal about those making the assumptions (and their own ethnic-cultural discourses) as those about whom assumptions are being made.[3]

So, if 'ethnicity is relational and processual: ...not a 'thing', but an aspect of a social process' (Eriksen 1995: 254), an instance of official or unofficial permanent exclusion from school, as a critical moment, can demonstrate what happens when the state's blunt instruments encounter what might be perceived as an essentialised cultural identity, whether this is on the basis of nationality, ethnicity, culture, religion, or language. Solomos and Back explain that, '[o]ne of the fundamental criticisms of the sociology of race and ethnic relations is that it has too often focused on the victims rather than the perpetrators of racism' (2000:21). Thus whilst it is difficult to talk about 'race' or ethnicity without essentialising the experience of those discussed, it is a much more easily identified and less objectifying task in the context of this book to focus on the 'perpetrators' of racism; to describe the institutional racism experienced by young people and their parents in the midst of an experience of actual or threatened permanent exclusion.

INSTITUTIONAL RACISM IN ADMINISTRATIVE PRACTICES OF REPRESENTATION

By 'institutional racism', I am referring to that racially motivated prejudice which the Macpherson Report in 1999[4] on the murder of the black London teenager Stephen Lawrence found throughout the police force. It constitutes the effects of an institutionalised indirect or direct prejudiced treatment of a person on the basis of essentialising representations of their ethnicity, 'race', or cultural identity. In order to think about the situation in Enway, I am using the concept of institutional racism to refer to a weight of administrative occurrences or representations that consistently push against the anti-prejudice actions of those who are reflexive about administrative prejudice within the local authority (see also Christian 2005).

The occurrences of systemic racist representation can be described as 'institutional' because they do not necessarily constitute the viciously direct prejudice of one person, but the deeper effects of a sometimes subtle blend of instances of exclusion or resistance to inclusion (such as 'gatekeeping' practices), or resistance by neglect. In this sense, institutional racism is similar to the concept of 'objective violence', whereas direct interpersonal prejudice could be thought of as 'subjective violence' (Zizek 2008, discussed above in chapters 5 and 6). As Sivananden (2005) states, 'the racism that needs to be contested is not personal prejudice, which has no authority behind it, but institutionalised racism, woven over centuries of colonialism and slavery into the structures of society and government.' This goes some way towards explaining why young people at risk of being or actually permanently excluded are sometimes negatively represented in Enway as a result of their 'race' or ethnicity, as described below.

Hall explains, 'We all now use the word representation, but, as we know, it is an extremely slippery customer. It can be used ... simply as another way of talking about how one images a reality that exists 'outside' the means by which things are represented' (1992:253). Thus the young people discussed at the Pupil Placement Panel can be posited as having been constituted as *relatively* 'outside', and the Panel itself is 'the means by which things are represented': representation, when used by a dominant power, becomes an 'othering' device, increasing the already heavy negative pressure on a young person at risk of or subject to a permanent exclusion (see also Rattansi and Donald 1992; Blair 2001). As Eriksen (1995) explains, '[e] thnic classification ... has something to do with the creation of social order in the environment by providing a division into 'kinds' of people.' (252). However, Hall's exposition of the politics of representation posits these institutionalised, administrative practices as powerfully constitutive:

[H]ow things are represented and the 'machineries' and regimes of representation in a culture do play a constitutive ... role. This gives questions of culture and ideology, and the scenarios of representation - subjectivity, identity, politics - a formative, not merely an expressive, place in the constitution of social and political life.

1992:254

As described in the ethnographic data below, 'formative' representation may constitute a response to an unfamiliar name on a document, or a person's religion, national 'identity', 'foreign' name, language, refugee or asylum status, or appearance. And it relies on a representation that constitutes a perceived difference between 'those who are from here and/or who are like us', and 'those who are not from here and/or like us'- described by Hall (1992) as 'belongingness and otherness' (255). Building on Hall's (1992) concept of 'formative' representation, and fundamental to the theoretical framework of analysis in this book, is the idea that the extended body incorporates the experience that 'formative' representation can produce. It is not static or only visual or linguistic: it is entangled kaleidoscopically with a subject's own identity, embodied characteristics, and biological processes, and creates a deep level of affect (see the discussion in chapter three referring to Blackman and Venn 2010).

The dangers of Hall's (1992) 'binary system of representation' - that framework which relies on a concept of 'belongingness and otherness' (255) - were crystallised in comments made to me by James, the former Chief Inspector for Ethnic Minority Achievement in Enway. Having successfully helped to raise the attainment of 'black boys' in Enway, James was made redundant. The new focus of concern in Enway was 'white boys', and a conference held on 'white boys' achievement' was held in Enway towards the end of 2006–07 school year. 'Ethnic minority achievement' was now seen as an outdated concept; the 'Ethnic Minority Achievement Service' had had its name changed to the 'Home-School Liaison Service'. James told me that his redundancy was the result of the administration's failure to see (or represent) 'white British' as 'an ethnicity', and that it constituted a process of 'othering'. It has been established that 'the embattled, hegemonic conception of 'Englishness' ... does not represent itself as an ethnicity at all' (Hall 1992:257; see also Osler and Vincent 2003: 17). In an effort to disrupt this 'white/non-white' dichotomy, instead of describing instances of institutional racism towards specific groups or 'ethnicities', or presenting any given pupil's experience as representative of any specific group, I will try to use the ethnographic methodology to 'study up' (Nader 1972): to expose a narrative of institutional racism in Enway.

SELF REPRESENTATION

Part of the reason why it has been difficult for me to purport to discuss individual young people's experiences of racism within the deconstructed, anti-essentialising post-modern theoretical framework of this book is that ethnic identity has been described as relational, flexible, self-determined and context-sensitive, whilst concurrently vulnerable to being fixed in place through stereotype or external representation (Eriksen 1995; Ball *et al.* 2002; Gillborn and Youdell 2000).[5] This tension is a good example of what can happen within the contested space of the extended body, and exemplifies the push-pull between self-identification (or dis-identification; Skeggs 1997) and imposed (and subsequently experienced) representation. Compounding this problem within the context of a discussion about permanent exclusion from school, 'issues of identity and inequality are central to understanding young people's relationship to education since identities can provide important sites of resistance to participation in education' (Archer and Yamashita 2003:116). Thus pupils can be trapped in a double-bind: the very ways in which they represent themselves as 'an expression of resistance'- within a system based on a hierarchy characterised by the existence of permanent exclusion as a sanction- can become a 'reason' for the administrative forces to turn against them and a cause of permanent exclusion.

GENDER, 'CLASS' AND INSTITUTI.ONAL RACISM

In Enway, as in some other parts of England (Evans 2007), thinking about educational attainment and exclusion could currently be said to be 'located within wider contemporary panics about boys' educational 'underachievement' ... (which are partially attributed) to the rise of feminism and the 'overachievement' of girls' (Archer and Yamashita 2003:116; see also Osler and Vincent 2003 and chapter five). And concerns focused specifically on boys can serve to exclude a discourse that tackles inequity on the grounds of 'race' and ethnicity within gender and class groups. Tomlinson (2005) has identified the fact that 'anxieties in England about 'boys' underachievement' were in fact about white male underachievement, and the overall improvement in girls' school performance masked the educational difficulties of significant numbers of girls from minority backgrounds' (161; see also Wright 2005; Osler and Vincent 2003). Whilst concerns focussed on gender can illuminate or obscure deeper understandings informed by thinking about racism, it must be noted that 'class, migration, and ethnicity are integrally connected concepts' (Archer and Yamashita 2003: 122). It is not that we must conflate 'race' or ethnicity with social deprivation - this can have the effect of distracting attention from institutional racism and classism (see chapter six). But studies of the effects of a person's 'race' or ethnicity on their educational success acknowledge that the 'class fractions' found within an 'ethnic group' are importantly revealing and constitutive of a person's experience (Blair 2001; Ball *et al.* 2002; Francis 2005).

So the focus of this chapter should be read within the context of the previous chapters on gender and 'class', with an acknowledgement that experiences to do with 'race' and ethnicity are inextricably intertwined with 'class' and gender. However, stories of institutional racism can usefully demonstrate the kinds of struggles taking place within the contested space of an excluded pupil's extended body. These stories illustrate the extended body's vulnerability to being channelled into a sustained experience through external forces of representation.

INSTITUTIONAL RACISM: THE INVISIBILITY OF 'ETHNICITY' IN OFFICIAL REPRESENTATIONS OF EXCLUSION IN ENWAY

In looking at potential links between permanent exclusion and institutional racism, it is important first to investigate the Enway professional and policy approach to 'race' and ethnicity.

In the multicultural district of Enway any underachievement exacerbated by institutional racism was conflated with (and thus its quality of exacerbation by racism made invisible through) discourses of social deprivation (Tomlinson 2005; see also chapter six). This very conflation was presented to James, the Chief Inspector for Ethnic Minority Achievement introduced above, as the reasoning behind his redundancy and replacement with a new Chief Inspector for Vulnerable Children. And at a children's services conference in Enway in October 2008, the new Director of Children's Services gave an address in which the multicultural composition of Enway was not mentioned once. Instead, we heard about 'our most vulnerable children'; 'looked after children' (in foster care); 'those young people for whom school is proving too problematic'; 'young people involved in offending behaviour'; and young people who were 'NEET'.[6] The Director also explained that 'The Enway Statistical Profile of Children and Young People [was] the basis of our Needs Analysis and [five year] Enway Children and Young People Plan'. In one report collated by a policy officer and fed into the Enway Statistical Profile, it was explained that the 55 pupils who were 'white' out of the 94 pupils permanently excluded in 2005–2006 constituted 'an overrepresentation' of 'white' pupils: 59% of the total excluded.[7] But although the statistical breakdown of 'white' had revealed a large differential in the rates of exclusion between pupils of 'white British', 'Traveller Irish', 'Traveller Gypsy Roma' and 'white other' backgrounds, this had not been identified as worthy of inclusion in the 'Enway Children and Young People Plan 2008–2011'. This demonstrates a version of non-colour-coded institutional racism in action. So whilst the Director had told us in her speech, 'every number is a child … you will have me on your back if the data is not accurate and robust and timely', statistics, in Enway, were as vulnerable to interpretation and representation as the extended body. Another policy officer I spoke to in Enway told me that in order to look into the effects a pupil's ethnicity had on the likelihood of exclusion, a five year sample would be needed to achieve the requirements of statistical significance, and that whilst this information would be available, they had never been asked for it. I felt that this neglect also constituted an element of institutional racism.

Osler and Vincent (2003) assert, 'institutional racism needs to be considered as one explanatory factor in … exclusion rates' (26). They also state that 'Teachers need to be sensitised to the everyday racisms of school life and to their impact on minority ethnic students' (ibid). The following ethnographic section offers an example of how 'institutional' and 'everyday' racisms can be linked.

Conflict at Ennon Grand Academy

As in Enway's official statistical data and policy pronouncements, an understanding of issues surrounding 'race' and ethnicity was not detectable in professionals' talk and actions at Ennon Grand Academy. Some of the white boys I supported into new schools from Ennon Grand had found themselves at risk of permanent exclusion due to conflicts they had become involved in with large groups of Somali pupils. Each one of the families separately described how their child had been chased all the way home by these groups, who had then thrown sticks and bottles at the house, threatened to break windows, and made sexually violent threats against the boys' mothers and sisters. The families themselves spoke using racist language and complained that the Somali children were 'getting all the attention' at school. I was concerned that this situation may have been exacerbated by a manifestation of a fear of the local Somali population invoked by emerging media discourses about Islamic terrorism. And as I explained in chapter five, the Enway 'Hard to Place' Pupil Placement Panel often conflated 'Somali' with 'gang member'. As Archer and Yamashita have identified,

> Working-class, inner-city and certain minority ethnic young men have been positioned as high-profile 'problems' within current social and educational policy discourses … Within popular discourses, too, these young men are frequently portrayed in 'folk devil' terms, being associated with inner-city social problems such as crime, deviance and unemployment, the causes of which have been linked to the boys' problematic subcultures and/or class/ethnic cultures and their 'anti-education' masculine identities.

2003:115

I was anxious to address this as a possible explanation for what I thought of as a rise in race-related conflict at Ennon Grand. But the school was proud of the recent award it had won for challenging bullying, and despite repeatedly voicing my concerns that Somali children may be grouping together for mutual support in a hostile environment and retaliating to racist comments made by white children, putting both groups in danger from each other and the police, I was told by members of the senior management that there was no problem; everything had been dealt with and they had never heard of any racism at the school.

Travellers

Both institutional and direct racism towards Traveller pupils were even more difficult to identify, name and discuss than the Ennon Grand violence, because they were often characterised by a school's neglect towards instances of school absence. Instead, institutional and direct racism towards Travellers was something revealed in the 'gaps' and 'silences' (Blackman 2001:8). Travellers attending Enway schools did not tend to get permanently excluded. This was partly because it was not only difficult to get some Traveller children to attend secondary school, but it was often difficult to get secondary schools to accept Traveller children in the first place. One Gypsy Roma family from Romania still had four children out of school after several months of applications to the Admissions service because the head teacher of Cherry Tree School decided that she did not want them to attend. From the school's point of view, they had attempted to contact the family on numerous occasions to bring them in for an interview. But as Emily, the Senior Traveller Education Consultant in Enway, explained, the family had been abroad to see relatives, where the mother had fallen ill. They had since returned, but needed translation and transport to get to the school for an interview. 'The school', as my colleagues in Children's Services saw it (actually the head teacher),[8] was unmoved at this report.

I observed that, in Enway, if a Traveller pupil did get into a Secondary school, he or she would often just leave if the school was not welcoming. One Romanian boy was given a six week trial period and threatened with permanent exclusion before he had even arrived. An Irish Traveller boy I took into Forrest Boys' School only attended for two days. I was not surprised at this: on his first day, we walked together to the reception desk to announce his arrival, and I stood aghast as the receptionist told him 'you aren't to go outside at lunchtime, you'll probably thieve from the boys' coats'. He told me later, 'I don't really feel welcome here'. I had been given a reading book about a Traveller family to work on with him but we never got beyond the third page, as he stopped attending.

The Traveller Education officer told me later that one of the Traveller pupils had once gone for a walk with her and seen a horse in a field and used an old seatbelt he found in the hedge to catch and ride it bareback. We talked then about the possibilities these amazing skills held for engaging with learning, and afterwards we met with senior managers and drew up an exciting Traveller Plan for Enway. It involved the establishing of an artist- or writer-in-residence to work on the visibility of Traveller communities in Enway, and proposed to draw on teachers who had developed expertise in working with Traveller families to educate professionals in other schools around Enway. But three years later, the Plan had not moved ahead; the senior managers did not carry out their agreed actions and I felt that there was no will to do so.

In 2007, Enway published a 'Welcoming Diversity' report. A page entitled 'Education for All' discussed Traveller children, describing a photography project that had taken place at Church Forest School. The Church Forest head teacher had put huge amounts of effort into building relationships with the Traveller community in Enway and had a fantastically empathic Inclusion team, including several Learning Mentors who spent their time working to address barriers to learning. Part of the Traveller plan we had put together involved the prospect that some of these staff might disseminate their expertise around working with Travellers to other schools in Enway. As the report boasted,

A particularly successful photography project went a long way towards bringing the communities together by allowing the school to demonstrate to the Travellers that they are a valued part of the local community. Attendance at the school has become more regular, and Traveller children are showing greater levels of attainment.

What the report did not mention was that Church Forest School was to close at the end of the academic year 2008–2009, in order to allow the building of a new Academy, run by Enway College, on the Church Forest site. There were no further plans to cater for the specific needs of Traveller children.

A confusing picture emerges: whilst Enway's 'White Boys and Achievement' conference was held earlier in the year, James, Chief Inspector for Ethnic Minority Achievement, indicated that the borough had failed to see 'white' as constituted of a range of ethnicities. Planning with reference to 'race' or 'ethnicity' was omitted from the Enway Children and Young People Plan and ignored as a feature of dangerous bullying at Ennon Grand Academy. Traveller pupils were consistently under-served. But at the same time (as will be shown in ethnographic detail, below), institutional racism continued to cause difficulties for pupils and to remain evident in a significant proportion of the professional discourse.

'RACE' AND ETHNICITY IN THE ADMINISTRATION OF EXCLUSION FROM
SCHOOL IN ENWAY

Language Issues

Statistical significance   Some of the 'ethnicity-linked' pressures on Panel pupils derived from statutory requirements with unintended consequences. For example, because of the nature of the ways in which pupils were 'counted' in the statistics-gathering exercises that result in a school's allocation of funding and its placement in the league tables, some pupils who came through the Enway Panel were automatically disadvantaged because of the level of their English. Schools can obtain extra money by taking in pupils who have only been educated overseas in non-English-speaking countries, and because these pupils' GCSE results are not counted in the 'five A* to C GCSEs including English and Maths' league table benchmark, there is less perceived 'risk' inherent in taking in such pupils. However, if a pupil has spent any time enrolled in a British school, their grades are counted in the league tables.

The Panel one day discussed a Pakistani boy, and whether he should be placed at a mainstream school. One head teacher, reluctant to take the pupil on roll, said, 'If they come from overseas, never having been in a British school, they don't count on our statistics so we don't mind- well, some of us don't- but if they've been in any British school they count; they've got a UPN (Unique Pupil Number)'.

Another head teacher replied, 'Not to put too fine a point on it, we took fourteen Nepalese last year and all got A*s in maths [GCSE]; couldn't speak a word of English;[9] if I talk to my governors we'll never take a Nepalese again; (because of) these ridiculous statistics!'

'The Nepalese are lovely people in general', added the third head teacher.

And an Inclusion manager told me, 'The ones I like are the Nepalese kids; they're like meerkats; they all look out for each other; in the morning there are about forty of them [in the refectory], and if one looks up they all look up, like meerkats'. This exoticised and essentialising view of Nepalese pupils both demonstrates the occasional 'front-line' eruption of professional talk about people in terms framed by their 'ethnicity', and the power of state-required statistics. Teachers' comments would lead one to believe that Nepalese pupils are delightful to work with; but they still would not be welcomed, simply because they are less likely to excel at GCSE English.[10]

This systemic racism is discussed by Osler and Vincent (2003):

Where the focus is on meeting the needs of individuals, there is sometimes a tendency to overlook or challenge systemic weakness. It is critical to remember that exclusion does not operate in a political vacuum ... policy and legislative frameworks which require schools to operate within a (quasi-) market mean that some students, such as those with SEN or ESL, who are likely to cost more to educate, become less attractive to schools.

43

Panel pupils who are perceived as less desirable due to the fact that they have been at risk of or subject to a permanent exclusion, then, are less likely to be welcomed on roll at a mainstream school if their language or lack of experience with an English National Curriculum means that they are less likely to get five A* to C GCSEs including English and Maths. As Wright *et al.* (2000) suggest, in a marketised education system, some pupils are regarded as 'more valuable' than others, and this often has something to do with their perceived ethnicity.

Translation   When a pupil is permanently excluded, or moved due to the threat of exclusion from school, their parent will probably have already been through several school meetings. Some of these meetings will have required the parent to make difficult decisions about, for example, which school they would like their child to move to. If that parent's first language is not English, they may have had to make these decisions based on information they have not fully understood and so would have struggled to ask questions about. Often the excluded child or young person in Enway was asked to translate difficult and emotionally risky information for their parent, and of course the situation in which they found themselves may have precluded them from making a totally accurate translation.

Schools often did not identify the need for a translator: one school administrator was thoughtful when I suggested that there may be possible translation needs for a Syrian parent, telling me doubtfully, 'there's nothing on the form.' I also noticed that parents often pretended that they knew more English than they did, nodding and smiling, and on checking the situation, found that this was because they were embarrassed to ask for help, or did not know it was available. Translation services were in any case expensive and difficult to arrange. Even where a school qualified for free translation support (and in Enway there was funding for this), inclusion staff may not have known about it; there was often only one translator available for the required language, and they were often unavailable when they were needed. When they were available and able to attend a meeting, it was frequently difficult for the translator to understand the complexities and objectifying nature of the disciplinary process through which schools were taking their pupils, and this caused further problems. Sarama's story, below, illustrates something of this effect.

Sarama   Sarama, an Eritrean pupil at Enway College, was at extreme risk of permanent exclusion. At twelve years old, she was at risk in many other ways, often spending the night walking the streets with friends, drinking alcohol, and getting into cars with people she did not know. At school she spent the day restlessly walking the corridors, screaming at teachers, and refusing to go into lessons. I first met her when Ayanna, one of the Home-School Liaison Officers, an older Somali Muslim woman, asked me to meet Sarama's mother, Zula, at home. I sat listening in her tidy, warm living room, an Eritrean flag on the wall and an Arabic TV channel playing on a large set in the corner. Speaking Arabic through Ayanna, and quietly weeping as she told her story, Zula told me that she had experienced the trauma of war and had escaped Eritrea when Haile Salassi invaded the country from Ethiopia. She had travelled across the Red Sea to Saudi Arabia with her four children, where she had consolidated her knowledge of Arabic, and then to England, where she had been housed in Enway. Her husband had 'gone away'. She was a Christian, and had not found any Eritrean or Christian friends from Eritrea, or the surrounding countries, in Enway. Zula's isolation was vastly compounded by the fact that her youngest child, a boy aged nine or ten, was severely physically disabled, in a large powered wheelchair, and unable to speak or feed himself. He was in and out of hospital, and every time Zula had tried to enrol in an English class, he had fallen ill, and she had been unable to continue the classes.

Sarama's older brother and sister had been moved out of Enway College on to a vocational course project as they too had experienced difficulties at school, and both were involved in what was described by police as local 'gang' activities, often roaming the streets with large groups of other young people, getting in trouble with the police and in danger with each other. Zula told me that as her children had grown older, whilst they could understand her mother tongue, Tigrinya, and Arabic, they refused to speak anything but English, of which she could only understand a few words and phrases. This had compounded her children's behaviour problems because they often pretended not to understand her and would not answer her when they did. When they translated for her into English, both with me at their home and at school meetings, they often treated her crossly, as a mother might an annoying child. This is perhaps caused by the imbalance of power presented to a child when they are asked to translate into the dominant language (in this case, English) and their parent is engaged in a discussion about that same child's misdemeanours with an authority figure.

The Enway College Inclusion manager told me that she thought Zula could understand everything that was said to her in English. But it was clear that she did not understand the important finer details. She thought, for example, that her older two children had had no choice when they were moved out of Enway College into the vocational programme, because she had missed the fact that they were not actually permanently excluded, but only being threatened with permanent exclusion. As Osler and Vincent (2003) explain, '[i]n reality, parents have very limited rights which only come into operation when a student is permanently excluded and when the exclusion is carried out according to the official guidelines' (36).

A translator was finally obtained for a crisis meeting about Sarama, amidst hopes that it would be a turning point for Zula's understanding and ability to advocate for her children. The translator that arrived at the school was a Saudi Arabian Muslim man, neatly dressed in a grey suit, and he spoke Arabic. His mouth fell open and he started to shake his head as the teachers described how Sarama would shout at teachers and refuse to go into class, appalled at her behaviour, and broke off in the middle of the meeting to turn and instruct Zula bossily in what she should be doing as a parent. Zula, tears streaming down her silent face, was clearly irritated by this and unable to concentrate on the discussion, patting her yellow head wrap and turning away from him, shaking her head. She did not want him to translate a second time, and asked for an Eritrean, a woman, or a Christian translator, none of which the Enway Translation Service could locate. It seems that despite having gone through the process twice with her older children, Zula's lack of English had deeply affected her ability to advocate on behalf of her third child, and prevent, as she desired, yet another move to a vocational education placement. Despite her hopes, none of her children achieved a GCSE, although her older daughter did well at the vocational placement. Zula and Sarama experienced a deeply unsatisfying experience of the system of support and discipline because of a systemic failure to ameliorate difficulties arising from their circumstances, and this amounts to institutional racism, exacerbated by the shadow of a threatened permanent exclusion from school.

Kim   Whilst most of the inclusion staff I met in Enway schools did not know that a translation service was available, they often relied on multilingual teachers- and sometimes on other pupils- to translate at meetings. Kim, a Vietnamese pupil from Pope John Paul Catholic School, came through the Panel for a managed move following an incident of theft. All the other head teachers at the Panel were very angry with Kim's head teacher for effectively excluding a pupil for what they saw as 'a one-off incident'. Of course there was no governors' hearing or appeal, as there was no permanent exclusion; so there was 'no clear or immediate means of redress' (Osler and Vincent 2003: 36). Kim was placed at Ennon Grand Academy, and the school was asked to arrange a Vietnamese interpreter to support her father at the reintegration meeting. Unfortunately, upon arrival at Ennon Grand, we found that the interpreter had not been arranged. The Head of Year told me that he had a 'straight-A student' in the Sixth Form who could speak Vietnamese, and invited him into the meeting. Kim and her father did not want to reschedule the meeting in order to ensure a Vietnamese translator could be there, as they were anxious to get her started at the new school. Kim told the meeting what happened:

'Me and my girls we went into the changing rooms and nicked an i-Pod', she explained. The Sixth Former's eyes bulged at this. Kim's dad sat at the table blinking. The Sixth Former did not say a word, and Kim translated for her father. Through Kim, he told us that the family was Catholic and that he was very upset and angry and disappointed that Kim had to go to a non-Catholic school, and felt that even perfect students make mistakes. For him the fact it was a one-off incident with no prior issues was the problem.

On the way out of the building after the meeting Kim told me that her head teacher at Pope John Paul had been 'racist'. I asked Kim what had happened to make her think this and she said that he had told her that if she 'told the truth' she may be able to stay at Pope John Paul. So she did. And she and one other (white English) pupil were pushed into a managed move to another school anyway. I explained that she was not officially permanently excluded, but it did not matter to Kim that she had not had the governor's meeting required to ratify or quash all official permanent exclusions. To her and her father, the result was that she had been excluded, permanently.

Kim's experience demonstrates the extra vulnerability of an unofficially excluded pupil whose parent does not speak English. Her 'translator', a pupil at her new school, could potentially have left the room and told all his friends about 'the new Vietnamese thief' entering their school. And her father had been much less able to advocate on her behalf, or to access the information he needed to challenge a managed move made under the threat of permanent exclusion.

Age Assessments

Another barrier to appropriate support for Enway pupils was that if they were not recognisably British they were often viewed with suspicion at the 'Hard to Place' Pupil Placement Panel with regard to their age. When young people enter the country without identifying paperwork, often as asylum seekers, they have their age assessed by a doctor and entered onto their arrival papers by immigration officials. These young people arrived in Enway with paperwork stating an age which some teachers suspected to be false. This situation was compounded by the fact that pupils from other countries were usually the only ones whose cases came to Panel with a photograph[11] attached to the paperwork. I always worried that the photograph was unnecessary, but that perhaps the parents of these young people had been asked for their passports so many times that they felt they must send a copy in with their school placement applications. But these photographs only confused and distracted Panel members further. Once, during a lengthy, harrowing and complicated set of cases, my colleague, shaking with suppressed hysterical laughter, silently passed me a photo of a particularly tired-looking young man on which he had drawn a moustache.

Stories about age-fraudulence abounded at the Panel. The Head of Admissions and others often discussed the idea that Nigerian families sometimes presented their sons as only fourteen or fifteen years old when they were suspected to be in their twenties in order to 'take advantage of the free education on offer' in the UK.

One young woman whose case came to Panel, a war-traumatised refugee from Afghanistan, was said by the head teacher at the PRU, who had worked with her before, to be twenty-three or twenty-four years old when she arrived in Enway and was placed in a mainstream school in Year 10.[12] Her violent behaviour - hitting and punching her classmates - led to her being permanently excluded from school, and she was placed in New Start, an alternative education placement on Enway High Street. When she attacked a member of public outside New Start, she became one of the very few pupils they permanently excluded, and was quickly placed at a second alternative education placement. This pupil, had she been viewed as actually fifteen years old, might have been referred for CAMHS[13] services to help with anger management. But because of her perceived age, her placement needs were simply seen as 'containment' until her papers said she was sixteen and she was no longer the responsibility of the local authority. If she was actually in her twenties, she would have been better served by adult services focusing on employment than on a children's service focussed on containment.

Assessing age was felt very much to be something the Panel had no control of - it was something done by Immigration officials, shadowy in their absence -[14] but it did not stop the speculation. This speculation and the effects it had on placement decisions can be seen as an example of institutional racism and an effect of the existence of permanent exclusion from school as an option.

Jed: Not Allowed to Claim Racism

Jed's case is a good example of how it is probably more useful to talk about institutional racism through the attitudes towards 'race' and ethnicity of those in authority than the essentialised experiences of particular groups of pupils.

I observed a sense of relief amongst Panel members when a 'Hard to Place' young person was contained in a young offender's institution. On exit, these young people presented the Panel with a reluctant responsibility to find a school place. Jed's paperwork, which identified him as a 'WBRI'[15] boy of fifteen, was introduced to the Enway Panel by his youth offending team officer. He was coming out of a secure unit where he had been serving a sentence for robbery, and wanted to go to Knightsdown College because he had heard that it was 'a good school'. Panel members were reluctant to give him a placement at mainstream school as he had been in a Pupil Referral Unit (PRU) before the secure unit. Since leaving what everyone called 'secure', Jed had spent several weeks sleeping rough, and had run away from his foster carer to go home to his heroin addicted mother. He was now to be placed with his Nan, and was keen to get his life back on track.

Jed was already contending with a history not usually looked on kindly by the Panel. But when I saw in the paperwork that he had said that other white boys at the PRU had been racist to him, my heart sank in anticipation. I knew that the Panel would question his 'right' to claim racism. Jed's friends were all reported to be 'BCRB' or 'BOTH'[16] and he liked to dress and talk like his friends and listen to rap and hip hop music. It was because of this that his white peers had bullied him and that he had complained of racism. But this above all else was what the Panel-members derided in their reading of the papers. The claim to having been a victim of racism was seen as more problematic than Jed's wish to try mainstream school after years in PRUs and a secure unit. Jed was subjected here to what can be identified as a racism drawn towards a white person's association with black people (Blair 2001), something often experienced by the white mothers of what some practitioners call 'dual heritage' children. His youth offending team worker told me that he was extremely frustrated by the Panel's lack of empathy and understanding. He felt that Jed had learned to 'manage himself' in the young offender's institution and deserved to make 'a fresh start'.

Cultural Attitudes to Mental Health Services: Ibrahim

Mental health services were often indicated in order to help a pupil develop the skills needed to 'manage themselves'[17] within an education system developed for an 'ideal', normed (white, English-speaking) set of pupils (Blair 2001). Another of the problems experienced by permanently excluded pupils whose parents may have grown up in a country outside Western Europe was to do with what was seen as a cultural stigma about these services. This was something I thought I could see happening in the case of Ibrahim, a fourteen year old boy permanently excluded from Ennon Castle School for sexually assaulting two girls in his year group. At Ibrahim's reintegration meeting at Forrest Boys School, he was asked to fill in the same standard set of paperwork completed by all entrants to any new school: name, address, emergency contacts, and so on. Part of this process also required the young person to self-identify their 'ethnicity' from a list, with the option to in write their 'ethnicity' below the tick boxes. Ibrahim, who had been born in England to parents born and raised in Nigeria, wrote 'Nigerian' on the dotted line. But he quickly scribbled this out and changed it when his mother in great embarrassment slapped him on the arm and said in her strong Nigerian accent, 'No, Ibrahim, you are British!' It is possible that Ibrahim was self-identifying as something 'other' than the teaching establishment[18] as an expression of 'resistance to participation in education' (Archer and Yamashita 2003:116). I theorised that his parent wanted him to claim the validating quality of 'Britishness' she had gained for him by giving birth to him far from her family home.

Ibrahim's story exemplifies the idea, introduced above, that '[a] person may ... switch situationally between being a member of an ethnic minority and a member of a nation' (Eriksen 1995: 266). It demonstrates how ethnic identity can be described as flexible, self-determined and context-sensitive, whilst concurrently vulnerable to being embedded deep into the extended body through external representation (what Ball *et al.* 2002 and Gillborn and Youdell 2000 refer to as 'fixing in place'). The 'embedding' was done both by Ibrahim's mother, under pressure in a hierarchy of nationality and ethnicity, and by the school paperwork requirement to identify an ethnicity. In any case, it was clear that Ibrahim's 'ethnic' or national 'identity' was affected by context. As will be shown below, what his father wanted or did not want for him was seen by Enway professionals as being affected by his own 'Nigerian-ness', whilst his mother hoped he would gain fair treatment by virtue of his 'Britishness'.

Because he had been convicted of the assaults for which he had been excluded, Ibrahim was required by court order to attend sessions with a psychologist. At a multi-agency meeting for Ibrahim, I asked Harold, his forensic psychologist, an erudite Zimbabwean man, about how the sessions were going.

Harold told me that they were 'Difficult, informative, problems in relationship with dad, irritated, angry and inability to speak up in front of dad- is very loyal and doesn't want to upset his dad, who didn't sign up to the idea of having sessions.'

Jacques, my youth offending team colleague,[19] who identified as British-Jamaican, interjected, 'Stigma?'

Harold replied, 'Mainly, yes; culturally, in Nigeria, therapy is for people who are extremely mad and off their rocker and if there is a problem you should talk to family and anyway just do what your parents tell you ...'

Jacques answered, 'so culturally ...'

Harold cut in, 'We did try a session with father who felt very bruised by it and said he didn't like being put on the couch as he put it, it wasn't about him. Eighteen or nineteen sessions is huge. It halted because family therapy had to happen [and the parents wouldn't engage.]'

Ibrahim said that he had 'found it helpful to talk to someone.'

Ibrahim had received a lengthy period of therapy, but his progress was said to be limited when family sessions were halted by the inability of his father to agree to engage with the therapeutic process due to his 'ethnicity'. There did not seem to be a way to find out how Ibrahim and his father could heal their differences through a means acceptable to him as 'a Nigerian'. The only option, it seemed, was to require him to fit into the British system: a hierarchical system topped by psychology, as noted in chapter six on class. So an effect of the immersion into the 'support services' surrounding a permanent exclusion from school could be seen here to be the emotional 'bruising' of a parent and an inadequate attempt at family therapy. These effects were perhaps due to an exacerbation of institutional racism expressed through a failure to acknowledge the possible need for an alternative approach based on cultural sensitivity. As with the 'working-class white girls' described by Skeggs (1997) and discussed in chapter six, I felt that the pathologising route (that is, an official recording of Ibrahim's 'problems' as being based on some kind of deficiency in him, rather than in his environment or experience, and perhaps leading to 'psy' techniques (Rose 1999) offering therapeutic input) was an 'authorising narrative' (Skeggs 1997: 167), and the only way Ibrahim could counter the invisibility his experience as a 'Nigerian-British person' encountered in the mainstream school system.

Ishaq's story, below, illustrates the slippery power of authorising narratives. His family sought to counter the invisibility of institutional racism by naming and challenging it. However, it seems that they were not authorised to adopt that narrative.

Ishaq: a Legacy and a Right

Ishaq was introduced in chapter three as the boy described as having hit a friend on the legs with a hockey stick in order to maintain his position within a 'street' hierarchy. His mother had been born to a white English mother and a Rastafarian Jamaican father, Moses. Moses was a well-educated education activist who gave lectures on inclusive education for the Open University and had been involved in several community youth schemes. The family was proud of their heritage and Ishaq had been named after an ancient Egyptian prince. Every male member of the family played in their successful semi-professional jazz band. Ishaq, who played the trumpet in the family band, was a tall boy with a charming smile, and had been attending Ennon Castle School for two years. Now in Year 9, he was beginning to wear the patience of his teachers, and was often in trouble for running down the corridors during lesson times, climbing out of windows, threatening his peers, and walking away from senior teachers when they were telling him to calm down. Because of this he was deemed at risk of permanent exclusion for persistent disruptive behaviour and his mother was called into several school meetings to discuss what could be done.

Moses would sit in these meetings and patiently explain that he thought his grandson was 'a victim of institutionalised racism' characterised by 'a curriculum that does not hold Ishaq's attention' and a set of teaching strategies 'not designed to cope with his physicality'. He and his daughter were tenacious in their assertion that Ishaq had a right to a relevant school experience; one which would catch and hold his attention, empathise with his lived experience, and offer a constructive focus for his energy.

The school and the family were polarised in their views: Ishaq's head of year and inclusion manager told me that he was 'a cheeky boy of medium intelligence who's allowed to do as he pleases at home'. They complained that his mother totally undermined their authority by challenging every instance of alleged misdemeanour and the processes through which Ishaq was being supported. They had never heard Ishaq play the trumpet and felt that the family was exaggerating his musical abilities. They had brought in an educational psychologist as his mother had asked repeatedly for this, but felt that this was unnecessary and that Ishaq was 'taking up valuable EP time'. They broadly ignored Moses and the intellectualised deconstruction of events he offered at every meeting. They were highly suspicious of the family, who over the weeks and months appeared to be becoming increasingly upset. For example, following one meeting, I wrote in my field notebook:

> Ishaq's mum has been banned from Ennon Castle School for screaming at the head of year and threatening her with witchcraft ... and there are rumours that she has been body piercing some of his classmates and getting evidence from them of bad practices and racism at Ennon Castle. At the PSP meeting the deputy head had a list of things Ishaq said, including threats to shoot people ... he also queried a possible referral to Safeguarding ... he said it may amount to emotional abuse, the undermining of education and lack of boundaries.

> Field-notes, June 2008

The complex mixture here of things said and threatened amount to a projection into the extended body. The possibility that Ishaq's mother had unearthed evidence of 'racism' at Ennon Castle was undermined by the deputy head's exoticised image of her as a witch who pierced the bodies of innocent schoolchildren, drawing them in to her piercing shop to delicately extract damning information. The institutional reasons behind the level of anger which prompted her to mention witchcraft was something I would have wanted to investigate as a deputy head teacher. On the other hand, Moses and Ishaq's mother felt that teachers were 'always picking on him' because of his demonised 'reputation'; that Ishaq was the victim of constant and unrelenting surveillance; that he was 'always the first pupil the teachers blamed' for any problem; and that he was highly intelligent and underserved by a curriculum and an education system not developed for 'Black Caribbean-British boys'. They also felt that the systems in place to support Ishaq were inadequate and poorly applied. As I had recorded in my field-notes:

> Pastoral Support Plan meeting: Moses, Ishaq's mum and aunt were all very concerned with: systemic inequities; unfair application of school rules

(uniform, etc.), communications from different school staff and wanting one trusted person, inconsistency ... Moses also concerned about largely unfounded behaviour logs following children around- made me think- ... is there a way families could go through a behaviour log and counter or agree with each item or explain them?

Field-notes: June 2008

Behaviour logs represent a 'prosecution case' against a pupil. In a courtroom environment, the defence would have had a chance to view this and to explain or counter each item. But in school, I see the paperwork as a representative domain flooding the contested space of the extended body and largely owned by the professionals.[20] As Osler and Vincent (2003) found, '[c]hildren can be permanently excluded from school without having any opportunity to defend themselves, highlight an injustice, or challenge the decision' (36).

The gulf between the school and family was broad and deep, and after three years of monthly meetings Ishaq was permanently excluded. His family scraped the money together and sent him to a boarding school in Scandinavia rather than allowing him to go to the Enway Pupil Referral Unit. They felt that as 'a Black Caribbean boy living in England', a quality education was a key to success for Ishaq.

The concerns raised by Ishaq's grandfather- that the English school system was not designed for Caribbean-English boys- are echoed in Blair (2001), who explains that '[t]he racial legacy of Europe generally and of Britain's specific historical relations with many parts of the world can still be found in our schools today' (8). Blair (2001) also identifies the development of assumptions about a perceived 'essential criminality of black people' (37), echoing Gilroy (1987) and Osler and Vincent (2003) and one of Moses' greatest concerns:

The representation of black men as having particular tendencies ... has ... justified their closer surveillance by the police and in school; has justified their exclusion from school and their constant presence before the criminal justice system ... It is not the crime, but the criminality which has been the focus of attention. It fed in teachers ... the widespread belief that ... Afro-Caribbean pupils were especially prone to threatening teachers' authority.

Blair 2001: 37–38

Ishaq's racialised gender and his family's ethnic identity provided them with a critical framework for understanding the difficulties he was having at school. It was a discourse not enjoined by his teachers, and this may have been one of the factors that resulted in his ultimate exclusion from school. Even if Ishaq's behaviour was difficult to deal with, engagement in a frank discussion about ethnicity in the education system would have offered an element of visibility to the ethnicity element of Ishaq's experience and would have helped the school to work collaboratively with the family, to share a critical language, and to turn a critical eye on its on its own processes. But this would have meant challenging the institutionally norming technique of pathologising the young person to avoid attention being turned on institutional failures (Foucault 1977; Thomas and Loxley 2001; Rendall and Stuart 2005; Cooper 2002; Slee 1995; Rose 1989; introduced in chapter one). The family and the school parted company with the school convinced that Ishaq was being seriously educationally neglected by his family through a perception that they were 'undermining' the school's disciplinary procedures, and the family unconvinced that the school was committed to offering an effective, empowering education for their son.

Ishaq's case really exercised my understanding of the extended body as contested space. His extended body was swarming with experienced representative labels from both his family and the school. Looking through my field-notes, I found a lone, forgotten yellow Post-it note randomly stuck to one of the pages. I had written to myself, 'Ishaq- he's in the middle of these people battling over him'.

CONCLUSION

There is a well-developed discourse in the literature explaining the process of 'othering' and the relationality of 'ethnic' representation and identity (Gilroy 1987; Hall 1992; Rattansi and Donald 1992; Eriksen 1995; Blair 2001). In fact, investigating this prompted me to go back and to think about gender and 'class' in a similar way. Issues of class fractionality across ethnicities and the gendered nuances of ethnicity were also comprehensively framed in the literature (George 2007; Archer and Yamashita 2003; Tomlinson 2005; Wright 2005; Blair 2001; Ball et al. 2002; Francis 2005). But despite the high visibility of 'race' and ethnicity in the literature, I found a high level of invisibility in Enway's educational policy discourse. So it was difficult to get senior management interested in issues such as increasing incidents of what families identified as 'black Somali/white British' conflict at one of the bigger schools, or the specific educational needs of Traveller children.

At the beginning of this chapter I introduced Eriksen's (1995) idea that 'the focus of research' into ethnicity and racism in schools 'ought to be the social boundaries between groups' (251). The administration of exclusion from school in Enway revealed a series of 'social boundaries between groups' related to ethnicity that can be seen as affecting pupils at risk of or subject to permanent exclusion: language; border practices, such as age assessments; and cultural opinions on psychology, for example.

So the high statistical currency of the English language was shown to exacerbate the negative effects of an instance of exclusion. Lack of translation facilities were shown to undermine the participation of parents in exclusion and inclusion processes. The issue of age assessments for immigrant and refugee children can also be seen to pre-empt Panel attitudes to individual cases. And access to the psy techniques (Rose 1999) necessary to develop the skills required to survive in an education system designed with a 'normed' set of pupils in mind was not necessarily effective for some of the pupils who could have most benefited from them. This was because culturally, it seemed that psy techniques were not wholly acceptable, and the institutions were unwilling to adjust their approaches accordingly. The system had not been designed for 'borderland' children (Anzaldua 1987; Pomeroy 2000). 'White' children were seen as a homogenous, non-'ethnic' group, excluded from being understood as engaged in difficulties to do with ethnicity. And Ishaq, whose grandfather was not 'authorised' (Skeggs 1997: 167), to explain the effects of institutional racism to school staff, did not benefit from the theory, but became trapped between his family and the school, his extended body not just a contested space, but a battleground.

NOTES

[1] As described in the Education Act 1996, Section 7, parents may choose to educate their children at home, as long as they can show evidence that it is adequate and appropriate to the Education at Home officer on her yearly visits.

[2] This is a similar effect to the opaque treatment of class described in chapter six.

[3] This approach is a feature of the 'studying up' (Nader1972) approach I am taking (see chapters one and two).

[4] The Stephen Lawrence Enquiry: report of an enquiry by William Macpherson of Cluny presented to Parliament by the Secretary of State, February 1999.

[5] This can also be applied to class and gender, but emerges with a greater degree of clarity and power in the literature on 'race' and ethnicity.

[6] 'Not in Education, Employment or Training'; a government term.

[7] These figures omit unofficial exclusions and pupils who do not finish Key Stage 4.

[8] 'The school' was often used as a possessive nomenclature for possibly unpopular decisions, but often meant 'the head teacher'. In some ways this conflates individual racism with institutionalised racism.

[9] This is clearly untrue, as due to the text content of the exam papers it would not be possible to get an A* in maths without 'a word of English'.

[10] Or perhaps disproportionately likely to excel at GCSE Mathematics.

[11] Albeit a blurred photocopy of their passport photograph.

[12] Most pupils in Year 10 are fourteen to fifteen years old.

[13] Child and adolescent mental health services.

[14] As explained in chapter two, Nader (1972) discusses the effects of remote 'policy makers' as a feature of interacting relationships sometimes omitted from localised ethnographies.

[15] 'White British' in the standard local authority codes.

[16] 'Black Caribbean or 'Black other' in the standard local authority codes.

[17] This is an example of the use of psy techniques to ensure that subjects internalise authoritarian power (Foucault 1977; Rose 1999; see chapter three).

[18] Who are mostly white English (Blair 2001).

[19] Mentioned in chapters five and six.

[20] This idea is developed in detail in chapter eight.

CHAPTER 8

POLICY AND PAPERWORK IN
THE ADMINISTRATION OF PERMANENT
EXCLUSION FROM SCHOOL

Deconstructing the Machinery of Institutional Prejudice

Like bureaucracy (of which it is a major accessory), policy can serve to cloak subjective, ideological and arguably highly 'irrational' goals in the guise of rational, collective, universalized objectives.

Shore and Wright 1997: 11

Why does permanent exclusion, caused in part by and exacerbating institutional prejudice on the basis of gender, class and 'race', exist as an option in a framework ostensibly built on a policy of inclusion? Why was there an Exclusions Officer in the Enway Children's Services Inclusion Service? Why did the Head of Inclusion sometimes have to recommend exclusion? Why was the Head of Admissions a vociferous gatekeeper, often attending the Panel to advise on how to refuse admission to a school? As a Pupil Support Officer, why was I under pressure to implement non-supportive protocol? Fundamentally, I wanted to find out why apparently inclusive, reflexive professionals (albeit labouring under the subjective weight of their own extended bodies) continued to deliver a 'weak' version of 'inclusion' policy focussed on individuals (Viet-Wilson 1998 in Macrae *et al.* 2003: 90; see chapter one) which channelled rather than challenged institutional prejudice. In order to understand these paradoxes, I thought I might be able to trace the route of institutional prejudice. This required me to investigate the techniques of power behind the delivery of policy.

It is helpful to understand 'policy' as a 'dignified myth'- a rational systems model, whereby 'policy is represented as a neat linear process of 'problem identification', 'formulation of solutions', 'implementation', and 'evaluation'' (Shore and Wright 1997:15; see also Fielding 2001:143). With this in mind, the New Labour government's policy of 'inclusion', introduced in chapter one, will be investigated here. It will be suggested that inclusion policy is not necessarily a bedrock on which to implement inclusive education practice, but perhaps a field of shifting sands.

In seeking to deconstruct the machinery through which the normalising pressures of institutional prejudice are delivered, this chapter will address the nature of policy as being constructed of a 'lexicon'- a 'rhetoric' (Ball 2001: 46; see also Fielding 2001; Whitty 2002; Edelman 2004) - and a cultural text (Shore and Wright 1997:15) within an international 'policyscape' (Ball 1997:46). New Labour education policy will be seen to have caused some of the problems it attempted to deal with (Fielding 2001; Ball 2001), as will the means by which its efficacy was measured (Miller 2003). The status of 'permanent exclusion' as a product of policy will be questioned. Permanent exclusion will instead be posited as a result of the production of pupil behaviours- behaviours seen as problematic because of their placement on a normed scale (Walkerdine 1998; Slee 1995). It is this normed scale which has been imagined through a lens of institutional prejudices.

So- if policy statements and normed scales are not objectively 'true', but infused with the prejudices and beliefs of those who constructed them, how do policy-makers manage to persuade policy-deliverers that their ideas are worthy of being considered to be common sense; that they are simply a helpful guidance on protocol? This chapter will provide ethnographic examples from central government policy dissemination events and local Enway conferences to illustrate some of the key modes through which policy suffuses the activities of those in the employment of local government with the letter and the spirit of central governmental authority, or as Foucault (1977) puts it, 'the gradual extension of the mechanisms of discipline ... their spread throughout the whole social body' (209). Descriptions of these conferences and of some of the Enway Inclusion documentation and forms will exemplify an attempt to explain governmental authoritarian power as a field of contested space. This will be seen to be a space in which frontline workers and professionals, with parents and pupils, can try to challenge institutional prejudice through a 'critical bureaucracy': to exercise their agency and deliver a socially justified service *despite the current policy*.

POLICY CONTEXTUALISED AND DECONSTRUCTED

'Liberal Communism': A Political View

As I explained in chapter one, the educational inclusion policy developed by New Labour was bolted onto an existing global 'policyscape' (Ball 2001: 46) which the preceding Conservative government had co-opted as appropriate to a New Right agenda and which was viewed by that government as 'the only possible response to globalisation' (Whitty 2002: 126). This incorporated the neoliberal features of choice, commercialisation and regulation that have been identified in this book as exerting pressure on young people at risk of exclusion. We can see the flavour of neoliberalism in, for example, issues around school and GCSE 'choice' (discussed in chapters four, five and six), the cost of permanent exclusion and its alternatives (discussed in chapter four), and the effects of SAT scores, linguistic ability and league tables on the chances of a fresh start in a mainstream school for excluded pupils (discussed in chapters four and seven). New Labour added to this a 'social equity' discourse which has been called 'largely cosmetic' (Whitty 2002: 127) without dismantling the conditions causing social inequity in the first place. Zizek

(2008) has termed this choice/commercialisation/'social equity' discourse paradigm 'liberal communism', explaining:

> While they fight subjective violence, liberal communists are the very agents of the structural violence which creates the conditions for the explosions of subjective violence. The same philanthropists who give millions for ... education in tolerance have ruined the lives of thousands through financial speculation and thus created the conditions for the rise of the very intolerance that is being fought.

> 2008: 31

Thus through the promotion of 'Inclusion' policy, policy-makers appear to be asking teachers and children's services workers to implement a strategy to deal with problems which may partly have arisen due to their neo-liberal 'strategy' in the first place. In this respect, neoliberal policies can be understood as a form of objective violence within the wider socio-political system. This is a self-defeating policy paradigm: the blanketing of the cause of the problem with a cosmetic/linguistic solution goes some way to ensuring that the objective violence itself remains unquestioned.

How Can a Self-Defeating Policy Paradigm be Addressed?

Shore and Wright (1997:20) explain that 'although some discourses are deeply embedded in institutional policy and practice ... they are constantly contested and sometimes fractured'. Thus the field of authoritarian governmental power can be understood as a contested and contestable space. In this space, pupils' lived experience interacts with some of the parents' and frontline workers' discourses of care and empowerment. Pupils' extended bodies are also constructed and experienced through the managers' and policy-makers' discourses. These discourses are based on their professional gaze and role (all experienced by them as embedded within their own extended bodies) as implementers of the political technology of power. The 'spatial' quality of the policy-field in which parents, pupils, frontline workers and Children's Services managers operate lends itself, as explained in chapter two, to an ethnographic approach, with what I think of as the 'policy-community' being amenable to detailed description.

The field of inclusion policy in which I worked as a Pupil Support Officer to assist pupils at risk of permanent exclusion included sub-policies designed to support Inclusion: multi-agency working, 'early intervention', law,[1] Every Child Matters (DCSF), 'youth participation', 'joined up government', and the development of a 'Children's Workforce'. In addition to these, and often interpreted to work at cross-purposes to inclusion policy were the anti-social behaviour agenda and the attainment agenda. Every Child Matters, with its exhortations to help children and young people to 'Stay Safe' and 'Enjoy', also asked that children and young people 'Achieve'. These three goals could be viewed as unsupportive of each other. For example,

'Health and Safety' has in this book (in chapter six) been identified as a reason cited by head teachers to permanently exclude a young person, but the exclusion itself can cause damage to the young person's chance to 'achieve' academically or her own emotional safety and wellbeing. As Ball (2001) explains, '[t]he explicit commitment to tackling exclusion does not seem to be matched by efforts to maximise inclusion ... the excluding effects of educational processes themselves remain unaddressed' (46–47). The inclusion rhetoric does not fulfil the needs of the inclusion project.

Is Permanent Exclusion a Policy?

Whilst there has occasionally been reference to the 'need' to allow head teachers to maintain the 'right' to permanently exclude (Lipsett 2008), I understand the act of permanent exclusion itself as originating outside the realm of policy. There could of course be a policy to *not* officially permanently exclude; and there are rules about how and when an official exclusion can be implemented. But exclusion itself is, as I understand it, an expression of abjection as opposed to an aspirational policy statement.

In this book I have been thinking particularly about those children and young people who transgress gender norms (discussed in chapter five); fail in their attempt to utilise an 'authorising narrative' (Skeggs 1997) from outside their ascribed social class (discussed in chapters six and seven); or whose racially ascribed status embodies the 'social boundaries between groups' (Eriksen 1995: 251; discussed in chapter seven). From within this paradigm, permanent exclusion can be read as the maintaining of boundaries through the expulsion of that which does not belong. Butler (1999) explains that '[t]he boundary of the body as well as the distinction between internal and external is established through the ejection and transvaluation of something originally part of identity into a defiling otherness' (170). The body that is the school, in the case of a permanent exclusion, then, establishes its identity partially through what it excludes. Because state funded schools can be seen as an expression of state governance, a school's abjected other is also a government's abjected other. Wright *et al.* (2000) frame similar concerns about the meaning of permanent exclusion within concepts of the 'marketability' of pupils, suggesting that 'unmarketable children' were more likely to be excluded because of the effect they may have had 'upon the overall image of the school' (105). In Enway, a pupil excluded from Pope John Paul Catholic School for 'causing death to a living creature',[2] in becoming excluded, re-established the projected ethic of the school as one that chooses life over death, no matter what the context.

If permanent exclusion does not originate as a policy aspiration, how does 'weak' inclusion policy operate to produce exclusion? Some of the members of the education policy-community were brought together in real space at government 'conferences' focussed on the policies of 'Inclusion' and the related policy of 'integrated multi-agency working', several of which I was required to attend in my role as Pupil Support Officer. As explained in chapters two and seven, Nader (1972) discusses the effects of remote 'policy makers' as a feature of interacting relationships sometimes omitted from localised ethnographies. Prompted by Shore and Wright's (1997:4) question in the introduction to their edited volume on the 'Anthropology of Policy', 'What are the mobilising metaphors and linguistic devices that cloak policy?', I have tried to understand the way in which policy operates in its interaction with Enway pupils and professionals by looking for examples of these at the conferences I attended. Revealing the influence of 'mobilising metaphors', I felt, may hold a key to understanding the impetus behind the powerful adherence to most professionals' belief in the 'absence' of institutional prejudice. It was this absence which I found in the 'gaps and silences' (Nader 1972) wherever I tried to explicitly discuss racism, heteronormativity and classism (in chapters five, six and seven). This could explain their nearly consistent delivery of a 'weak' version of inclusion which did not address institutional failures.

THE GOVERNMENT POLICY CONFERENCE: 'MOBILISING METAPHORS AND LINGUISTIC DEVICES' (SHORE AND WRITGHT 1997:4)

Understanding the way in which policy works requires what Fielding (2001) has described as 'the philosophical task of delving beneath the surface of clear charts, crisp paragraphs and confident cameos' (143). It also requires an understanding of the techniques of self-representation used by policy-makers (Miller 2003:72). Miller's ethnography of a government inspectorate describes 'Best Value' inspections of local authorities. These inspections required local authorities to represent all aspects of their services in a way that demonstrated 'value for money' partly through evidence of consultation with the public.[3] Apart from the problems inherent in measuring service-user satisfaction in pounds Sterling, this gave rise to a series of representational abstractions that amounted to Miller's theory of 'Virtualism'. These abstractions are those that:

> arise from the scale of the institutions; ... from ... taking factors out of the frame of reference during evaluation; ... that result when the representation of the act of consulting comes to replace the purported aim of consulting as a reorientation to users; ... [and] that follow from an exaggerated respect for hard quantitative data over soft qualitative data.

72

Abstraction creates an effective screen on which to project description, propaganda, and mobilising metaphors. Like the extended body, also a field vulnerable to the expression of authoritarian power, the field of local government abstraction is[4] perhaps engaged in without the ongoing awareness of the actors. Thus, in the minds of local authority research officers, consultation may not be consciously 'pretend'; there may actually exist the intention to consult.

The first policy technique I will be discussing, and perhaps (because it is a construct) something we could call a form of abstraction (Miller 2003), represents one of the ways in which policy-makers identify themselves: 'The Collective "We"'.

The Collective 'We'

In November 2007, along with other children's services inclusion staff, school inclusion managers and children's centre managers, I attended a conference of the Children's Workforce Development Council (CWDC), at which I identified the policy-making body's propensity to describe itself as a collective 'we'.

An example of the collective 'we' was embedded in part of a speech made by the National Development Manager for Integrated Working. She explained, 'we are a sector skills council ... a workforce reform body ... a delivery agent for the DCSF... partners of government ...' This technique functions to distance herself personally, repudiating any hint of subjectivity in policy-making, and separates the conference attendees as a collective 'you'. It sets up a dichotomised, hierarchical relationship between the dominant governmental discourse and the subordinate discourse of 'us', the policy-implementers (or as Wright and Shore term 'us', the 'street-level bureaucrats' (1997: 5)). This, however, appears to be a slippery relationship, with the CWDC oscillating between appearing to be working 'with' us policy-implementers- 'listening'- and then 'pulling rank' to coerce us.

Oscillating Alignment

Us and them The oscillating alignment demonstrated by policy-makers is exemplified in their propensity to voice what is thought of as the popular view, but to concurrently push the policy objective. For example, they might talk about government as if it is a fascistic master in order to buy empathy, coercing policy-implementers to implement policy through their propensity to solidarity. This functions as a device which distances the policy-maker (in this case, the CWDC) from the centre of power, aligning itself with the 'subjects of power'. Exemplifying this, the National Development Manager for Integrated Working explained at the conference that in October 2006 the CWDC was given responsibility by the Department for Children, Schools and Families (DCSF) for implementation of a massive raft of time consuming initiatives. These included the Common Assessment Framework and the Lead Professional, Information Sharing and multiagency working initiatives.[5] Ostensibly seeking developmental feedback, she asked plaintively, 'we've only just got used to these (documents) ... don't change them radically ...' By pleading that she had been pushed into working with this large number of difficult documents by a higher body, the National Development Manager for Integrated Working made a case for the audience to refrain from radical change.

Asking or telling? The National Development Manager in the example above made a case for the audience to refrain from radical change. This was despite her later comment that 'we are at the very early stages, and as such we are keen to have your thoughts.' Corroborating this 'consultation' role, the conference pack stated that the event was intended to 'hear about and share experiences of integrated working' and to look at the 'challenges and barriers to integrated working'.[6]

This oscillation between presenting the policy as a non-negotiable package on the one hand, and inviting the expression of the democratic mandate on the other, was also demonstrated at a 'Westminster Briefing' on implementing Inclusion policy, entitled 'Promoting Discipline, Respect and Good Manners: Implementing Government Strategy to Improve Children's Behaviour'. The introduction to the conference handbook read, 'The aim of this morning's Briefing is not just to be a one-way flow of information, but an opportunity for discussion and debate, where views and ideas can be aired and shared.' There is nothing immediately negative about inviting such debate, and the absence of a debate would in some senses be a more vociferous expression of governmental authority. But that would have represented an outdated expression of authoritarian power: as Foucault (1977) explains,

> He who is subjected to a field of visibility, and who knows it, assumes responsibility for the constraints of power ... he becomes the principle of his own subjection. By this very fact, the external power may throw off its physical weight ... it is a perpetual victory that avoids any ... confrontation and which is always decided in advance.

202–203

Thus in feeling that we have 'had our say', we are less likely to question that which we are discussing. By bringing representatives from the Anti-Bullying Alliance, Unicef, and the 'Headmaster' of a 'Full Service School'[7] into the Westminster Briefing, the policy-makers were offering an open discussion of *methods* to deliver a *policy* they were not willing to question.

Mobilising Metaphors: Persuasive Tropes

The representatives from Unicef and the Anti-Bullying Alliance at the Westminster Briefing could be seen as constituting 'mobilising metaphors'; powerful tropes capable of persuading professionals to deliver inequitable policy without questioning the underlying normative prejudices enfolded into it. Another example of a 'mobilising metaphor' concerns the familiar big statements that can be seen at these policy conferences. 'TDA:[8] developing people, improving young lives', proclaimed the banner at the foot of every massively projected PowerPoint slide at the November 2007 CWDC conference. And in her introductory speech, the National Development Manager for Integrated Working indicated her strategic and laudable aspirations, explaining that 'the goal' was 'to create a world class workforce for children, young people and families', and that 'Integrated Working', as a policy, was designed to involve 'everyone supporting children and young people working together effectively to put the child at the centre, meet their needs and improve their lives' and to be 'championing children'. She later introduced the Children's Plan, the new DCSF department, and the Children's Workforce Strategic Action Plan as vehicles- 'key documents; key drivers' to 'embed', 'humanising' this prerogative a few minutes later with the statement that 'change is fundamentally about people and practice, not just common systems and procedures.'

These grandiose statements make it very difficult for a voice of dissent to make itself heard. As one of the 'policy implementers' attending this conference, I was sitting in the audience, exhausted from a long week of trying to support young people living in the midst of extreme domestic violence and permanently excluded from school for sexual assault, unable to get a social worker interested in one of my cases because the young person was over fourteen years of age and this fell outside Enway's funding boundaries for intensive social worker involvement. I had a nagging feeling that 'Integrated Working' (actually implemented as a cheaper alternative to the funding of social workers) was failing these children. But as Whitty (2002) explains, 'to suggest that current policies might not be the best way of doing better, or asking whether we are clear about what we mean by doing better, [is] too often regarded as treachery' (137). In other words, voicing my concerns would run the risk of positioning me as someone opposed to these big statements: opposed to the mobilising metaphors of 'improving young lives' and 'championing children'.

The Child as mobilising metaphor   When policy and public work is concerned with children, it makes the mobilising metaphors inherent in their policy discourse especially difficult to challenge. Edelman (2004) discusses a series of public appeals made by US President Clinton 'on behalf of America's children' (2) during which one of the television advertisements showed Clinton saying, '"We're fighting for the children. Whose side are you on?"' (ibid). Edelman explains that 'the Child' as a metaphor is 'an ideological mobius strip ... so obviously unquestionable' and is what 'distinguishes public service announcements [what I read as 'policy discourse'] from the partisan discourse of political argumentation' (2).

The reason that 'the Child' is such a powerful metaphor is that it embodies potential: it represents a future. Marshall (1996) locates the ancestry of this mobilising metaphor in the nineteenth century, where 'fears of urban disorder in the context of industrialisation can be understood to have produced a focus on the child as a key point of reform and progress through education' (93). Because policy - the public service announcement of politics - 'works to affirm a social structure, which it then intends to transmit to the future', the Child 'remains the perpetual horizon of every acknowledged politics, the phantasmic beneficiary of every political intervention' (Edelman 2004:8). At the same time, there is an undercurrent of accepted wisdom that 'degeneracy could be nipped in the bud, by regulating the development of children in order to ensure their fitness as adults' (Walkerdine 1998:165). This might partially explain the policy-wave of 'early intervention strategies' (for example, the Common Assessment Framework and its application to children still in the womb,[9] or the 'Healthy Lives, Brighter Futures' child health document (Department of Health 2009), which offered increased access to contraception for teenagers),[10] filtering down through children's services departments. Not only are they cheaper to implement, but they represent an investment in the future: the 'production of the democratic citizen' (Walkerdine 1998:176).

The power of 'the Child' as a mobilising metaphor also insidiously distracts our attention from those things a government may want to conceal, including the reduction of public spending and the restriction of civil liberties. Later in this chapter I will make an ethnographic account of the capturing of the stories and extended bodies of young people in Enway's official documentation. At this point, however, it is important to mention that there are more and more data-capturing mechanisms in place, and that these have been implemented in response to devastatingly sad cases of child death, such as those of Victoria Climbie in 2000 and Baby P in 2007 (discussed in chapter one), both followed by extensive media coverage documenting a perceived failure of public services to collaborate sufficiently to stop the extreme neglect and abuse. This might be seen as a clue to the problem of interagency professional conflict which I have raised in this book, but the perceived answer to this 'failure to collaborate' has been in part to develop more and more detailed and time consuming data-capturing opportunities. Data captured as an 'early intervention strategy' could be used later to 'predict' a person's likely misbehaviour. But as Edelman (2004) explains, 'our enjoyment of liberty is eclipsed by the lengthening shadow of a Child whose freedom to develop undisturbed ... terroristically holds us all in check' (21). Lightfoot (2009) demonstrates this, reporting that '[a]mong a proliferation of government databases, the three causing concern over legality, privacy and consent were set up to protect children' (1). Lightfoot's Guardian Education article was written in response to a Joseph Rowntree Reform trust report, *Database State* (Anderson 2009). It stated that following the loss of two CD-Roms containing names and addresses from the Child Benefit database in October 2007,

> [t]he old line 'if you have nothing to hide, you have nothing to fear' was given a very public rebuttal. The millions of people affected by this data loss, who may have thought they had nothing to hide, were shown that they do have much to fear from the failures of the database state.

4

'The Child', then, as a mobilising metaphor, generates a particularly potent mixture of insidious power and danger to civil liberties. It is also perhaps the basis of the 'within-child' approach with its pathologising adherence to discourses of 'need' (Thomas and Loxley 2001; discussed in chapter three; see also Walkerdine 1998, discussed above) and its link to the gatekeeping practices of the 'Hard to Place' Pupil Placement Panel described in previous chapters.

CHAPTER 8

Self Evaluation as a Technique to Internalise the Technologies of Power

In order to further internalise the big statements of policy which are 'mobilising devices' and a technology of power, those who deliver policy into practice are asked to track and measure their progress. Thus the technique of 'self-evaluation' is often discussed at the conferences. The concept of 'self-evaluation' is fully in line with the techniques described above- particularly the 'oscillating alignment: us and them' technique. In self-evaluating we are expected to undertake a discursive, iterative process, but in reality we are led by the spectre of the ultimate performance of our results.

At the CWDC conference, the National Development Manager for Integrated Working projected onto the massive screen at the front of the room a visual model of 'a workforce reform model' consisting of concentric circles, with 'children, young people and families' at the centre, wrapped around with 'specialist skills and expert knowledge'; 'common skills: Common Assessment Framework'; 'change management; local workforce'; and 'partnership working for senior managers'. Having effectively placed the pupil's extended body at the centre of a hierarchy of power, the Manager for Integrated Working then advised that in order to manage this model, there would be 'guidance for local areas', with a 'self assessment tool' and 'guidance for Children's Services workers on using the self assessment tool'.

The genealogy of the strategy of self-assessment is described by Rose (1999) as deriving from the nineteenth century's new focus on the limiting of state's rights to interfere in the private lives of citizens. Like water flowing to fill an empty space, authoritarian power found its way into 'private citizens' through other means. Forcible policing techniques were no longer needed if the individual now saw itself as 'in a contract in which individual and society would have mutual claims and obligations ... Each individual was to become an active agent in the maintenance of a healthy and efficient polity, exercising a reflective scrutiny over ... conduct' (Rose 1999: 228).

Rose (1999) describes these post-Rousseau individuals as being 'obliged to be free' (218). Children's Services workers are thus charged not only with tracking a child's extended body through the hierarchy of power, but of recording and judging their own performance in this endeavour. I have replicated a tracking sheet: the 'Pupil Placement Panel referral contact report sheet', (Fig. 1, page 225 below in the section on documentation) on which I was responsible for recording the interactions and various methods of recording judgments and interventions made on behalf of a young person who had been permanently excluded, and which illustrates this point. Self-evaluation, self-assessment, or even 'reflective practice' can seduce policy implementers into feeling that they are in charge of their own destiny. Their responsibility to discharge their own duties and to improve or 'not see' inequity is easier to implement if it is thought of as 'a choice'. In fact, self-evaluation is not a matter of choice. Rose (2007), in later work, describes the identification and confinement of 'intractable individuals unable to govern themselves according to the civilised norms of a liberal society of freedom' (249).

A Splendid Environment

A splendid environment also often seduces the policy implementers attending these conferences into accepting policy as something which "clearly'... inescapably ought to be done and 'stands to reason' and cannot be negotiated or bargained over' (Shore and Wright (1997:20).

The Westminster Briefing was held in a large, deeply carpeted hotel, with a massive marble staircase sweeping up towards the seminar rooms, and a full three course lunch with exquisitely delicate panna cotta tartlets for dessert served by experienced waiters in long starched aprons. The CWDC event was held at 'Rendezvous@Novotel', a large, shiny conference centre in a hotel at the heart of London, and we were given little sausages in a light, buttery pastry, and free pads of creamy olive paper on which to write our notes. Dazzled by the big city surroundings, and sleepy after a large, carbohydrate-laden lunch, the 'We/you' hierarchy; the confusingly oscillating alignment, now with the workforce, then with the government, now asking our opinion, then telling us what to do; the grandiose statements; and the obligatory soul-searching 'self-evaluation' technique all serve to develop a policy-implementer identity aligned with that of the policy-makers. Shore and Wright explain that 'when people failed to identify with the policies of their rulers, the normative power of modern government lost its ideological grip' (1997:31). Maintaining an ideological grip requires the foregrounding of some things ('Championing Children') and the eclipsing of others: for example, the problems of normative institutional prejudice; and the search for value for money.[11]

Hidden Agendas

Value for money was not foregrounded at the CWDC conference, but the hidden agenda seemed to be to remove a significant caseload from the more expensive remit of Children's Services social workers whilst ostensibly promoting the 'Lead Professional', 'Common Assessment Framework', and 'Information Sharing' protocols. It was not an easy task for the policy-makers to obfuscate this 'value for money' goal, as children's services staff-members across the country were deeply concerned that these 'Integrated Working' tools would add massively to their workloads. This concern was reflected by a report at the conference on a pilot study in Peterborough which had found that 'the Lead Professional Role adds five to eight hours a week to the workload.'[12]

But 'cost-effectiveness' is promoted amongst public services workers as an ethical concern, to the point at which it is shamelessly foregrounded as a justification for inclusive action. The head teacher at the 'Full-Service School' who attended the Westminster Briefing explained how his school's strategies saved money in the long term. The school had supported a student through street-art- based re-engagement tactics, and the head teacher explained that: 'In normal circumstances he would have disappeared. We saved a young man who is now a tax payer.'[13]

The techniques described above go some way towards answering Shore and Wright's question, 'How are normative claims used to present a particular way of defining a problem and its solution, as if these were the only ones possible, while enforcing closure or silence on other ways of thinking or talking?' (1997: 3). They represent techniques of political 'spin'. It is this 'spin' which may have functioned to overcome disbelief and ideological discomfort to achieve the conflicting aims of 'inclusion' and 'attainment' (Whitty 2002). It may also be partially at the root of professionals' lack of subjective reflection on the norming structures of prejudice I have laid out in previous chapters.

Once we are away from the controlled environments of these government conferences, however, how is policy embedded and enforced?

LOCAL AUTHORITY EVENTS

Enway Council sets up its own internal conferences and these could be said to be an attempt to translate government policy into local context and embed it into practice.

Giving a Good Impression

At the Children's Inclusion Services (CIS) annual conference in October 2006, staff-members were told that a Joint Area Review of Enway was being planned. This was an OFSTED-type review of 'integrated' health, social care, education, and youth justice services by a team consisting of OFSTED, the Healthcare Commission, the Audit Commission, and three other similar bodies. The Director of Children's Services told us that the team would be looking at case studies of vulnerable children, and that we needed to consider:

How do we make sure the inspection team get a good first impression?

How do we make sure we tell them a consistent story? Let's not pretend- we need to showcase here.

They will be looking for evidence of impact on outcomes.

Don't grind your own axe- you will be asked what you've done about it.

Field-notes, October 2006

It was not clear whether senior managers really wanted actual 'evidence'. What was certainly wanted, however, was a 'showcase'- for the department to be telling the inspectors the 'consistent story' that they wanted to hear. Impression and experience were collapsed into an officially mandated 'story', the 'truth' of which was much less important than the production of a laudable depiction of the 'truth'. This exemplifies two of Miller's (2004) 'abstractions' leading to an attitude of 'Virtualism': that which arises 'from the scale of the institutions', and that which arises from 'the practice of externalisation taking factors out of the frame of reference during evaluation' (72).

During the evaluation period, which lasted about three weeks, individual Enway workers were called into several meetings with inspectors. In these meetings, they were asked to give their opinion on or justify 'evidence' (paperwork). The feverish preparation for this inspection was such that walking into the Enway Inclusion office during the first week, I kept expecting to see clipboard-carrying inspectors in pale shirts and ties peering over our shoulders as we wrote emails, made calls to schools and filed away a variety of descriptions of young people's behaviour. We had even been asked to tidy our desks.

What actually happened felt somehow more sinister. Our managers would suddenly be asked to 'go upstairs' to the Director's office to answer inspectors' questions. They would often be seen running out of the office, looking flushed and anxious. The effect was to place them on a similar hierarchy to ourselves; they would be pulled out of the kinds of important meetings and telephone calls they would never usually be able to leave. There was a marked disjunction between the need to, for example, stay and discuss a child in crisis with assembled professionals, and the need to leave that crisis meeting to go upstairs and relate the efficiency with which such crises were generally managed. It effectively reduced the fruitfulness of the meeting they had been obliged to leave. This was indicative of both Miller's 'practice of externalisation' (2004:72) and of the gap between the Director's request for a 'consistent story' and the unfolding narrative of the child about whom the meeting downstairs was being held. Although they usually showed good intentions in their work, this did not matter to the managers, as the Director had given them their first priority: to give a good impression. This coaching in abstraction served to distance professionals from the effects of their actions on young peoples' experience, privileging 'impressions' over reflexive action.

Aligning with the Frontline Workers

Another seminar at the same Enway Children's Services event involved the dissemination of information about the newly introduced 'Common Assessment Framework' (CAF) and 'Lead Professional' (LP) role initiatives. These were the government's attempts, described above, to promote integrated services for young people falling just below the threshold of need qualifying them for the support of a (comparably more expensive) social worker. The Enway CAF Coordinator told us,

This is yet another form, another layer of bureaucracy.

Does it really help or improve multiagency, collaborative working?

There is already confusion around the idea of keyworkers- are these designated social workers? Or Lead Professionals?

Field-notes, October 2006

By complaining about bureaucracy and confusion and thereby aligning herself with those of us 'training' to implement the new integrated working policies, the CAF and LP Coordinator was using a similar tactic to that used at the CWDC conference. At the same time, verbalising an alignment with 'frontline workers' could be thought of as serving to 'encompass diversity through presenting dissenting opinion. This sets the scene for dealing with dissent as a minority view' (Strathern 2005:472). A similar effect is achieved through a demonstration of 'youth participation' decision-making activities.

'Voice' and Consultation

I heard that the Assistant Director of Children's Services, Leslie, was chairing a 'Youth Participation' steering group. On joining this group, however, I became disconcerted with the methods used to gather the 'youth voice'. Although a youth conference, face to face interviews, and participation events had been organised, the majority of the report which was to be submitted by the Youth Participation Panel as part of the Children's Plan development exercise was derived from a questionnaire sent out to hundreds of school pupils. The questions I looked at seemed to me to be overly directive. For example, young people were asked cheerfully, 'Do you feel that questionnaires like this one help us to understand your opinions about services for children and young people?' The pupils whose voices were most likely to be silenced (those who spoke English as an additional language, 'looked after' children moving from one school to another as their foster care placements changed, dyslexic students, and excluded pupils not present at school to fill out the questionnaire, for example) would not have been involved in this exercise.

Leslie's team was (perhaps without awareness) less concerned with collecting the actual views of young people than with the appearance of having done so. This could be read as a form of Zizek's (2008) 'objective violence' (see chapter six), perpetuating disadvantage by failing to unearth genuinely useful feedback from the most disadvantaged children. But the semblance of youth 'participation' in decision-making was a mobilising metaphor, lending the validity of the 'service-user's voice' to the policies to be produced, and distracting attention from the deep veins of institutional prejudice.

Mobilising Metaphors in Enway

The October 2006 internal conference was also an opportunity for Enway's own policy-makers to implement the policy that central government had asked them to implement. To do this, Enway made use of its own mobilising metaphors. The Enway Children's Inclusion Services (CIS) Plan gave the Directorate Mission statements:

- Children first
- Deliver the 5 Every Child Matters Outcomes
- Integrated service delivery
- Listen to children, young people and their families

Again, opposition to the subsequent details of the CIS Plan would have implied that workers were not aligned with the big aspirational statements- for example, putting children first, or listening to families. However, over the following three years in Enway, I observed that finances, schools' league table positions, and 'health and safety' were often put first, rather than children. Service delivery had not by September 2009 become integrated. And although efforts to genuinely listen to children, young people and families had started to blossom in isolated patches, they had not become embedded deeply and broadly into practice.

Use of Statistics

It has been shown in this book and elsewhere that the existence of league tables has caused head teachers to be more likely to welcome previously excluded pupils into their schools if a good set of GCSE results is to be expected (chapters three and seven; Osler and Vincent 2003; Cooper 2002; Rendall and Stuart 2005; Ball 2001). This illustrates the problems that can be caused on the 'front line' when policy-makers borrow the validating gloss that can arise from the quoting of a statistic. This gloss, it could be suggested, does not merely distract attention from institutional prejudice, but actively produces it.

At the CIS conference, documentation printed on high quality paper and neatly bound offered delegates a selection of interesting statistics together with a written analysis of them. In every age-group, the most underachieving groups were those labelled as 'Black Somali', 'White Other', and 'Gypsy Roma'. 'Black British' pupils were shown to be improving fastest, achieving at two percentage points above their 'White British' counterparts. However, as discussed in chapter seven, three years after these statistics were disseminated, the Chief Inspector for Ethnic Minority Achievement had been made redundant, having been told he 'should be happy' as he had 'done his job', and the new policy was focussed on 'White Working-class Boys'. There was no specific policy to support Gypsy Roma and Somali pupils, and in fact the Enway school most familiar with and successful in educating Gypsy Roma children was earmarked for closure to make way for a new academy, due to its low attainment rates. Quoting the statistics gave the impression that policy was being arranged to organise for improvements. It is an example of another of Miller's (2004) 'abstractions', as it follows 'from an exaggerated respect for hard quantitative over soft qualitative data' (72). As I described in chapter seven, during the next round of statistics-gathering in Enway, in 2008, an Enway policy officer told me that they had 'not been asked' for a report on Somali and Gypsy Roma children.

A reliance on statistics has been called by Fielding (2001) 'the idolatry of measurement' (146). He concludes,

> The worry here is that strength of conviction about the necessity of measurement blinds its proponents to the limitations of current instruments and we all end up not only mismeasuring the measurable but misrepresenting the immeasurable or elusive aspects of education which so often turn out to be central to our deeper purposes and more profound aspirations.
>
> 146

The Enway school whose inclusive ethos welcomed and educated the children of Traveller families was one of the fatalities of this misrepresentation of the 'immeasurable'; victim to its own deeper purpose and profound aspiration. It follows that the reliance on and 'idolatry' given to a chosen set of statistics is a feature of institutional racism, in the case of the group of Traveller pupils attending the closing school.

Butler (2004) identifies 'governmentality' as operating 'through policies and departments, through managerial and bureaucratic institutions … diffusely … in relation to specific policy aims' (52). These diffuse operations are evident in the description, above, of the oscillating alignments of those charged with making and embedding policy. They are also evident in the theatrical staging (the self-representation; what Miller (2004) terms 'Virtualism') intrinsic in the hidden agendas barely concealed by irrefutable mobilising metaphors; in the dazzling policy conference environments; in the vast range and idolatry of statistics; and in the representation practices inherent in surveillance regimes reliant on the internalising of authoritarian power through a requirement for official self-evaluation.

I have described in this book the ways in which the extended bodies of pupils at risk of exclusion can be represented in documentation,[14] and this is also one of the ways in which authoritarian power and policies are situated 'not only in the inextricability of a functioning, but in the coherence of a tactic' (Foucault 1977: 139). As Foucault later adds, '[t]he examination that places individuals in a field of surveillance also situates them in a network of writing; it engages them in a whole mass of documents that capture and fix them' (ibid, 189). The next section penetrates the mechanisms of normative authoritarian power further, and looks at an area of specific activity involved in the administration of permanent exclusion from school: documentation.

CHANGING POLICY: CHINKS OF VULNERABILITY IN THE ENORMITY OF THE
SURVEILLANCE TASK

The Paper Trail

The officially mandated bits of a pupil's extended body, subjected to the critical event of a threatened or actual permanent exclusion, makes its passage through databases, filing cabinets, and document shredders. For example, Mahad[15] had his behaviour logged at school in 'Incident Slips' and then collated by an administrator and re-logged onto an electronically held database called a 'Behaviour Log'. This Behaviour Log was printed out and photocopied for the permanent exclusion Governors' Hearing. Following the hearing, after permanent exclusion had been ratified, a letter was written to Mahad's mother explaining the exclusion, a copy of which was held in his school file. For the Pupil Placement Panel, the Behaviour Log and related letters were collated and stapled with a cover sheet for the Panel, detailing Mahad's name, address, parents' names, ethnicity, a précis of the behaviour history and of related interventions (such as fixed term exclusions or referrals) to date. This was copied to the twenty-five Panel members, some of whom left their copies at the end of the Panel meeting piled up on the Formica table for shredding. A few copies were retained, for example by me, in order to carry out the reintegration meeting at Mahad's new school placement. A copy was also sent to the new school. This was inserted into a file, which would also contain a new set of paperwork completed by Mahad's parent during the reintegration meeting. This school paperwork included another form requiring addresses and contact details, another form requiring ethnicity data, doctors' contact details, preferred subjects, and details of involvement with other services. Later that month Mahad and his mother met me at a CAMHS[16] meeting, where a longer history of Mahad's life was taken, with teachers and family members present to add to the narrative. These case-notes were retained at the CAMHS Centre, together with the bundle from the Pupil Placement Panel. Back in the Enway Children's Services offices, a copy of the whole file was kept in a locked filing cabinet whilst further copies from the Panel lay unsecured in bin-bags waiting to be shredded by the young volunteer who came in on Fridays. She would sit, totally absorbed, reading every detail within each stack of papers, before feeding them nosily into the shredding machine. Paper dust hung in the air around her as paper facsimiles of bits of Mahad's and other children's extended bodies were nonchalantly shredded in what might be seen as an act of objective violence (Zizek 2008; see chapter three). In the meantime, Mahad's progress from one school to another and details of referral to the Panel and to CAMHS were held on an Admissions Department database, which I had access to. Notes from teachers, Admissions officers, administrators and other professionals which had arrived by email or attachment in electronic format were saved in the notes section of this database (excluding details passed on orally or in handwritten notes), and were often used to write reports or to give information to other professionals such as social workers, who might call to ask what was happening with the case. The whole trail was recorded on its own special handwritten tracking sheet (replicated with identifying details changed below):

Table 1. Contact Report Sheet

Pupil Placement Panel referral contact report sheet		Sheet no. 1
Pupil Name Mahad xxx	Provision Forrest Boys	
d.o.b. xxx	Year Group 10	
Contact no. home xxx xxx xxxx	Mobile no. 07xxx xxx xxx	
Date	Notes	Initials
7.6.07	Panel→ dual registered with Church Forest or Forrest Boys & PRU	AC
8.6.08	Exclusion paperwork arrived from Ennon Castle School. Poss. Mixed school inappropriate.	AC
11.6.07	Letter to school in file	AC
26.6.07	As Church Forest felt unable to support reintegration, has been placed at Forrest Boys- letter in file	AC
14.8.07	Letter from admissions and Head of Inclusion to get reintegration moving- in file	AC
4.9.07	Call from xx at Forrest Boys- Rtg Fri 7/9 at 9.30am	AC
"	Spoke w/ mum- will be attending	AC
"	Called PRU to speak to home school liaison officer who will speak w/head teacher and may attend, or call XX at Forrest if nobody can come	AC
"	Spoke w/ Youth Inclusion Support Project- will refer→emailed. Take consent form to meeting to sign and fax	AC
5.9.07	Spoke w/ head teacher at PRU- xx at Forrest can call her Fri PM to discuss protocol if necessary	AC
"	Left message/emailed w/ Young Minds project manager and CAMHS doctor	AC
6.9.07	Referral to CAMHS completed	AC
7.9.07	Review set for Oct 17 9am	AC
"	Fax to Youth Inclusion Support project (signature page)	AC

It can be seen from the tracking sheet above that the paperwork, carrying Mahad's story, had its own journey to make. Emails and phone calls were also made and logged. Thus a multitude of documents, including Behaviour Logs, Pastoral Support Plans, admissions documents, records of academic scores, and attendance tracking print-outs were all called into service when the Enway 'Hard to Place' Pupil Placement Panel tried to make a decision on where a permanently excluded pupil should be placed.

Behaviour Logs were particularly significant as they worked to 'capture and fix' normative representations of the pupil in a paper form which became darker and grainier and more difficult to read as it was repeatedly photocopied as 'evidence'. The Behaviour Log privileged one part of a young person's extended body (the 'badly behaved' representation above all the other kaleidoscopic elements (for example, the 'motherless child' part). The Log did not include a space requiring the pupil to put his or her side of the story, and was always viewed by staff as a justification for discipline rather than as a source of information to assist in planning for support.

At the same time, the observation/record-keeping nature of Behaviour Logs could be read as a 'modern pedagogic practice' related to the historical adoption in schooling of child study and observational record-making in alignment with 'developmental psychological principles ... so taken for granted that it is difficult to see precisely what could be questionable about them' (Walkerdine in Henriques 1998:150; see also Rose 1989:145–154). The link between psychology and discipline made so clearly by Foucault (1989) is clear.

In a Behaviour Log distributed at Mahad's permanent exclusion Governors' Hearing, there were nine pages of comment. Each page was divided into two columns: on the left, a narrow column recorded the date of each incident. On the right, teacher comments described a story of Mahad's life at school from September 2004 until March 2007. A sample of these comments read:

Table 2. Behaviour Log

Date	Summary of Incidents/Behaviour
12.02.05	Letter home (Geography). Concerns over Mahad's lack of work and disruptive behaviour in recent lessons. Also his lack of cooperation with the teacher.
19.02.05	Incident Slip (ICT). Mahad smashed down the keyboard on the desk causing the space bar to fall off. This was the final straw in a lesson where he had done no work, was continually out of his seat and constantly disturbing others. Removed by Senior Management.
10.4.05	Incident Slip (History). Late to lesson. Mahad had knocked down chairs in the dining room. One hit a meal supervisor. Mahad refused to apologise. Mahad refused to put his shoes on all lesson. Had no equipment. Did no work. Put head on desk to sleep. Sent out. Refused to follow instructions. Would not answer any questions for 20 minutes. Banging on the wall.
16.4.05	Seclusion (2 days). Urinating against a door when sent out of lesson.
18.6.05	Incident slip (lunchtime). Mahad was up a tree in the playground. He refused to get down despite being asked 3 times. He said 'shut up you ****ing ****'. He got down eventually and started shouting 'shut up', 'you don't know my name anyway'. Mahad spoken to and warned.

All nine pages of comments such as these were limited to negative incidents and did not describe Mahad's own view of each story or possible contextual reasons behind each incident. For example, the Log does not mention that in 2005 his mother had come out of prison after several years. Some of the more 'disturbed' behaviour (urinating against a classroom door, for example) should perhaps have warranted an investigation into all of the overlapping contexts in which Mahad lived. The Log amounted to around sixty recorded events each year. But by the time Mahad was permanently excluded in 2008 for sexually inappropriate behaviour and 'sexual assault', nothing, beyond tracking, had been done to address the context in which Mahad was growing up, or the relationships he had with staff. On 12.2.05, he was said to demonstrate a 'lack of cooperation' with the teacher. But cooperation is not a one-person endeavour. The Behaviour Log, with its 'within-child' focus, can be seen as a punitive tool of an 'audit culture' (Strathern 2000). It is so taken with the procedures of recording and auditing - with Fielding's (2001) 'idolatry of measurement' (146) - that it constitutes a kind of 'tyranny of transparency' (Strathern 2000b). The behaviour log in this case can thus be described as a virtualist abstraction (Miller 2003) concealing the real task of helping Mahad behind a picture-wall of recorded observations infused with institutional prejudice but considered to be a 'true' picture because of the lengthy and official way in which they had been recorded.

As I explained in chapter three, Blackman and Venn (2010) point out a preferable view of the body-as-process as opposed to one discussed solely as a reductive, static representation. The representations 'captured and fixed' (Foucault 1977:189) in a behaviour log have the effect of excluding from the young person's story important details which, if accepted, would affect the ways in which the child or young person was supported. Behaviour logs, such as a second example below (again, taken from Mahad's Log), are a place in which a young person's extended body can, to their detriment, be described and fixed in that description:

Table 3. Behaviour log

Date	Summary of incidents/behaviour
22.9.05	Incident slip. Mahad was reported to have been threatening a year 7 boy. Mahad had apparently broken a window after school and the owner had come out and grabbed another boy. He wanted to know who Mahad was. Mahad got to hear about this and had threatened to get the boy for giving his name over. Head of year spoke to Mahad and warned him re fighting. [1]
25.9.05	Seclusion (lunch + one lesson) Mahad slapped another student for no reason. Uncooperative/unacceptable behaviour. Mahad in seclusion until Dad came up at the end of the day. Mahad then excluded for 7 days. [2]
5.10.05	Mahad was slapping other students around the head as they entered the building. Mahad denied doing this but it was witnessed by an adult. It was also reported by other students. [3]
8.10.05	Geography: challenging and disruptive behaviour. Told the teacher he didn't have his planner and wouldn't give it to her even if he did have it. The teacher noted that his behaviour "seriously affects the achievement of the class". Mahad was given 15 minutes detention. He climbed out of the window. [4]

One of the confounding problems with this kind of document[17] is that those who use it are standing in various roles: for example, that of 'pastoral nurturer', that of 'police investigator', and that of 'subject teacher'. The 'pastoral nurturer' is evident in the head of year's actions (paragraph 1 in the example above) in speaking to

Mahad and warning him about fighting. Although the burden of proof in school investigations is usually held 'on the balance of probabilities', the teacher in the role of 'police investigator' tries to use legalistic 'beyond all reasonable doubt' language- for example, Mahad's behaviour 'was reported' (paragraph 1) and 'was witnessed' (paragraph 3). And the 'subject teacher' worries about 'the achievement of the class' (paragraph 4). The Behaviour Log document brings all these roles together into one corporate or institutional personality. This corporate personality would later be discussed in the Panel meeting as 'The School': 'The School has recorded in the Behaviour Log that Mahad "seriously affects the achievement of his classes"'. All of this amounts to the vulnerability of the Behaviour Log and similar electronic or paper documents to the establishing of unqualified but nonetheless calcifying judgements. As Lightfoot (2009) mentions in her discussion of the New Labour government's Contact Point database[18] on all children of school age: 'It is not just factual information that is being logged. People who work with children are being compelled to make judgments about them and their families that they are not qualified to make ... '[t]ittle-tattle' will be entered on the system and treated as gospel' (1).

Even positive comments, if abstracted and decontextualised, could result in inappropriate or misguided decisions. Mahad's head teacher was at the Panel meeting and described him as having 'a bubbly personality', saying that he was popular with teachers and staff. It was this comment (later recorded by myself, fixed in place in document form, in a referral to CAMHS) that prompted the head teacher of Forrest Boys School (also attending the Panel that day) to cheerfully offer Mahad a placement following his permanent exclusion. Unfortunately, he was unable to cope at another mainstream school and was excluded a second time, finally finding his academic feet at the Enway Pupil Referral Unit. Had this comment not been seized upon, some months at Forrest Boys would not have been wasted and Mahad may have received the more intensive support he needed much sooner.

ONSET forms Another document in which Mahad's extended body was described and fixed was the ONSET[19] Referral and Screening Youth Inclusion Support Panel (YISP) form. YISPs had been established across the country from 2003 to try to predict and stop criminal or young offending behaviour. They were formed as 'fair access panels' (which function as funding distributors); collaborations between Youth Service teams (who run diversionary activities, such as youth clubs); local and school-based policing teams; and Youth Offending Service teams, who were responsible for the support, surveillance and enforcement of young people under court orders for offences already committed. YISP referrals are of special note because they are intended to be acted upon by 'prevention teams'. As such, they are an embodiment of the 'early intervention' model discussed above in relation to Edelman's (2004) conception of 'the Child' as a mobilising metaphor. This metaphor is capable of prompting activities that limit current civil liberties in order to secure the 'wellbeing' of 'the Child' in a future which will never arrive (as 'the Child' will be ever-present in policy-making activities: 'the Child' will never grow up). ONSET forms can be downloaded from the internet[20] and following yet another capturing of basic date-of-birth and address details, take the referrer through a series of check-box statements. In carrying out its task of predicting the need for input from a young offending 'prevention team', the form asks the referrer to confirm, among other things, whether the young person 'is separated from either or both of his or her parents', 'does not use spare time constructively', 'seems to be suffering from emotional problems', 'displays inappropriate self-esteem', 'displays discriminatory attitudes against others', or 'gets easily bored'. There are five 'Positive factors' to be chosen from, and thirty-two negative factors, grouped under headings such as 'Living and family arrangements', 'Neighbourhood and friends', 'Emotional and mental health', 'Perception of self and others', and 'Thinking, behaviour and attitudes'. Each heading asks for a few lines of 'evidence' (from non-police professionals, as with the Behaviour Log) for the boxes ticked. In Mahad's ONSET form, the Behaviour Log was quoted as 'evidence':

> Behaviour report states that "Since his father became his main carer after he spent time living with his mother, this has had an impact on Mahad's social development. This in turn caused changes in Mahad's behaviour. He was a bright bubbly boy who underperformed due to these circumstances. Behaviour changed when his mother came into his life after a three year break. Mahad ended Year 7 excluded. On his return in Year 8 he seemed to have matured and was happier, however his behaviour soon became a cause for concern again. Mahad's behaviour is a real cause for concern and often disturbing".

Reading this comment, one might add to the roles of those charged with entering notes onto a Behaviour Log, described above, a further role: that of 'psychological expert'. It details the type of case history and 'professional judgment' one might find in highly confidential mental health case-notes, but which has been written by a teacher (not a psychologist), and then copied and recopied and distributed to school governors, Inclusion officers, Panel members, administration workers, and those who shred documents after Panel meetings. The language in the form explicitly invites this type of comment on 'behaviour', 'attitudes' and 'self-esteem', three of the extended body 'attributes' I have mentioned (in chapter three) as vulnerable to drawing descriptive attention.

Whilst it might feel sensible to assess and target-fund the needs of young people who have been identified as suffering 'from emotional problems' or to re-educate young people who display 'discriminatory attitudes towards others',[21] the ONSET form does represent significant civil liberties issues. For example, would an adult be happy for a referral form to be completed stating that he or she 'does not use spare time constructively' and therefore needs to be referred for diversionary activities? The procedure looks like something George Orwell (1949) might have written about in *1984*, or close to the activities of the 'Precrime' team on those who have featured in predictive dreams of violent attack in the Spielberg (2002) film interpretation of a Philip K Dick short story, *Minority Report*. Further, as has been noted by Anderson (2009) in his report *Database State*,

> All of these systems have a rationale and a purpose. But ... in too many cases, the public are neither served nor protected by the increasingly complex and intrusive holdings of personal information invading every aspect of our lives ... [the] systems ... have significant problems with privacy ... Sharing [data] can harm the vulnerable, not least by leading to discrimination and stigmatisation.

4

Fundamental to the problems with this type of information-gathering exercise is that the people entering the data are not necessarily qualified to make the judgments they are recording. This is particularly problematic given the validating power of an 'opinion' once it has been captured as 'fact' on an official form.

Documentation, then, is a powerful tool for the delivery of a policy framework that allows the permanent exclusion of disadvantaged children and young people within a system built on a 'weak' model of inclusion.

'Critical bureaucracy': using documentation to support self-actualisation in the field of authoritarian power   Noticing the propensity for documentation to 'capture and fix' (Foucault 1977:189) pupils inside a policy framework, I tried early in my work as a Pupil Support Officer to change some documents. My goal was to find out if a purposely constructed pro-forma, used by all staff in a permanent exclusion incident, could steer towards more genuinely inclusive practice. I chose to use the Reintegration Support Plan (RSP) document. This document was used in meetings between new heads of year, parents, pupils, professionals from other agencies (such as social workers) and support staff, to discuss and plan for a successful reintegration into school, after the placement had been made by the Panel. When I first saw this blank form (Form 1), it provided plenty of space for the concerns of the school, but no space specifically inviting the concerns of the pupil.

Thinking about making space for the voices of the pupil and parents or carers,[22] and viewing the management of behaviour as something that needed to investigate school environment factors as closely as the pupil him or herself, I changed the form to guide the process. Pathologising the individual takes attention and responsibility for positive change off the institution (Foucault 1977; Thomas and Loxley 2001); I wanted to reposition the 'problem' as one which included the institution's possible culpability and potential for ameliorating action. This was a reconfiguring of documentary and thinking space, and an act of what we might call 'critical bureaucracy'

Form 2 included a larger space for the concerns of parents and pupils to be recorded; and each target now required a corresponding commitment from the school, reminding staff of the need for positive reinforcement, and designating a named support person. The form guided the meeting to see support planning as a

Table 4. Form 1: A Form that 'Tracks' a Situation

Reintegration Support Plan				
Date: Meeting attended by:		Plan completed by:		
Name:	Date:	Year:	M/F:	Last or current school:
Date permanent exclusion upheld, if applicable: Pupil Placement Panel:			Date considered by	
Named school: Plan No:			Start date:	
Interim arrangements:				
Long-term arrangements:				
Additional considerations:				
Pastoral and educational objectives:				
Pupil targets, based on objectives 1 2 3			Target met at review? Please comment:	
Signed:	Parent		Local authority	
School	Pupil		Agencies	
Review date (four school weeks):				

joint endeavour, placing responsibility within the group collectively, rather than monitoring the pupil's own progress towards pupil-based targets. It became a place where it was possible to add the opinions of people other than the 'professionals', challenging the 'supposed empiricism' Foucault (xii: 1989) identified in the medical, pathologising 'gaze' (see chapter three). This form became somewhat of an action research project, as over the following two years I gradually expanded the space for pupil comments and added the 'Agencies' signature box to promote the participation of social workers and other involved professionals in the school-based process. The form also became something schools began to use independently of local authority involvement.

The development of the second Reintegration Support Plan form described above was an attempt to ameliorate the inequitable quality of the recorded information that was capturing and fixing pupils, and to support and reintegrate rather than pathologise, label and mark out as lacking the qualities required to belong. As Walkerdine (1998)

Table 5. Form 2: A Form that 'Deals with' a Situation

Reintegration Support Plan			
Date: Plan completed by: Meeting attended by:			
Name: Date: Year: M/F: Last or current school:			
Date permanent exclusion upheld, if applicable: Date considered by Pupil Placement Panel:			
Named school: Start date: Plan No:			
Interim arrangements:			
Long-term arrangements:			
Additional considerations Parent/carer: Pupil: School: Other agencies:			
Pastoral and educational objectives:			
Targets, based on objectives	School support strategies, including positive reinforcement:	Person responsible for providing support and monitoring progress:	Monitored by LA Officer at review:
1			
2			
3			
Signed: Parent/carer Local authority			
School Pupil Agencies			
Review date (four school weeks):			

explains in her discussion of nursery record cards on which teachers recorded their child study observations of the developmental stages of play, 'the apparatuses of the pedagogy are no mere application but a site of production in their own right' (157). If the pedagogical apparatus of the first Reintegration Support Plan form (above,

Form 1) was the 'site of production' of a pupil held solely responsible for his own educational and social failures, then perhaps Form 2 could be a 'site of production' of a pupil-parent-professional collaboration taking equitable responsibility for supporting a successful period of schooling.

Walkerdine's (1998) Foucauldian conception of 'regimes of truth created by psychology ... internally related to shifts and transformations in pedagogic practice' (158) is particularly important here because this book focuses on young people whose 'behaviour' has often been pathologised to the detriment of reflexivity about the objective violence of institutional prejudice. Thus if documentation is understood as a space in which authoritarian power can be exercised through the describing or representing of selected aspects of the extended bodies of young people (sometimes known as 'labelling'), a change in the documentation can also provide a reconfiguration of that space. This could then become what Allen (2009) calls 'a space of critical enunciation', and is a space in which young people can potentially exercise their 'voice', or flex their agency, both in their extended body and in public space in the contested space of the field of authoritarian power.

VULNERABILITY IN THE SIZE OF THE TASK OF AUTHORITARIAN SURVEILLANCE: CRITICAL MASS?

The ways in which documentation can be altered can help to find a space for the strategic use of power ('critical bureaucracy'), through privileging the 'voice' of those disempowered within the children's services system. By requiring positive input from all engaged parties, the new version of the Reintegration Support Plan document can in itself reveal some vulnerabilities in the objective violence (Zizek 2008) of pathologising institutional practices.

An example of critical bureaucracy in use as a power-rebalancing strategy is apparent in the case of the OFSTED inspection of one of the Enway schools, Cherry Tree. This school had during the 2000s made great strides in terms of its 'value added' results. In other words, it succeeded in raising the educational attainment of its large population of pupils 'with English as an additional language', and was particularly successful in terms of supporting refugee children in settling into education, and including children with physical disabilities. But when OFSTED made its inspection, this school found itself on the 'National Challenge' list of schools 'at risk' because it did not have 30% of its pupils receiving the gold standard of at least five GCSEs at grade C or above including English and Maths. Whilst 'value added' scores (i.e. the measure of the increase in attainment) are *recorded*, they are not *taken into account* when a school is designated as 'failing' or not. So a school where all the children begin in Year 7 with average to above average standardised test scores (linked to the level of cultural capital- see chapter six) is measured in exactly the same way as a school where most of the Year 7 pupils begin with very low to low average test scores. Cherry Tree, like most schools (and like Enway in the Joint Area Review described above), however, had grown to understand what OFSTED wanted to see. So having been given two days notice of their next inspection, staff, in an act of critical bureaucracy, organised for the twelve most disruptive pupils to climb into a minibus and go on an educational and diversionary school trip on the two days when OFSTED inspectors were in school. Because the OFSTED inspection regime relies heavily on a self-evaluation system - schools must complete a 'self-evaluation form' (SEF) which is then used as the basis of the OFSTED inspection - schools have first become accustomed to and then developed an adeptness at representing themselves in a way to which OFSTED responds favourably. Foucault's (1977) understanding of the development of internalised surveillance is clearly in action here (see also Rose 1989), but there may be space to see this kind of internalised surveillance as more 'knowing'; more cynical.

Has the universalised internalisation of authoritarian power reached critical mass? Has it become so large that surveillance has become perfunctory, relying too much on internalised surveillance as a strategy, reading a show of surveillance as evidence of an adequately surveyed organisation; throwing shadows and making islands of resistance more easy to implement? If the internalisation of authoritarian power has become a globalised phenomenon, perhaps global problems do not warrant global solutions but small local solutions; little tweaks not picked up in the blunt instruments of auditing tools designed to cover all situations, such as the second Reintegration Support Plan form, above, redesigned with attention to detail in order to reconfigure discursive and descriptive space. Small local solutions rely on the existence of local agency. The Reintegration Support Plan form demonstrates that this agency is available to be activated in documentary space. The next section will focus on finding other spaces for resistance through critical bureaucracy.

The Field of Authoritarian Power as a Contested Space

As I explained at the beginning of this chapter, policy is 'an expression of intent'. We have found possibilities for agency inside the extended body of the permanently excluded pupil. This requires a contest where pupils have been supported to self-advocate in the face of the dominant authoritarian discourse.[23] Similarly, the field of authoritarian power represents a space in which contests over inclusion and exclusion can be held, where the instruments of government (which are also subjects, according to Foucault 1977) learn to self-advocate alongside the subjects of government.

Could we really think of the field of governmental administration as a contested space? In thinking and talking through this book, I have often been confronted with the idea that I am presenting a doom-laden account of the business of working with young people at risk of school exclusion. What of the empathic LSU and PRU teachers described in chapter four; the facilitator of the 'boys' group' described in chapter five; those who teach with an ethic of care; those who are actively anti-sexist and anti-racist? What of the Anti-Bullying Alliance; the Unicef drive to promote schools run along 'Rights and Responsibilities' lines; and the 'Full Service School', where the head teacher chose to close the gap between professional cultures and spend funds on an in-school social worker?

The Paradox Inherent in the Lack of Evil Intent in Technologies of Power

I have described the cul-de-sacs we can wander down when confronted with Shore and Wright's (1997:4) seductive '[m]obilizing metaphors and linguistic devices' of policy. For example, the Unicef representative at the Westminster Briefing used a mobilising metaphor ('the universality of human rights ... challenging injustice, inequality and poverty in the world') to justify what might be seen as the internalisation of the technologies of power- teaching young people 'to become active global citizens': the kinds of active citizen acceptable to government (Biesta 2011). Always seeking to disrupt hegemonic wisdom, Zizek (2008) challengingly suggests that '[h]uman rights emerge as a false ideological universality which masks and legitimises the concrete politics of Western imperialism ... domination ... and neocolonialism' (126). However, he clarifies that simply because the universality of human rights bullishly foregrounds the ways of a dominant culture, it does not mean that they are not necessary in some circumstances. From my orientation towards social justice, I understand this to mean that perhaps teaching young people about their rights can give them a more equal footing in their interactions with the technologies of power. If policy is then a feature of the government's field of authoritarian power, and we 'study up' (Nader 1972; chapter two) on it, then it is a contested space; and this indicates room for the expression of agency and a subsequent rebalancing of the power inherent in the politics of social space.

POLICY AND PROTOCOL: A CAUSE OF PERMANENT EXCLUSION FROM SCHOOL?

Through looking at the mechanisms which help to implement inclusion policy and the administration of permanent exclusion from school, this chapter has attempted to deconstruct the machinery of institutional prejudice. The institutional prejudice and neglect that contributes to the causes of permanent exclusion from school can be found hidden, justified and enacted in policy pronouncements, surveillance regimes, and the documentation which is designed to deliver them. But it is in identifying the workings of these techniques that we can understand how this prejudice and neglect can also be challenged.

The next chapter draws together some of the causes and impacts of permanent exclusion from school investigated in this book, and lays out a range of suggested local and general recommendations to ameliorate them.

NOTES

1   Children's Act 2004; Equality Act 2010.
2   Suffering from the throwing tic which is often a part of Tourette's Syndrome, he threw a frog at a wall. See table 4 in chapter 6.
3   See the discussion of the 'youth participation steering group', below, for an example of this happening in Enway.
4   Like other fields of panoptic power described by Foucault (1977).
5   These initiatives were designed as an early intervention package to investigate and plan for the needs of children and young people who fell below the threshold for safeguarding and social care (and thus to save the expense of a social worker), and concurrently to centralise and track the gathering of information on individual children from across agencies (problems with which are discuss in this chapter, below).
6   This exemplifies one of Miller's (2004) 'abstractions': that which results 'when the representation of the act of consulting comes to replace the purported aim of consulting as a reorientation to users' (72)
7   A school which employs as permanent staff all the members of a multi-agency team, including for example a psychologist and a social worker.
8   Training and Development Agency for Schools.
9   Truly an early intervention.
10 An even earlier intervention .
11 Although 'value for money' was at the time of research a hidden agenda, the current coalition government has adopted 'austerity' as a motivating metaphor.
12 And in mentioning this, the organisers were oscillating again to align themselves with the policy-implementers.
13 For the head teacher, this pupil would have simply 'disappeared'. But the story prompts the thought that this might have happened through a process of abjection. The word 'disappeared' encapsulates for me the status of what I could call 'the abjecting event' not as a chosen series of actions but as a natural extrusion from a body of something that does not belong, as in the way a wood splinter, left to resolve itself, is naturally pushed out of the soft skin of a padded fingertip. Thus permanent exclusion does not constitute 'a policy'.
14 For example, in the case of age assessments made by border control officials, described in chapter seven.
15 The Turkish boy who had been permanently excluded for sexual assault, whose mother had been in prison, described in chapter five.
16 Child and Adolescent Mental Health Services.
17 And an indication of the stresses under which school and children's services professionals are working.
18 Introduced in 2009 and removed in 2010 amid criticisms of the infringement of civil liberties.
19 The standardised referral and assessment framework designed by the youth justice board to help prevention programmes to identify if a young person would benefit from early intervention, and to determine the risk factors that should be reduced and the protective factors that should be enhanced in order to stop him or her offending or committing anti-social behaviour.
20 Youth Justice Board (2003).
21 A constructive approach to this is suggested in the concluding chapter.
22 And acknowledging that some young people may have carers rather than parents.
23 See chapter three.

CHAPTER 9

SOME CONCLUSIONS AND RECOMMENDATIONS

In this book, I have attempted to excavate the significance of the causes and impacts of permanent exclusion from school as a disciplinary option for schools. I have also considered what a focus on permanent exclusion from school can reveal about weaknesses within the children's services system, particularly where professionals from a variety of agencies interact with school staff. Through an ethnographic methodology, these focusing questions led to the collection of a range of examples of institutional prejudice on the basis of class, gender, and ethnicity. In chapter eight, I looked at the machinery of this normative prejudice through a deconstruction of the ways in which policy becomes protocol. The nefarious, pervasive qualities of 'policy work' helped me to understand some of the reasons why professionals with positive intent continue to run an inequitable system.

THE CAUSES AND EFFECTS OF PERMANENT EXCLUSION FROM SCHOOL

This book has developed the idea that institutional prejudice underpins some of the causes of permanent exclusion from school, and involves the exercising of normative power. This is expressed through the (mis)representation of children and young people at risk of or subject to permanent exclusion, a process which results in a lack of privilege given to self-representation and is characterised by conflict in the extended body.

The stress and exhaustion of teachers and other professionals, some of which derives from the conflicting policy agendas of attainment and inclusion (Osler and Vincent 2003; Cooper 2002; Rendall and Stuart 2005; Ball 2001; chapter one), embodied partly within the all-powerful league tables, can result in a lack of consistent reflexivity about the expression of institutional prejudice. The 'easier' way is sometimes taken, representing a 'weak' form of inclusion (Viet-Wilson 1998 in Macrae *et al.* 2003: 90; see chapter one), and often materialising as a discourse of need (Thomas and Loxley 2001) deriving from psy disciplinary structures and distracting attention from what institutions might need to change (Sellman 2002; Foucault 1977; chapter three). Within this 'weak' form of inclusion, horizontal violence (Freire 1970) between young people, oppressed under the weight of normative institutional prejudice, is often identified by schools as 'the reason' for an exclusion.

The Impact of Permanent Exclusion from School as an Option

Because it represents the possibility of 'giving up', the existence of permanent exclusion from school as an option available to those professionals charged with supporting young people in crisis might be seen to prevent the development of a 'strong' version of inclusion; one which requires institutions to change the way they work (Viet-Wilson 1998 in Macrae *et al.* 2003: 90; see chapter one). Permanent exclusion from school also contributes to the perpetuation of inequity, crystallising the effects of institutional prejudice into a critical incident. This has been demonstrated throughout this book in stories about a range of young people such as Nama (chapter five), Ibrahim, and Ishaq (both chapter seven).

The causes and effects of permanent exclusion from school are circular. Those who are the recipients of objective violence (Zizek 2008) expressed partially through normative institutional prejudice are oppressed. Oppressed young people might engage in subjective horizontal violence (Zizek 2008; Freire 1996; chapter three) as they jostle for position, for which they can then be permanently excluded. And the permanent exclusion process intensifies, condenses and focuses the effects of institutional prejudice.

Weaknesses in the System Revealed Through a Study of Permanent Exclusion from School

One of the major weaknesses in the children's services system[1] appears to be a deep seam of institutional prejudices on the bases of gender, class and 'race'.[2] These are expressed in different and specific ways (see chapters five, six and seven) and become both a tool and a result of institutional norming. Inter-professional conflict can exacerbate these effects,[3] but professional collusion[4] on the basis of prejudice demonstrates its nefariousness.

The lack of clarity around the meaning and policy of 'inclusion' (introduced in chapter one) leads partially to the problems with the discourse of 'need' (Thomas and Loxley 2001) discussed in chapter three and throughout the book. This, along with professional stress, (discussed in chapter four) results in a lack of reflexivity on the part of the practitioners delivering the institutional norms. More specifically, there is a lack of collaboration between local authorities (discussed in chapters four and six), which is especially damaging to transient children such as those who have been in 'secure accommodation'.[5] The very existence of exclusion as an option is a weakness in the system. If the government made a policy-aspirational statement to abolish permanent exclusion from school, it could push professionals to maintain a more constructive focus on supporting young people in crisis.[6]

RECOMMENDATIONS

Dealing with Institutional Prejudice

An official enquiry into institutional prejudice in children's services, including schools, would, perhaps, inform a professional awareness of the problems of (mis) representation. This might include an enquiry into children's services policies and practice on a range of issues. For example, much would be revealed through an overview of how schools consider and deal with families that need translation services (discussed in chapter seven), bullying that leads to sexual assault (discussed in chapter five), and the links between attainment and social class (discussed in chapter six).

Understanding institutional prejudice could help teachers and other professionals to move away from the pathologising view of behaviour management encapsulated in the 'needs' discourse and consider institution-changing strategies such as 'increasing motivation by broadening the curriculum and making it more pertinent to the real lives of our pupils and communities' (Searle 1996: 47). This might include the recognition of cultural capital (Bourdieu 1977) as a foil to the 'fairness' discourse cloaking the overarching policy of meritocracy (Radnor *et al.* 2007: 297; chapter six). This could also deal with some of the roots of 'subjective horizontal violence' (Zizek 2008; Freire 1996; chapter three).

Removal of Permanent Exclusion as an Option

Another institutional change would involve the removal of permanent exclusion from school as an option. Searle (1996), who carried out an experiment to test this idea in the school at which he was a head teacher, states that '[a]fter four years without a single permanent exclusion we found an improvement in our GCSE results … a significantly reduced truancy rate; a big increase in the post-16 staying-on rate and a growth in overall school numbers' (47). Assisting in this goal might involve the inclusion of careful arrangements for alternative education on the mainstream school site, combining the benefits and reducing the disadvantages of such places (discussed in chapter four).

Cultural Capital

Youth voice strategies have the potential to redress an inequitable social hierarchy through the development of cultural and social capital. A lack of social and cultural capital can keep young people oppressed and therefore more liable to 'horizontal violence' (Freire 1996; see chapter three). Changes in institutional frameworks can make a difference to the socio-economic chances of working-class pupils. At a conference at the University of Pennsylvania's Centre for Urban Ethnography (29.2.08) I heard Hugh Mehan, Professor of Sociology, talking about a University of California San Diego programme that had taken 'low-income' pupils, chosen on a lottery basis, out of their neighbourhoods to teach them at a purpose-built school (The Preuss School) inside the walls of the university campus (Alvarez and Mehan 2006). Their strategy was to challenge what they called the 'radically pessimistic' view that schools can make no difference to pupils' socio-economic chances against a context of 'social deprivation' and 'family background'.

Mehan explained that the project wanted to ask, 'Can cultural capital and social networks be assembled and enacted in a non-habitus institution- the school? Can schools make a difference to low-income students of colour?' going on to explain that CREATE (the Centre for Research Education Access and Teaching Excellence) and The Preuss School were testing the 'school hypothesis". The team decided to teach only 'Honours' classes.[7] Cultural and social capital were consciously embedded into the curriculum. Alvarez and Mehan (2006) explain that at the school, 'students take courses at the university and intern on campus, giving them access to the library and professors, thereby increasing their cultural capital and connecting them to valuable social networks'(84). Where their pupils seemed to be struggling, instead of offering a 'vocational' or 'dumbed down' version, the teachers decided that 'instead of holding time constant and varying the curriculum' they would 'vary time and maintain the curriculum.' So they taught the pupils who needed it for longer- until they were able to pass the Honours classes. The results included a set of much higher grades than their counterparts at other local state schools, and an 87% enrolment rate at 'four year' colleges.[8]

The strategies above rely on either empathic policy-makers, or practitioners who are aware of how to work (sometimes subversively) within the policy framework in which they find themselves situated. Wholesale and swift systemic change does not seem wholly practicable. It is likely to meet with resistance, and to be viewed as an unprecedented undermining of institutional value systems without the benefits of immediately improved behaviour in schools (Slee 1995). In addition, at the time of writing, school and other children's services professionals have had enough of the slews of rapid policy changes (Ball 2001) and are subject to reductions in funding commensurate with the economic downturn.

Given these difficulties in achieving whole-system change (although not rejecting the possibilities), I wanted to also establish some recommendations which might be thought of as deliverable on a more immediate basis, and despite policy: 'policy-proof' strategies.

Critical Bureaucracy? Room for Agency within the Contested Space of the Field of Authoritarian Power

Chapter eight considered the possibilities for critical bureaucracy, and this idea really underpins the concept of policy-proof practice. During my work as a Pupil Support Officer whilst concurrently conducting the ethnographic research at the heart of this book, I often asked myself whether, as a 'street-level bureaucrat' (Shore and Wright 1997:5), I could align an ethic of social justice with models of policy and practice which appeared inequitable.

However, despite the inequities, there are pockets of possibility. The dedication to fair outcomes for children and young people, for example, was evident amongst staff and management in the Enway Children's Services Inclusion Section. I tried to consider how this might fit within Foucault's (1977) conception of the internalisation of authoritarian power. There are many examples of attempts to work creatively within the policy framework. This is what I have called 'critical bureaucracy', close in nature to critical pedagogy. Enway's Head of Inclusion, for example, gave me free rein to develop the new, more inclusive Reintegration Plan form (see chapter eight).

Another focus for 'critical bureaucracy' might be to consider the possibilities for 'youth voice'. This is a general term related to various forms of listening to the opinions of young people, and is associated with 'citizenship, democratic participation and social inclusion' (Milbourne 2009). Searle (1996) recommends a 'general democratisation of school life ... which puts power and responsibility to the pupils on a day-to-day basis' (48–49). The struggle in the extended body, in the context of permanent exclusion from school, is often between professionals and young people (chapter three). This democratisation approach might serve to rebalance the struggle and transform it into a collaborative dialogue of the kind recommended by Freire (1996). However, 'youth voice' is a problematic concept: as Milbourne (2009) explains, 'such strategies which imitate existing systems fail to question structures and institutions that perpetuate exclusion of potentially marginal groups' (351). In Enway, despite institutional attempts to ask young people what they thought through questionnaires and related events, the opinions of young people were difficult to detect in the theatre of permanent exclusion (discussed in chapters two and eight). Given this, and to challenge the dominance of the institutionally prejudiced view, a key recommendation is the careful embedding of effective 'youth voice' or 'participation' strategies in school governance arrangements. As Slee (1995) recommends, '[p]olicy-making ought to enlist the constituents of the policy impacts into the development, implementation and evaluation phases' (179). However, Milbourne (2009) cautions,

> (e)ven where responsive service models are apparent, which value and respect young people's views, it is questionable whether this increased participation from young people can be transformative, involving longer-term cultural change and greater impact on existing institutions (351).

The final chapter lays out a model for the implementation of this goal which attempts to address this challenge.

The Contested Space of the Field of Governmental Authoritarian Power

Just as there is potential for 'voice'- where people can express representations of themselves in the contested space of their own extended bodies- I think that there are many other spaces for teachers and children's services officers to help families negotiate contested space in the field of governmental power. For example, an opportunity for the strategic use of power is presented through an understanding of the ways in which workers are persuaded to align themselves with aspirational policy statements to the detriment of a focus on institutional prejudice. In this model, critical bureaucrats might adopt for themselves the mobilising metaphor of 'the

Child' (Edelman 2004; discussed in chapter eight) to help children and families to access scarce services or to persuade senior managers to set up a better model for service-user participation, for example.

Within the institutional framework that currently exists, with its focus on the pathologising view (Thomas and Loxley 2001), the strategic use of power could also be delivered through the reflexive adoption of the authorising narratives (Skeggs 1997) of pathologising discourses, and child-centred pedagogical approaches suffused with empathy (such as the approach used by CAMHS and described in chapters six and seven). This is not without its dangers: Walkerdine (1998) explains, 'child-centred pedagogy satisfied those concerned with juvenile crime, with psycho-analysis, with freedom, with 'keeping the masses in their place' and more, all at the same time and in contradictory ways' (198, note 29). But used consciously (for example, through the Boys' Group described in chapter five), the strategy has the potential to help young people avoid permanent exclusion. It is concerned with understanding the consequentialist tools of normative authoritative power (mobilising metaphors; authorising narratives of pathology), and using them deontologically and reflexively, and with the goals of social equity in mind.

As Back (2008) has identified, it is our responsibility to 'pay attention' to the details of an extremely complicated field if we are to promote social justice in the delivery of children's services. In order to take advantage of the possibilities inherent in the contested-space nature of the field of authoritarian power, it will be important to promote opportunities for in-depth collaborative and critical thinking across the children's services workforce, and to support the development of practices of local critical pedagogy and critical bureaucracy. This will require frontline workers to pay attention to the ways in which the development and delivery techniques of 'policy', infused with institutional prejudice, might be obfuscating the important issues. They could share their insights with parents and young people, providing opportunities for them to creatively grasp the power gained from 'studying up'.[9] The final chapter offers one possible model for the delivery of this endeavour.

NOTES

[1] For the purposes of this book, this includes local authority and/or school processes as well as those of other agencies involved in 'supporting' children and young people.

[2] This may not be an exhaustive list, but provided a useful set of foci comparable with other studies on permanent exclusion from school (Archer and Yamashita 2003; Ball et al. 2002; Skeggs 1997; Tomlinson 2005; Wright et al. 1999; Wright 2005; see also chapter one).

[3] For example, in the account of Becky's support planning meeting in chapter four.

[4] For example, in chapter five in the discussion about professional collusion on the basis of heteronormativity.

[5] Such as Billy, whose story is described in chapter four.

[6] Although I acknowledge the recent (2010) Conservative/Liberal Democrat coalition government is unlikely to do this.

[7] Equivalent to GCSE and A level classes, and in which the only available grades are A, B and C.

[8] University level.

[9] Nader 1972; chapter two.

THE ILLUMINATE STUDENT RESEARCHERS PROJECT

A Model for Addressing Institutional Prejudice and Reducing Permanent Exclusion from School

As explained in chapter nine, 'youth voice' concerns 'young people's political and civic education (and) addresses concerns about voting and the wider democratic deficit' (Milbourne 2009: 350–351). It sometimes involves the setting up of 'Youth and Schools' Councils, organised conventionally to mirror government decision-making structures' (ibid). However, it is important to acknowledge that a version of youth voice that underpins the hegemony is very different to one which underpins a 'strong' version of inclusion (Viet-Wilson 1998 in Macrae *et al.* 2003: 90; see chapter one) forcing an institution to rethink its own practices. As Milbourne (2009) cautions,

> (t)ransformative outcomes would imply the potential for ... youth-led projects to create sites of resistance and a radical collective habitus (Bourdieu, 1992) based on wider developmental aims. By contrast, wider research ... suggests that recent projects may be confined to generating only new sites and forms for young people's accommodation of, and adaption to, normative models of social and political institutions (351).

Facilitators must thus be willing to support young people to develop the tools to unpack the problems of normative institutional prejudice and representation, for example, and respond constructively to their ideas (Hart 1992) to develop new models of institutions. Youth participation programmes should not focus merely on mining organisations for 'gifted and talented' children to create well-behaved, well-organised articulate 'prefects' or 'school ambassadors' who have mastered 'their will in the service of character through the inculcation of habits and rituals of self-denial, prudence, and foresight' (Rose 1996: 32) in the image of existing management personnel. This is fundamentally different from 'mastering one's desire through bringing its roots to awareness through a reflexive hermeneutics in order to free oneself from the self-destructive consequences of repression, projection, and identification' (ibid).

I wanted to rise to these challenges and to try to develop a model for 'youth voice' which addressed these problems and delivered a reflexive and self-liberating approach. The 'Illuminate Student Researchers' programme was developed in response to the findings of the research into school exclusion.

The basic approach of the programme involved the training of young people in critical research and presentation methods and the subsequent development of institutional or systemic changes in schools as a result of their findings. This approach concurrently focused on developing young people's cultural, linguistic and social capital (Bourdieu 1977; see chapter six) through the learning of research and presentation skills in partnership with teachers and university staff. Its goal to embed an effective approach to youth 'voice' as a strategy for positive institutional change can be considered as an example of 'strong' inclusion. Compare this approach with the children's services questionnaire sent out to pupils and discussed in chapter eight as an example of 'weak' inclusion (Viet-Wilson 1998 in Macrae *et al.* 2003: 90; see chapter one). This questionnaire was claimed as an example of the facilitation of 'youth voice', gathering a range of opinions about the experience of living in Enway and receiving Enway services, but failed to investigate ways in which institutions might be changed to challenge the inequities they experienced (Nader 1972; chapter two).

This chapter explains the Illuminate method and details its potential for ameliorating some of the negative effects of permanent exclusion from school.

The Process

The language and content of the stories available to student researchers are of course subject to their own mechanisms of power. So I will be describing a process, below, through which young people conducted participatory research in such a way that it purposefully borrowed the power of existing policy mandates around school 'improvement'. The process of the Illuminate Student Researchers' Project has been informed by Foucault's (1977) conceptions of the technologies of power. Thus in understanding how powerful constituencies construct effective discourses (see chapter eight) and in borrowing some of these strategies, it became clear that it might be possible to use these technologies to design and then insert the Illuminate method into processes of school governance. The Illuminate approach might be thought of as somewhat subversive in this regard. This is rooted in its Freirian (1996) design. Of particular importance is Freire's understanding that pedagogy should be designed in response to investigations about the experienced world by 'teacher-students' and 'students-teachers' (74) together.

The chapter will proceed with an overview of the theory underpinning the design of the Illuminate method. It will explain how Illuminate can be established as an activity in schools and colleges which is seen as important, where it is linked with senior management team interests. I will then describe an Illuminate project in one school with some of the findings related to the student researchers' chosen focus on the strengths, challenges and aspirations in a new vertical tutoring system. The final section of the chapter will critically analyse the Illuminate approach, and its use as a tool for critical bureaucracy.

Essentially, this chapter describes investigations made by Illuminate Student Researchers but focuses on analysing the Illuminate project itself as a form of research into student voice. In particular I will be looking at the tensions inherent in the adoption of a combination of post-modern theories of governance and an ethic of social justice in designing a model for student voice. The school involved chose to investigate an area apparently unconnected substantively with permanent exclusion school. However, it can be seen in the analysis that the model is designed to disrupt the imbalance of power which underpins institutional prejudice, and which has been seen throughout this book to be a cause of school exclusion. This is an attempt to deliver a 'strong' version of inclusion (Viet-Wilson 1998 in Macrae et al. 2003: 90) which addresses governance structures and administration mechanisms, as opposed to a 'weak' version which merely exists to include the excluded (ibid; see chapter one).

Context

Following my departure from the pupil support role at Enway I began working in a university Department of Educational Studies, with part of my role being to educate new secondary school teachers on a PGCE[1] programme. As I have explained in this book, conducting an ethnography at work became a profound strategy for reflective practice, and I wanted my research to continue to inform my work. My positioning in terms of the research based around the Illuminate projects, then, was that of a critical pedagogue. In designing the Illuminate approach, I was attempting to deliver on earlier research recommendations in a way which was oriented politically against powerful institutions and concerned to mediate creatively and constructively between the needs of student teachers, school students, and education managers. Primarily, though, I wanted to develop a model of student voice which could borrow the technologies of power (Foucault 1975) to deliver an emancipatory pedagogy (Freire 1996). The next section expands on the theoretical basis for the Illuminate project.

THEORETICAL BACKGROUND

Governance, Participation and Critical Bureaucracy

School-student participant research projects were the subject of a large scale ESRC[2] funded project about 'students-as-researchers' (Fielding and Bragg 2003). Building on this key and comprehensive exemplification of the potential for student researchers, the theory underpinning the Illuminate model emerges from three areas: Foucault's (1975) theories of governance and docility; Hart's (1992) ideas on youth participation; and how Freire's (1996) understanding of critical pedagogy links to 'critical bureaucracy'.

Foucault's (1975) 'capillaries of power' I have described in this book how the ethnographic research into the causes and effects of permanent exclusion from school revealed underlying threads of institutional prejudice, and that these threads constitute and are interwoven with capillaries of normative power (Foucault

1975). The education hegemony is traditionally dominated by adult teachers, but as Fielding (2003) explains, '(y)oung people and adults often have quite different views of what is significant or important in their experience of and hopes for learning' (5). The Illuminate project, then, arose partially as an implementation of the idea that to challenge governance through hegemonic, normative prejudice requires a multiplicity of voices telling their own stories.

Hart's (1992) 'Ladder of Participation'

How children and young people might be supported to report and act on the content of their own heteroglossic (Bakhtin in Francis 2010) stories can be informed by Hart's (1992) 'ladder of participation'. This 'ladder' describes varying approaches to supporting children and young people to participate in decision-making, beginning with activities which represent 'mere tokenism', and developing into activities at the top of the scale which implement 'full citizenship'. The key element in Hart's model is that at the top of the ladder, decisions and activities are young people-initiated, but shared with adults. These projects empower young people while at the same time enabling them to benefit from the access, life experience and expertise available to adults. In constructing the Illuminate model, then, and to ensure that the projects could effectively draw on adults' resources, I 'studied up' (Nader 1972) on school governance systems, and endeavoured to add perceived value to student research projects with an infusion of what I thought might be important to school senior management teams.

School head teachers and senior management teams in England are responsible for ensuring that their institutions achieve a good OFSTED report, and I have reflected throughout this book on some of the effects of this regime. OFSTED inspections – part of a technology of power and surveillance (Foucault 1975) - are carried out in schools every one to three years, and funding and reputation is linked to the resultant grade. Each OFSTED report includes a set of recommendations, and in order to achieve what is known as 'a good Ofsted', schools need to be able to show that they have addressed these. To show that recommendations are being addressed, they form the basis of an action plan known as a 'SIP' (school improvement plan), and this is given to subsequent OFSTED inspectors as evidence, albeit a constructed piece of evidence that, as with other 'performances for inspection', merely represents on paper the notion that their advice has been taken (Ball 2003, Gillies 2008). Despite the distance between the SIP and action - an 'abstraction' leading to a culture of 'virtualism' (Miller 2003; see chapter eight) - a SIP does have the effect of fixing a school or college senior management team's focus. And the language of OFSTED favours the word 'impact': SIPs which identify a desired and preferably measurable 'impact' are seen as efficient and effective.

As I explained in chapter eight, Shore and Wright (1997:4) ask, 'What are the mobilising metaphors and linguistic devices that cloak policy?' I would argue that in the context of school governance, 'impact' is a 'mobilising metaphor'. 'Impact' is a tough, decisive word: it implies decision, action, and positive consequence. It suggests force, and effect. It is also heavily gendered. So I use the word 'impact' to engage the interest and commitment of school senior management teams in Illuminate research projects. So in brokering the offer to an educational institution of an Illuminate project, I ask whether there is a specific area for development; something the school would like to research – perhaps, even, an issue which can produce a tangible *impact* on the goals of the SIP. This is one way to deliver 'critical bureaucracy' in action: consciously using official protocol and language to lend legitimacy and power to the project. This strategy draws on the link with the resources of significant adults required by Hart's (1992) model for participation and citizenship.

Freire's (1996) 'Critical Pedagogy': the Roots of Critical Bureaucracy

The idea of 'critical bureaucracy', introduced above, is linked to Freire's (1996) concept of a critical pedagogy. As I have outlined in chapter three, Freire was interested in the power of dialogue and critical thinking and concerned that teachers should be asking questions about their own role in an inequitable system. He explained that '(e)ducation which is able to resolve the contradiction between teacher and student takes place in a situation in which both address their act of cognition to the object by which they are mediated' (1996: 74). In other words, a constructive, dynamic and socially just education requires teacher and student to consider and make decisions together about how and where learning and schooling takes place. In their discussion of the kinds of student-teacher research collaboration which aim to operate within these parameters, Fielding (1999 in Fielding and Bragg 2003) describes a process of 'radical collegiality' (55).

The development of a model for student 'voice' influenced by Foucault's (1977) understanding of hegemonic power and Freire's (1996) approach to emancipatory education, then, is the contribution that this research method, scheme of learning, youth voice strategy, and school project might be able to make to a more reflective, responsive and critical bureaucracy.

THE ILLUMINATE MODEL

An Illuminate project lasts about twelve hours, delivered across an academic term,[3] and tends to involve around twelve young people, divided into research teams of three. It can also be condensed into four half-day or two day-long sessions, if necessary, and this flexibility enhances its applicability across a range of settings, enabling its penetration into inflexible power structures. Each team is supported by a teaching student, or in some institutions, a teacher or a university ambassador (university students who undertake mentoring work in schools and colleges). The teams usually meet together for about an hour each week.

Research Briefs: Who Asks the Questions?

Crucially for Illuminate, whilst student researchers may be given a research brief, they must be supported to arrive at their own questions. This feature is designed to ensure that the research projects are important or relevant to them, and is designed with Freire's (1996) concern for working with rather than on students: that '(j)ust as the educator may not elaborate a program to present to the people, neither may the investigator elaborate "itineraries" for researching the thematic universe, starting from points which he has predetermined' (89, original emphasis). It could be argued that the research briefs are 'predetermined' starting points. But Freire (1996) also had a predetermined starting point: to develop an emancipatory pedagogy. What was important for him was the method for drawing out the detail with students. With the imperative to borrow the technologies of power identified by Foucault (1975) in the design of Illuminate (and thus to ask head teachers to identify an area requiring 'impact'), it became necessary to balance these points of tension. And in any case, the important thing was that students had the space to tell their stories effectively. It may be that the focus of a project is less important than the fact that Illuminate students are voicing their opinions. As Couldry (2010) explains, 'giving an account of oneself in a world in which one acts is a basic feature of what we do as humans, and so a possible starting point for recognising someone as a political subject' (109).

Once the research brief has been obtained from school staff, and the questions have been established by the students, during the first half of the project, the student researchers are trained in a variety of research methods and skills. They can choose which of these will best fit their investigations. The choice of methods includes interviews, questionnaires, focus group discussions, observations, journaling, and visual methods such as film and photography. Research skills learned include note-taking, making a focussed observation, positioning and bias, asking open and developing interview questions, ethics, and the triangulation of data.

As explained above, the Illuminate model is developed within a conceptual framework drawing on Foucault's (1975) approach to the technologies of power. In his work Foucault (1975) identifies the internalisation of authoritarian control amongst subjects who know that they may or may not be under surveillance at any time. The research methods training is in some sense a way to make available to the subjects of institutional power – here, young people in schools and colleges– the tools of surveillance. Education institutions are now subject to a 'tyranny of transparency' Strathern (2000), and as such surveillance and inspection have become embedded methods for the 'improvement' of schools. It might be contested that the Illuminate model therefore only enhances the internalisation of surveillance and carries deeper the capillaries of power into the hands and minds of school students themselves. But Foucault does not see power as inherently evil or good. In this case, a technology of power (surveillance) is implemented in order to facilitate a meaningful collaboration with students. In doing this, Illuminate attempts to deliver what Freire (1996) defines as '(a)uthentic education… not carried on by "A" for "B" or by "A" about "B" but rather by "A" with "B", mediated by the world- a world which impresses and challenges both parties giving rise to views or opinions about it' (74). Decisions about school governance affect teachers and students, and both groups become interested in hearing each others' opinions.

In addition to training on research methods, student researchers are also trained in the coding and analysis of data- how to consider and lay out the evidence of the 'views' and 'opinions' of students and teachers identified as important by Freire (1996:74). They are supported in the implementation of research ethics on the basis of the guidelines issued by the British Educational Research Association Code of Practice. By the end of the first half of the project, student researchers will have developed their question and sub questions, and made a weekly research plan.

Once research questions and plans have been established, and research methods have been learned and practiced, during the second half of the project, the teams meet weekly for a dialogical (Freire 1996) research supervision session. In line with Hart's (1992) model, described above, adult helpers (teachers, student teachers, support staff or volunteers) act to brainstorm ideas; support access to materials, equipment, interviewees, and classrooms; and check on researchers' progress through their research plans. In the last two or three sessions, research teams gather their data together, code it and arrange it into a presentation format. This might be a film, PowerPoint, article, or notes. They present their research to the project coordinator (often myself), who writes up the findings into a research report with an Executive Summary, suitable for dissemination at senior management team or governors' meetings. The writing of an Executive Summary is itself a piece of critical bureaucracy: having 'studied up' (Nader 1972), I consciously made the decision to present findings to governors and head teachers in an accessible, time-saving format congruent with the style inherent in the technologies of power (Foucault 1975). The findings ideally become the basis of a set of continued professional development sessions for teachers in the school; or of a set of thoughtful systemic changes. The process is supported by a full set of teachers' notes and forms to guide the student teams through what they need to do, including for informed consent, taking observation and interview notes, arriving at a research question, and developing a research plan.

Critical Thinking to Challenge Stereotypes

The Illuminate framework is designed to support the development of a critical and reflective thinking orientation by student researchers. As Freire (1996: 69) explains, 'To exist humanly is to *name* the world, to change it'. Learning about research methods helps students to gather evidence to facilitate the naming of their world and their participation in meaningful dialogue about it. Further, the research skills learned are the kinds of transferable skills which could potentially enhance the cultural, social and linguistic capital (Bourdieu 1991) affecting other areas of students' lives, such as academic work or job seeking.

I will next describe an Illuminate project conducted at Coopers Technology College in Bromley, London. I had sent out a newsletter offering the project as a form of consultancy and a senior teacher at the school responded, asking if we could use it to evaluate their new vertical tutoring system. The project tests the Freirean and Foucauldian conceptual bases for the model in interesting ways.

ILLUMINATE IN ACTION

The Vertical Tutor Group System: Strengths, Challenges and Aspirations

This project was conceived in order to embed a deep level of student voice into the evaluation and continued improvement of the relatively new vertical tutor group system at Coopers Technology College. School students in England usually spend a short period in their tutor groups every day, often in the morning. 'Tutor group' is where they often hear notices about sports and other events, register their presence for the day, learn about personal, social and emotional issues, and build a relationship with a key member of staff. Tutor groups in most English schools consist of students in the same year-group, sometimes who achieve at an academically similar level; in these cases their constituency emerges from a system of academic tracking. At Coopers, however, the vertical tutor groups consisted of a few students from each year group. The aim was to develop a family-like relationship between the students, where older students could develop their mentoring capabilities and younger students would benefit from the advanced experience of their elders. The system had been in place for around a year when the Illuminate project was employed to evaluate and improve it.

The research was carried out by Year 9^4 History students. They were trained and supervised by staff-members David Lucas and Vikki Horsley and by myself as research coordinator. One entire History class (around thirty young people) was trained in research methods and supervised through the research process. The Student Researchers were divided into six teams, and supported by the two dedicated members of staff. The staff-members had a central role in supporting the Student Researchers in accessing classrooms, pupils and teachers to observe and interview, and equipment and materials to support their investigations. They also provided an objective listening ear during weekly supervision sessions, and helped the teams to plan for each week and analyse their data. Research questions to be used in interviews and surveys emerged from the Student Researchers themselves.

Findings
Team 1

Team 1 asked: what are the strengths of vertical tutor groups, in students' opinions? For this team, the main form of research involved the use of a survey asking students various questions about Vertical Tutoring and their tutor groups. 81 students across all year groups returned their surveys. The team also interviewed students from younger and older years.

Data Around 75% of pupils surveyed and interviewed liked the new system. Most students socialized in their tutor group with older and younger years and appreciated that this was something that usually would not happen. One student explained that 'it's a chance to get along with other students'. A student who did not like the system said that students from older year groups could 'be annoying and swear and talk about rude stuff'. One student was repeatedly teased about her American accent by year 7[5] students.

The system made students feel as if they were 'part of a community', which made school 'more fun' for academic reasons. Group quizzes and other social activities made tutor group time more entertaining and educational. Generally, it was felt that the system had had a huge positive impact on tutor group time.

Recommendations Students said that they would like to keep the vertical tutor group system if it could become more interactive. They also wanted to keep the system if bullying was effectively managed. Most suggested that all tutor groups should use a seating plan in order to further develop relationships between year groups and to protect younger students where bullying was a possibility. It was also suggested that older students could be given specific training in how to listen to and interact with younger students.

Team 2

Team 2 asked about the strengths of vertical tutoring in the opinions of staff. This team used online surveys and did interviews with staff to gather information. They also sent out a letter to all staff asking them to fill out the survey, receiving most of their responses from this. Altogether they received twenty responses.

Findings 60% of the staff respondents said they preferred vertical tutoring. One said 'it's nice to have a variety of different aged students'. Year 11[6] students sometimes appeared as if 'they can't be bothered any more'; staff felt that it was more fruitful to motivate four year 11 students than 30. The Year 11, 12 and 13 students, however, had spent most of their school lives in horizontal tutor groups, and so were often heard to compare the previous system favourably. However, most staff-members felt that the system helped older and younger students to socialise, reducing bullying. One staff-member said that 'younger students are supported and older students learn responsibility'.

The system enabled group work and the sharing of ideas. Younger students learned from older students during group discussions. For example, some Year 11s who were not on track to get C grades[7] in some of their GCSE exams could talk to Sixth Form[8] students who had felt the same way at exactly the same point in the year- but had gone on to nevertheless get the C grade. Younger students found this encouraging.

Recommendations Seating plans emerged strongly as the recommended way to manage the social mix between year groups.

Team 3

This team asked: What do students feel are the challenges of vertical tutoring? Information for this part of the project was collected via paper based questionnaires in class time and tutor group time. The group received 35 responses, mainly from Year 8 students, with some Sixth Form students participating. They also interviewed students to seek their opinions on vertical tutoring.

Findings Whilst more than half of the students surveyed generally liked vertical tutoring, about 90% of those surveyed had some sort of issue with the system. The research this group was undertaking was focussed on challenges, and the problems discussed related partially to year 7 students, either talking too much, or being disruptive or 'too immature'. Some younger students felt that older students in their form bullied them. In forms where there was no seating plan, students did not tend to talk to others outside their year groups, but instead would 'just sit with their friends'. Activities in form were felt to sometimes be boring or repetitive. Finally, students felt that whilst the vertical tutor group system was a positive change overall, and that they had developed form-group community identities, they had to some extent lost their year-group identity. Celebration assemblies were in 'house' teams, and (apart from subject lessons and sports day) students felt that they collaborated as year groups only in what they identified as 'bad' situations such as a 'Dedicated Learning Day' about crime, and admonishments about throwing ice-balls or conkers, or for fighting. They also missed out on guidance from tutors on choosing their GCSE options.

Recommendations As with the previous team, this group felt that seating plans should be reviewed in order to prevent bullying between year groups and to encourage mixing between year groups. They suggested that activities could be developed in partnership with students. Students felt that they would like the opportunity to give feedback on activities they had undertaken in their tutor groups. They also felt that there should be more ways to interact as a year group for celebratory rather than negative reasons. One of these occasions could centre around choosing GCSE options, where appropriate.

Team 4

This team looked at the challenges in the vertical tutor group system according to staff. The team created a paper survey which they put in staff pigeon holes. They also interviewed staff to get feedback face to face. Overall, thirteen staff members were surveyed.

Findings The team found that staff felt that older year groups could be inappropriate and disruptive and did not always act like role models. The age mix could be an issue as year groups were not evenly spread across forms and, as other teams found, where seating plans were not used it could be difficult to get year groups to mix. One teacher explained, 'it is natural for students from the same year group to stick together'. Sixth Form students, in particular, were often only in their tutor group room one day each week, because of their enrichment work (for example, reading with younger students or mentoring non-attenders). One Sixth Former said, 'I don't go because it's a waste of my time and I don't get anything out of it'. Staff also felt that there was not enough time to talk to students and there were too many notices for each year group.

Teachers also felt that 'the Consequence System'[9] was more difficult to follow during form time. Senior leadership was not always available and Sixth Form students tended to be sent out of class much more quickly than in regular lessons.

Finally, one staff member said that the curriculum provided for the system was 'not that inspiring'. Topics were boring for students, who found it difficult to concentrate, and they did not emerge in a logical sequence. For example, there was a PowerPoint about drugs which was succeeded by another on animals. Support materials were often limited to a list of a few websites. It was difficult to deliver a topic to years 7–11[10] as it was sometimes pitched too high or too low for some of the students.

Recommendations This research team recommended that the school should either place Sixth Form students in tutor group all the time or remove them completely. If they were to stay, they would need specific mentoring training to support the healthy development of their relationships with younger students. If they were to leave, there should be a facility to enable them to maintain contact with their tutors. It was also recommended that the school might be able to provide a space for year groups to spend more time together. This could be supplemented by a year group newsletter, web page or noticeboard for notices. There was a suggestion that the school might review the application of 'the Consequence System' during form time, and finally, develop a robust, flexible curriculum with a comprehensive bank of support materials. Some curriculum could be developed with the tutor groups themselves.

Team 5

This team asked: What are parents' aspirations for the vertical tutor group system? The group sent a questionnaire out to all the students in their tutor groups to give to their parents and also set up an online survey. In total they had fifteen responses. Both the survey and the questionnaire addressed the same questions.

Findings Most parents liked the vertical tutor group system. One parent said that 'it encourages different year groups to support each other'. The main aspiration for parents was that vertical tutoring should 'reflect a work place' in that it could be a realistic reflection of a world where different age groups mix. Most of those who responded felt that the system would help their child in the future through making new friends and getting them used to a range of age groups. Some parents felt that the system would become even better as it became embedded into the school and that it helped with confidence and prevented students from being worried about school. One parent felt that the topics delivered in form group would not necessarily help their child.

Recommendations   It was suggested that vertical tutoring might be better if the system only mixed years 7, 8 and 9 together. Parents also felt that the curriculum should be developed so that it better took students' needs into consideration.

Team 6

This team asked what aspirations staff and students had for vertical tutoring. The team collected their information through eight staff interviews and 117 anonymous online and paper student surveys.

Findings   Staff felt that the system had potential for 'continued interaction and to eradicate bullying across the school'. As with the previous team, this group found that staff and students felt that there was potential for a better and less repetitive curriculum resource for form time. 20% of students wanted to use the system to further befriend students in other years. 5% said they wanted to be more confident and that the vertical tutor group system might be able to help with this. Many other students said they would like to widen their knowledge and improve their reading in form. One said, 'I want good grades and other year groups can help'.

Recommendations   The team felt that there could sometimes be the opportunity provided to do independent work or revision during tutor group time, where perhaps older students could tutor younger students in specific areas. Because the tutor group curriculum is delivered to five year groups, it was felt that there should be enough to deliver for five years in order to avoid repetition. There should be silence during 'silent reading' time, or alternatively, 6th Formers in each tutor group could read with younger students in their own groups. Some form groups might choose to have a 'book club' and all read and discuss the same book together. The team also felt that there should be training regarding mentoring and listening skills for older 'befrienders'. In terms of activities, students asked for interesting speakers to visit their tutor groups. Some tutor groups thought they might like to play football games; intercommunity sports events were suggested. It was also suggested that some tutor groups may like to collaborate on a project to, for example, make a magazine together, or run a business-focused activity.

General Conclusions

The vertical tutoring system at Coopers Technology College was to a large extent accepted by students, parents and staff as an improvement to the original system. However, there were issues around relationships between students of different ages, tutor group activities and resources. Recommendations were put forward aiming to deal with these issues.

Areas identified for further research   Researchers and respondents suggested several areas for further research projects. They felt that it would be interesting to find out how people feel about staying in school until the age of eighteen;[11] thoughts on school uniform and planners;[12] students' health outside school; whether students like the school rules, and why; and what people dislike about going to school.

The Student Researcher and Staff Experience   All the students really valued the input from both the research coordinator and the Coopers staff involved with the project. Both students and staff enjoyed the opportunity to engage in independent learning. Participants felt that mutual trust and respect was built around activities where students had to 'go off and interview people on their own'. One student said that he felt better able to go and talk to teachers and older students. Another said, 'I have had a confidence boost'. Parents giving feedback at a parents' evening reported that they really appreciated their children's' involvement in the project.

The Illuminate project gave students a 'chance to ask people things and get their personal opinions'. One student said that it 'changed my view of what other people think- there is a wide variety of views on one little topic'. Although some people worried that 'not much will change', most of the Student Researchers said they felt 'listened to' and that their views would 'hopefully change (tutor group) time so that it can be more enjoyable for students'. One student said that 'if they use our ideas to make (tutor group) better then it will improve the opinion of the school'.

Some Student Researchers felt they worked well as a group and 'really believed in what we were researching'; others would have preferred to have been able to choose their groups. Students said that they learned 'psychological skills'; 'methodology'; 'to observe people'; 'speaking and listening skills' and 'how to show someone you are listening to them'; 'interview techniques'; 'how to be confident'; and 'presentation skills'. The project allowed one student to 'ask questions I would otherwise have been scared to ask'.

Some Researchers felt that the project 'helped all of us with our confidence' and 'will help us for the future to get the job we want'. One student explained that he is now 'considering going to university so that I can get a better job'.

There was also felt to be great potential for sustainability. Staff had the training and materials to deliver further Illuminate Student Researcher projects at Coopers.

The School's Response

I sent the research report off (containing the findings above) to the teachers involved in the Coopers project, and a few days later, I received an email in reply from David. He told me, 'I have copied you into our current plans . . . to show you we are moving forwards.' Attached to the email was a document listing the recommendations and the planned responses, including staff responsible for the changes.

The changes planned in response to the research included a commitment to 'create a programme of study for ... next academic year with student voice... ensure the work created is differentiated for staff to use with students... build in some project work, where over a period of time students have to research a theme and report back to the community / form... (and) develop a community magazine for each term'.

The response also suggested that because 'many of the negative comments were from sixth formers', the school would allocate 'specific roles' to sixth formers as '...a peer reader / peer mentor or Co-tutor. This role will involve training and will be monitored closely'. There was a plan to 'ensure each form group has a seating plan set up at the start of each term ... checked / observed regularly to ensure it is being used'. In response to the concern that the year group identity had been lost slightly, the response explained that whilst 'year assemblies were run this year' the school would '(n)eed to expand on this with a calendared assembly each half term for each year group'. Perhaps most sensitively, the school's response named a specific staff member who was to '...use student voice to run a review of 'the Consequence System'', promising further that '... the issues and how we can combat these will be discussed in detail during this review'.

ANALYSIS

Illuminate: 'Studying Up'; Challenging Institutional Prejudice with a Multiplicity of Voices

The Illuminate project described above constituted an effort in 'studying up' (Nader 1972). Investigating the mechanics of their educational institution, Coopers students were able to look at the pedagogy, behaviour management, time structures, and organising principles of the new tutor group system, and offer ideas on how each of these approaches felt to the young people in the classroom. Students, teachers and parents were involved in the research, and whilst students formulated and asked the questions, they had dedicated teachers to scaffold their approaches, respond to recommendations, and provide access to their field of research; and dedicated class time to carry out the work. Tentatively, it may be suggested that following Hart's (1992) 'Ladder of participation' model - where the most advanced form of 'youth voice' requires that decisions and activities are young people-initiated, but shared with adults - appeared to be an effective way to initiate a studying-up activity (Nader 1972).

Following Foucault's (1975) ideas about governmentality, I have explained above that to challenge a form of governance through prejudice and normativity requires a multiplicity of voices telling their own stories. In this project, students were able to give their opinions on issues of material importance.

Critical bureaucracy In terms of 'critical bureaucracy' – related in approach to Freire's (1970) 'critical pedagogy' – the Coopers Technology College Illuminate project appealed to senior management whilst crucially maintaining students' ability to ask the questions for themselves. This 'critical bureaucracy' approach supplements and could potentially replace elements of more formal, staff-led programme monitoring activities. The senior management team's involvement in designing the brief ensured that they were invested in the findings, and therefore more likely to take them seriously. The project appears to have caught the interest of senior management; and to have benefited from student voice backed up by staff action and a dialogic, collaborative valuing of student voice. The attempt to combine the theories of Foucault (1977), Hart (1992) and Freire (1970) in the delivery of an Illuminate project could therefore be said to have been achieved at Coopers Technology College.

Measures of success Because the Coopers project drew on student voice and resulted in substantial material changes and challenges to structures such as 'the Consequence System' and the conditions which sometimes caused bullying, it could be said to be successful in terms of the stated Illuminate goals of 'studying up' (Nader 1972) and drawing on student voice to inform material change for social justice. The work on 'the Consequence System' and the school's promise to '...use student voice to run a review of 'the Consequence System" where '... the issues and how we can combat these will be discussed in detail' was perhaps, in its focus on the behaviour management system, the most significant in terms of its potential effect on permanent exclusions. Because the project facilitated an open discussion between students and teachers about problems within a school's system of discipline and curriculum it might be said to have transcended a superficial form of 'voice' and consultation to offer one which opened up 'sites of resistance' (Milbourne 2009: 351).

The project was also notable in its breadth of data, if slightly limited in terms of methods. The breadth may have been partially due to the high level of staffing and the senior management team mandate as well as the fact that the Illuminate project was timetabled into the humanities[13] curriculum time. It might also be seen as having been effective as an exercise in Freirean (1970) dialogue. The project cannot be said to contribute to an academic discourse (as it is understood within the hegemony) on the subject of its investigations- vertical tutor group systems- as the Illuminate method does not include literature reviews and theoretical analysis. But maybe the goals of Illuminate should be restated here.

Firstly, in terms of exploring the efficacy of 'youth voice', this research has on a meta-level (that is, from my point of view as a post-modern youth voice and educational governance researcher) revealed something about what makes a genuine representation of young people's views difficult. Attempting to draw Freire (1970) and Foucault (1975) together has revealed the tension inherent in a post-modern reading of emancipatory pedagogy. The insidious nature of power identified by Foucault (1975) is difficult to shake even where a pedagogue is trying hard to operate with '*conscientização*' (Freire 1970:85).[14] I may be channelling the kind of grand narrative Foucault warns against: fetishizing marginality, for example; privileging a discourse of resistance which is as hegemonic in its persistent positioning as that which it is resisting. According to Gold and Revill (2003), marginalisation '...creates apparently purified and homogeneous spaces ... often created by conscious acts of social marginalisation and clearly articulated fears. However, fear also produces landscapes of marginalisation' (37).

Notwithstanding these arguments, Illuminate was designed to facilitate the telling of stories- the revealing of a multiplicity of experiences as an antidote to institutional prejudice based in stereotyping. The students who participated in the project engaged in a research skills and supervision programme in collaboration with a university, and as a result, details of their many experiences are evidenced here in this chapter. The Coopers project arguably demonstrates the potential for Illuminate where both Freirean and Focuauldian elements are present.

Approaches which may be called 'critical bureaucracy' involve making multiple incremental decisions in the delivery of policy, derived, not cynically, but pragmatically, from tactics unearthed as a result of 'studying up' (Nader 1972) on the techniques and 'mobilising metaphors' (Shore and Wright 1997:4) of those in power. As a model for critical bureaucracy, Illuminate projects present some interesting possibilities. Their criticality is embedded within the requirement that students must ask their own questions. Their effectiveness in an institutionally prejudiced bureaucracy is derived from the borrowed power procured through means and language motivating to senior managers. The inclusion of an executive summary in a research report; the way a research brief is given to students to elicit their own interview and survey questions; the 'branding' of the approach as 'Illuminate'; and the conscious use of the word 'impact' in inviting head teachers to participate are all the strategies of a critical bureaucrat. The aim of the Illuminate Student Researchers Project is to challenge a culture of institutional prejudice which leads to and is exacerbated by permanent exclusion from school, and Milbourne (2009) alerts us to the need for such activities to lead to 'cultural change' (351). Although it would be difficult to show a direct link between the use of an Illuminate approach to school governance and a reduction in school exclusions through the Coopers project, it is suggested here that the approach may function to improve student-teacher dialogue and thus to challenge the stereotypes at the root of the institutional prejudice which can lead to permanent exclusion from school.

NOTES

[1] Post-graduate Certificate in Education, providing students with a qualification enabling them to take up positions as Newly Qualified Teachers in schools.
[2] The European Economic and Social Research Council
[3] In England and Wales, there are three school terms in a year: September to December; January to April; and April to July.
[4] Aged thirteen to fourteen years old.
[5] Aged eleven to twelve years old.
[6] Aged fifteen to sixteen years old.
[7] Usually the lowest grade to be considered a valid 'pass', where other educational institutions such as further education colleges, and professional agencies, such as the Teaching Agency, are concerned.
[8] Year 12 and 13 students aged from sixteen to nineteen years of age. The Sixth Form is post-compulsory and students usually study an advanced level (A-level) pre-university course of academic study.
[9] The school-wide behaviour management and discipline system.
[10] That is, aged between eleven and sixteen years old.
[11] The UK government is currently suggesting that this will be phased in over the next two years.
[12] Diaries or schedules.
[13] Usually History and Geography.
[14] Critical consciousness

APPENDIX

Acronyms

ADHD	Attention deficit (hyperactivity) disorder
ARTI	At-Risk Teens Intervention
ASD	Autism spectrum disorder
AWPU	Age weighted pupil unit
BBC	British Broadcasting Corporation
BCRB	Black Caribbean(local authority ethnicity monitoring code)
BOTH	Black other (local authority ethnicity monitoring code)
BERA	British Educational Research Association
BESD	Behavioural emotional or social disorder/difficulties
BSU	Behaviour support unit
BTEC	Business and Technical Education Council
CAF	Common Assessment Framework
CAMHS	Child and adolescent mental health services
CIS	Children's Inclusion Services
CREATE	Centre for Research Education Access and Teaching Excellence (USA)
CWDC	Children's Workforce Development Council
DCSF	Department for Children, Schools and Families
DfE	Department for Education
DfES	Department for Education and Skills
ECM	Every Child Matters
EP	Educational Psychologist
FAPE	Free Appropriate Public Education (USA)
GCSE	General Certificate of Secondary Education
IRAS	Initial referral and response (Safeguarding)
JAR	Joint Area Review
LGBT(QI)	Lesbian, gay, bisexual, transgender/transsexual (queer, intersex)
LP	Lead professional
LSU	Learning support unit
NAHT	National Association of Head Teachers
NCLB	No Child Left Behind (USA)
NEET	Not in education, employment or training
OFSTED	Office for Standards in Education
ONSET	Standardised referral and assessment framework designed by the youth justice board .
PMS	Pre-menstrual syndrome
PSO	Pupil support officer
PSP	Pastoral support plan
PRU	Pupil referral unit
PTA	Parent-teacher association
RAC	Royal Automobile Club

APPENDIX

RE	Religious education
RSP	Reintegration Support Plan
SATs	Standard assessment tasks
SENCO	Special educational needs coordinator
TAC	Team around the child
TDA	Training and Development Agency
WBRI	White British (local authority ethnicity monitoring code)
WI	Women's Institute
YISP	Youth Inclusion Support Project
YOS	Youth Offending Service
YOT	Youth offending team

REFERENCES

Alheit, P (2005). 'Stories and structures: An essay on historical times, narratives and their hidden impact on adult learning' *Studies in the Education of Adults* **37**(2), 201–212.

Allen, JS (April 2009). 'Queer spaces of critical enunciation' Seminar: 'Race in the Modern World' Conference, Goldsmiths, University of London.

Alvarez, D and Mehan, H (2006). 'Whole-School Detracking: A Strategy for Equity and Excellence' *Theory Into Practice* **45**(1).

Amit, V (2000). *Constructing the field: Ethnographic fieldwork in the contemporary world.* London: Routledge.

Aldrich, R (2004). *Public or Private Education? Lessons from History.* London: Woburn Press.

Anderson, R, Brown, I, Doughty, T, Inglesant, P, Heath, W and Sasse, A (2009). *Database State*, York: The Joseph Rowntree Reform Trust Ltd [internet], available at http://www.cl.cam.ac.uk/~rja14/Papers/database-state.pdf (accessed 28 March 2009).

Anzaldua, G (1987). *Borderlands/La Frontera: The New Mestiza.* San Fransisco: Spinsters/Aunt Lute Book Company.

Archer, L and Francis (2007). *Understanding Minority ethnic achievement: Race, class, gender and 'success'.* London: Routledge.

Archer, L and Yamashita, H (2003). 'Theorising Inner-city Masculinities: 'race', class, gender and education' *Gender and Education* **15**(2), 115–132.

Arnot, M (2003). 'Male working-class identities and social justice: A reconsideration of Paul Willis's *Learning to Labour* in light of contemporary research' in Vincent, C (Ed.) *Social justice, education and identity.* London: RoutledgeFalmer, 97–119.

Association for Professionals in Services for Adolescents (APSA). 'Workshop Profiles' received at 'Come back and move on: A conference on re-integration- helping young people back into mainstream services after a period of exclusion', [conference literature] September 6–7, 2005, Reading University.

Atkinson, P, Coffey A and Delamont, S (Eds.) (2001). *Handbook of Ethnography.* London: Sage.

Atkinson, P and Hammersley, M (1994). 'Ethnography and participant observation' in Dankin, NK and Lincoln Y (Eds.) *Handbook of qualitative research.* Thousand Oaks: Sage Publications ,248–261.

Back, L and Solomos, J (Eds.) (2000). *Theories of race and racism.* Oxon: Routledge.

Back, L (2007). *The Art of Listening.* Oxford: Berg Books.

Back, L (2008). 'London calling: Multiculture and the war on terror's nervous system', Inaugural seminar of the Identity and Social Justice Group, Department of Educational Studies, Goldsmiths, University of London, October 7.

Ball, S. (2001). 'Labour, learning and the economy: A 'policy sociology' perspective' in Fielding, M. (Ed.) *Taking education really seriously: four years hard labour.* London: RoutledgeFalmer, 45–46.

Ball, S. (2003). The teacher's soul and the terrors of performativity, *Journal of education policy* **18**(2), 215–228.

Ball, S (2008). *The Education Debate.* Bristol: The Policy Press.

Ball, S, Reay, D and David, M (2002). ''Ethnic Choosing': minority ethnic students, social class and higher education choice', *Race Ethnicity and Education* **5**(4), 333–357.

Barker M and Beezer A (Eds) (1992). *Reading into cultural studies,* London: Routledge.

BBC News (2000). *Special report: Hijack at Stansted* [online] (updated 14 February 2000). Available at: http://news.bbc.co.uk/1/hi/uk/636375.stm [Accessed 14 May 2010].

BBC News (2000a). *Asylum pleas 'will not be met'* [online] (updated 10 February 2000). Available at: http://news.bbc.co.uk/1/hi/uk_politics/637729.stm [Accessed 14 May 2010]

Batty, D (2003). 'Q&A: Victoria Climbie Enquiry' *Guardian Online*, [internet] 30 January. Available at: http://www.guardian.co.uk/society/2003/jan/30/1 [Accessed 17 May 2010].

Bell, J (2005). *Doing your research project,* Maidenhead: Open University Press.

REFERENCES

Biesta, G (2012). 'Changing the discourse of education- interrupting the politics of learning' Keynote, *Discourse, Power, Resistance* conference. University of Plymouth [4 April 2012]

Blackman, L (2001). *Hearing voices: embodiment and experience.* London: Free Association Books.

Blackman and Venn (2010). 'Affect' in *Body and Society* **16**(7), Available at http://bod.sagepub.com/cgi/content/refs/16/1/7 [Accessed 16 June 2010].

Blair, M (2001). *Why pick on me? School exclusion and Black youth.* Stoke on Trent: Trentham Books Ltd

Blyth, E and Milner, J (1996). *Exclusion from school: inter-professional issues for policy and practice .* London: Routledge

Booth, T (1996). 'Stories of exclusion: natural and unnatural selection' in Blyth, E and Milner, J (Eds.) *Exclusion from school: inter-professional issues for policy and practice.* London: Routledge, 21–36.

Booth, T and Ainscow, M (2002). *Index for Inclusion: developing learning and participation in schools.* Bristol: CSIE.

Bourdieu, P (1991). *Language and Symbolic Power.* Cambridge: Polity Press.

Bourdieu, P (1979). *Distinction: a Social Critique of the Judgement of Taste.* London: Routledge.

Bourdieu, P and Passeron, J (1977). *Reproduction in Education, Society and Culture.* London: Sage Publications.

Britzman, D (1995). '"The question of belief": writing poststructural ethnography' *Qualitative Studies in Education* **8**(3), 229–238.

Butler, J (1993). *Bodies that Matter: on the discursive limits of "sex".* London: Routledge.

Butler, J (1999, first published 1990). *Gender Trouble.* Routledge: London.

Butler, J (2004). *Precarious Life: the powers of mourning and violence.* London: Verso.

Carlile A. (2009a). 'Bitchy Girls and Silly Boys': Gender and Exclusion from School *International Journal on School Disaffection* **6**(2).

Carlile A. (2009b). 'Finding space for agency in permanent exclusion from school *Power and Education* **1**(3), 2009.

Carlile, A (2010). 'Docile bodies or contested space? Working under the shadow of permanent exclusion' *International Journal of Inclusive Education* 24 August 2010 iFirst.

Carlile A (2011). 'An ethnography of permanent exclusion from school: revealing and untangling the threads of institutionalised racism', *Race Ethnicity and Education.*

Caputo, V (2000). At 'home' and 'away': reconfiguring the field for late twentieth century anthrolplogy in Amit, V (Ed.) *Constructing the field: Ethnographic fieldwork in the contemporary world.* London: Routledge, 19–3.

Children Act 2004. SI UK.

Christian, M (Jan., 2005). 'The politics of Black presence in Britain and Black male exclusion in the British education system' *Journal of Black Studies* **35**(3), 327–346.

Cohen, L, Manion, L and Morrison, K (2000). *Research Methods in Education (5th Ed.).* Abingdon: RoutledgeFalmer.

Conteh, J, Gregory, E, Kearney, C and Mor-Sommerfeld, A (2005). *On writing educational ethnographies: the art of collusion.* Stoke on Trent: Trentham Books.

Convention on the Rights of Persons with Disabilities (2006). SI United Nations [Article 24 (Education)].

Cooper, C (2002). *Understanding school exclusion: challenging processes of docility.* Nottingham: Education Now Publishing Cooperative.

Couldry, N (2010). *Why Voice Matters: Culture and Politics After Neoliberalism.* London: Sage Publications Ltd.

Csordas, TJ (1999). 'Embodiment and Cultural Phenomenology' In Weiss, G and Haber, H (Eds.) *Perspectives on Embodiment.* New York: Routledge 143–162.

Dankin, NK and Lincoln Y (Eds.) (1994). *Handbook of qualitative research.* Thousand Oaks: Sage Publications.

Convention on the Rights of the Child (1989). SI United Nations.

Delpit, L (1995). *Other people's children: conflict in the classroom.* New York: The New Press.

DePalma, R and Atkinson, A (Eds.) (2008). *Invisible boundaries: addressing sexualities in children's worlds.* Stoke on Trent: Trentham.

DePear, S and Garner, P (1996). 'Tales from the exclusion zone: the views of teachers and pupils' in Blyth, E and Milner (Eds.), J *Exclusion from school: inter-professional issues for policy and practice*. London: Routledge 149–158.

Department for Children Families and Schools (2003). *Every Child Matters*, SI Available at http://www.everychildmatters.gov.uk/ [internet] [Accessed 7 July 2007].

Department for Education and Employment (1999c). *Statistical First Release, SFR 10/1999*, 28 May 1999 (London, DfEE).

Department for Education and Employment (2001). *Statistical First Release, Special Education Needs in England- January 2001 (Provisional Estimates)* SFR 21/2001.

Department for Education and Skills (2003). *Green Paper: Every Child Matters*.

Department for Education and Skills (2005). *Supporting the new agenda for children's services and schools: the role of learning mentors and coordinators*. Nottingham: DfES Publications

Department of Health (2009). 'Healthy Lives, Brighter Futures- the strategy for children and young people's health', *Department of Health* gateway reference 10489, [internet] available at http://www.dh.gov.uk/en/Publicationsandstatistics/Publications/PublicationsPolicyAndGuidance/DH_094400 (accessed 28 March 2009).

Donald, J and Rattansi, A (Eds.) (1992). *'Race', culture and difference*. London: Sage Publications.

Dyck, N (2000). 'Home field advantage? Exploring the social construction of children's sports' in Amit, V (Ed.), *Constructing the field: Ethnographic fieldwork in the contemporary world*. London: Routledge 32–53.

Edelman, L (2004). *No Future: Queer theory and the death drive*. London: Duke University Pres.

Education Act 1996. [SI] UK.

Education (areas to which pupils and students belong) Regulations 1996 [SI] UK.

Equality Act 2010. [SI] UK.

Ellis, C (1997). 'Evocative Autoethnography: Writing emotionally about our lives' in Tierney, W and Lincoln, Y (Eds.), *Representation and the text: re-framing the narrative*, SUNY Press: Albany 116–139.

Ellis, T and Graham-Matheson, L (2008). *SEN and inclusion: reflection and renewal*. Birmingham: Nasuwt.

Enway City Director of Children's Services (May, 2007). 'Information pack'. Assembled by: Head of Inclusion (Behaviour). Supplied at: meeting of Enway City Secondary Head Teachers to discuss the rising Fixed Term and Permanent Exclusion rate

Epstein, D and Johnson, R (1998). *Schooling Sexualities*. Buckingham: Open University Press.

Epstein, D and Johnson, R (2008). 'Walking the talk: young people making identities' in DePalma, R and Atkinson, A (Eds.), *Invisible boundaries: addressing sexualities in children's worlds*. Stoke on Trent: Trentham 33–50.

Eriksen, TH (1995). Small *places, large issues: An Introduction to Social and Cultural Anthropology* . London: Pluto Press.

Estrich, S (1986). 'Rape' *Yale Law Jo* **95** 1087–1184.

Evans, G (2007). *Educational failure and working-class white children in Britain*. Hampshire: Palgrave Macmillan.

Fielding, M (Ed.) (2001). *Taking education really seriously: four years hard labour*. London: RoutledgeFalmer.

Fielding, M and Bragg, S (2003). *Students as Researchers: Making a difference*. Cambridge: Pearson Publishing.

Fletcher, W (2001). 'Enabling students with SLD to become effective target setters' in Rose, R and Grosvenor, I (Eds.), *Doing research in special education*, London:David Fulton Publishers 18–29.

Foucault, M (1977). *Discipline and Punish: the birth of the prison*. Harmondsworth: Penguin Books (Trans. A Sheridan).

Foucault, M (1989). *The birth of the clinic: an archaeology of medical perception*. London: Routledge (Trans. A Sheridan).

Francis, B (2005). 'Not/Knowing their place: Girls' classroom behaviour' in Lloyd, G (Ed.) *Problem Girls: Understanding and supporting troubled and troublesome girls and young women*. Oxon: RoutledgeFalmer 9–21.

REFERENCES

Francis, B (2010). 'Re/theorising gender: female masculinity and male femininity in the classroom?' *Gender and Education* **22**(5).

Freire, P (1996). *Pedagogy of the Oppressed*. London: Penguin Books.

Freire, P and Macedo, D. (1987). *Literacy: Reading the Word and the World*. London: Routledge and Kegan Paul.

Freud, S (1940). *Splitting of the ego in self defence*. London: Hogarth Press.

Gaine, C and George, R (1999). *Gender, "race", and class in schooling*. London; Philadelphia, PA: Falmer Press.

Geertz, C (1973). *The interpretation of culture: selected essays*. New York: Basic Books.

Geertz, C (1998). *Works and lives: the anthropologist as author*. Stanford, California: Stanford University Press.

George, R (2007). *Girls in a goldfish bowl: moral regulation, ritual and the use of power amongst inner city girls*. Rotterdam: Sense Publishers.

Gerwitz, S, Ball, SJ and Bowe, R (1995). *Markets, choice and equity in education*. Buckingham: Open University Press.

Gillborn, D (2009). 'Who's afraid of critical race theory in education? A reply to Mike Cole's 'The color-line and the class struggle'', *Power and Education* **1**(1), 125–131.

Gillborn, P and Youdell, D (2000). *Rationing Education: Policy, practice, reform and equity*. Buckingham: OUP.

Gillies, D. (2008). 'Developing governmentality: conduct and education policy', *Journal of Education Policy* **23**(4), 415–427.

Gilroy, P (1987). *There Ain't No Black in the Union Jack: the cultural politics of race and nation*. London: Routledge.

Gilroy, P (1998). 'Race ends here' *Ethnic and Racial Studies* **21**(5), 838–847.

Gold, R and Revill, G (2003). 'Exploring landscapes of fear: marginality, spectacle and surveillance' in *Capital & Class* **27**(27).

Graham, M and Robinson, G (May, 2004). '"The silent catastrophe": Institutional racism in the British Educational System and the underachievement of Black boys' *Journal of Black Studies* **34**(5), 653–671.

Haigh, G (2006). 'Where stories collide: book of the week': [Clandinin, Huber, Murphy, Murray Orr, Pearce and Steeves, *Composing diverse identities: narrative inquiries into the interwoven lives of children and teachers*. Routledge: London] in *Times Educational Supplement* (July 28 2006).

Hall, S (1992). 'New ethnicities' in Donald, J and Rattansi, A (Eds.), *'Race', Culture and Difference*. London: Sage Publications 252–259.

Hammersley, M (1995). 'Theory and evidence in qualitative research'. *Quality and Quantity* **29** 55–56

Hart, Roger A (1992). *Children's participation: from tokenism to citizenship*. Florence: UNICEF International Child Development Centre.

Heath, NL, McLean-Heywood, D, Rousseau, C, Petrakos, H, Finn, CA and Karagiannakis, A (2006). 'Turf and tension: psychiatric and inclusive communities servicing students referred for emotional and behavioural difficulties', *International Journal of Inclusive Education* **10** 335–346.

Henriques, J *et al.* (1998). *Changing the subject: psychology, social regulation and subjectivity*. London: Routledge.

Hinton, K (2008). 'A transgender story: from birth to secondary school' in DePalma, R and Atkinson, A (Eds.), *Invisible boundaries: addressing sexualities in children's worlds*, Stoke on Trent: Trentham 77–90.

Hymes, D (Ed.) (1972). *Reinventing Anthropology*. New York: Pantheon Books.

Izekor, J (2007). 'Challenging the stereotypes: Reaching the hard to reach, Black young men' in Sallah, M and Howson, C (Eds.), *Working with Black young people*. Lyme Regis: Russell House Publishing Ltd 64–74.

James, S and Freeze, R (2006). 'One step forward, two steps back: immanent critique of the practice of zero tolerance in inclusive schools', *International Journal of Inclusive Education* **10** 581–594.

Krumer-Nevo, A (2009). 'From voice to knowledge: participatory action research, inclusive debate and feminism', *International Journal of Qualitative Studies in Education* **22**(3), 279 – 295.

Lave, J and Wenger, E (1991). *Situated Learning: Legitimate Peripheral Participation.* Cambridge: Cambridge University Press.

Lawrence-Lightfoot, S (2003). *The Essential Conversation: what parents and teachers can learn from each other.* The Random House Publishing Group: New York.

LeBesco, K and Braziel, JE (Eds.) (2001). *Bodies out of bounds: fatness and transgression.* London: University of California Press.

LeBesco, K (2001). 'Queering fat bodies/Politics' in LeBesco, K and Braziel, JE (Eds.) *Bodies out of bounds: fatness and transgression.* London: University of California Press 74–87.

Lightfoot, L (2009). 'At risk from the registers?' *The Guardian (Education)* Tuesday 24 March.

Lipsett, A (2008). 'Academies under fire for rapid rise in pupil exclusions', *The Guardian* Tuesday 24 June, available at http://www.guardian.co.uk/education/2008/jun/24/schools.pupilbehaviour (accessed 1 March 2009).

Lloyd, G (Ed.) (2005). *Problem Girls: Understanding and supporting troubled and troublesome girls and young women.* Oxon: RoutledgeFalmer.

Lloyd-Smith, D and Davies, D (Eds.) (1995). *On the margins: the educational experiences of 'problem' pupils.* Stoke: Trentham Press.

Lunt, I and Norwich, B (1999). *Can effective schools be inclusive schools?* Institute of Education: University of London.

Macpherson, W (1999). The Stephen Lawrence Enquiry: report of an enquiry by William Macpherson of Cluny presented to Parliament by the Secretary of State, February 1999, [internet] available at http://www.archive.official-documents.co.uk/document/cm42/4262/4262.htm (accessed December 12, 2008).

Macrae, S, Maguire, M, Milbourne, L (2003). 'Social exclusion: exclusion from school'. *International Journal of Inclusive Education* 7 89–101.

Maguire, M, Wooldridge, T and Pratt-Adams, S (2006). *The urban prinmary school.* Berkshire: Open University Press.

Malinowski, B (1923). 'The problem of meaning in primitive languages' in Ogden, K and Richards, I (Eds.) *The meaning of meaning: a study of influence of language upon thought and of the science of symbolism.* New York: Harcourt, Brace and World 296–336.

Marshall, W (1996). 'Professionals, children and power' in 'Exclusion from school: the role of outside agencies' in Blyth, E and Milner , J (Eds.), *Exclusion from school: inter-professional issues for policy and practice.* London: Routledge 92–104.

McCarthy, C and Dimitriadis, G (2005). 'Governmentality and the sociology of education: Media, educational policy, and the politics of resentment' in *Race, Identity and Representation in Education.* London: Routledge 321–335.

McRobbie, A (1980). 'Settling accounts with sub-culture' *Screen Education* 34 37–50.

Mehan, H (2008). Educational Field Stations: a Model for Improving access to Higher Education (Conference paper), University of Pennsylvania's Centre for Urban Ethnography (29.2.08).

Meo, A and Parker, A (2004). 'Teachers, teaching and educational exclusion: Pupil Referral Units and pedagogic practice', *International Journal of Inclusive Education* 8 103–12.

Milbourne, L (2009). 'Valuing difference or securing compliance? Working to involve young people in community settings', *Children and Society* 23(5), 347–363.

Miller, D (2003). 'The virtual moment', *Journal of the Royal Anthropological Institute* 9(1).

Moore, H (2007). *The Subject of Anthropology.* Cambridge: Polity Press.

Nader, L (1972). 'Up the anthropologist: perspectives gained from studying up' in Hymes, D (Ed.) *Reinventing Anthropology.* New York: Pantheon Books 284–311.

Nicholas, C (2004). 'Gaydar: Eye-gaze as identity recognition among gay men and lesbians', *Sexuality & Culture* 8 1 60–86.

Normington, J (1996). 'Exclusion from school: the role of outside agencies' in Blyth, E and Milner, J (Eds.), *Exclusion from school: inter-professional issues for policy and practice.* London: Routledge 237–149.

Office of National Statistics: 'GCSE and Equivalent Average Point Scores for Young People by Ethnic Group, Referenced by Location of Pupil Residence (2004–2007)', [internet] available at http://

neighbourhood.statistics.gov.uk/dissemination/LeadTableView.do?a=3&b=276753&c=Greenwich &d=13&e=5&g=333611&i=1001x1003x1004&m=0&r=1&s=1226851538500&enc=1&dsFamily Id=1643 (accessed November 16 2008).

Ogden, K and Richards, I (1923). *The meaning of meaning: a study of influence of language upon thought and of the science of symbolism*. New York: Harcourt, Brace and World.

Ong, A and Collier, S (Eds.) (2005). *Global assemblages: Technology, politics, and ethics as anthropological problems*. Oxford: Blackwell Publishing 464–481.

Orwell, G (1949). *1984*. London: Penguin.

Osler, A and Vincent, K (2003). *Girls and exclusion: Rethinking the agenda*. RoutledgeFalmer: London.

Parsons, C (2008). 'Race relations legislation, ethnicity and disproportionality in school exclusions in England', *Cambridge Journal of Education* **28**(3), 401–419

Phoenix, A (2009). 'De-colonising practices: negotiating narratives from racialised and gendered experiences of education', *Race Ethnicity and Education* **12**(1), 101–114.

Pomeroy, E (2000). *Experiencing Exclusion*. London: Trentham Books Ltd.

Radnor, H, Koshy, V and Taylor, A (2007). 'Gifts, talents and meritocracy', *Journal of Educational Policy* **22**(3), 283 – 299.

Rattansi, A (1992). 'Changing the subject? Racism, culture and education' in Donald, J and Rattansi, A (Eds.), *'Race', culture and difference*. London: Sage Publications 11–49.

Reay, D (2008). 'Tony Blair, the promotion of the 'active' educational citizen, and middle-class hegemony' *Oxford Review of Education* **34**(6), 639–650.

Reay, D (1998). *Class work: Mothers' involvement in their children's primary schooling*. London: RoutledgeFalmer.

Reay, D *et al* (2008). 'Re-invigorating democracy?: White middle-class identities and comprehensive schooling', *Sociological Review* 2008 **56**(2), 238–256.

Redfield, M (Ed) (1963). *The social uses of social science: the papers of Robert Redfield, Volume 2*. Chicago: Chicago University Press.

Rendall, S and Stuart, M (2005). *Excluded from School: systemic practice for mental health and education professionals*. Hove: Routledge.

Rehabilitation Act 1973. SI United States of America.

Ridge (2005). 'Feeling under pressure: low-income girls negotiating school life' in Lloyd, G (Ed.) *Problem Girls: Understanding and supporting troubled and troublesome girls and young women* . Oxon: RoutledgeFalmer 22–35.

Roddenberry, G (Executive Producer) (1966–1969). *Star Trek: the original series*. Desilu Producations, Paramount Television, Norway Corporation.

Roddenberry, G *et al* (Executive Producers) (1987–1994). *Star Trek: The Next Generation*. Paramount Television.

Rose, N (1999). *Governing the Soul: The shaping of the private self* (2nd Ed). London: Free Association Book.

Rose, N (2007). *The politics of life itself: Biomedicine, power, and subjectivity in the Twenty-First Century*, Princeton and Oxford: Princeton University Press.

Rose, R and Grosvenor, I (2001). *Doing research in special education*. London: David Fulton Publishers.

Sacks, O (1996). *An Anthropologist on Mars: Seven Paradoxical Tales*. London: Picador.

Salamanca agreement 1994. SI UNESCO (United Nations Educational, Scientific and Cultural Organization).

Sallah, M and Howson, C (2007). *Working with Black young people*. Lyme Regis: Russell House Publishing Ltd,

Sanders, S (2008). 'Tackling homophobia, creating safer spaces',in DePalma, R and Atkinson, A (Eds.) *Invisible boundaries: addressing sexualities in children's worlds*. Stoke on Trent: Trentham 3–12.

Searle, C (1996). 'The signal of failure: school exclusions and the market system of education' in Blyth, E and Milner, J (Eds.), *Exclusion from school: inter-professional issues for policy and practice* . London: Routledge 37–52.

Sellman, E *et al* (2002). Thematic Review: A Sociocultural Approach to Exclusion, *British Educational Research Journal* **28**(6), 888–900.

Silverman, L.K. (1989). 'The highly gifted' in Feldhusen, JF, VanTassel-Baska, J and Seeler, KR (Eds.), *Excellence in educating the gifted* Denver: Love 71–83.

Shore, C and Wright, S (Eds.) (1997). *Anthropology of Policy: Critical perspectives on governance and power.* London: Routledge.

Shostak, M (2000). *Nisa: the story of a !Kung woman.* London: Earthscape.

Sivananden, A (2005). 'Why Muslims reject British values' in *The Observer*, 16 October, [internet] available at: http://www.guardian.co.uk/politics/2005/oct/16/race.world/print (accessed on October 19 2008).

Skeggs, B (1992). 'Paul Willis, Learning to Labour' in Barker M and Beezer A (Eds.), *Reading into cultural studies.* London: Routledge 181–196.

Skeggs, B (1997). *Formations of Class and Gender: Becoming respectable.* London: Sage.

Slee, R (1995). *Changing theories and practices of discipline.* London: The Falmer Press.

Slee, R (2001). 'Social justice and the changing dimensions in educational research: the case of inclusive education', *International Journal of Inclusive Education* 5(2), 167–177.

Sontag, S (1966). 'Notes On "Camp"' in *Against Interpretation and Other Essays.* New York: Farrar, Straus and Giroux.

Spielberg, Steven (Dir) (2002). *Minority Report* Perfs. Tom Cruise, Colin Farrell, Samantha Morton, Max von Sydow, Neal McDonough. 20th Century Fox/ Dreamworks.

Spindler, G and Spindler, L (Eds.) (1987). *Interpretive ethnography of education: at home and abroad*, New Jersey: Lawrence Earlbaum Associates.

Stewart, K (2002). *Helping a Child With Nonverbal Learning Disorder or Asperger's Syndrome.* San Francisco: New Harbinger Publications Ltd.

Stewart (2006). 'Teachers need to be part of university studies, former minister tells the British Educational Research Association Conference: Academics told: keep in touch', *Times Educational Supplement*, September 15 2006, **17**.

Strathern, M (2000a). *Audit Cultures: anthropological studies in accountability, ethics and the academy.* Oxon: Routledge.

Strathern, M (2000b). 'The Tyranny of Transparency', *British Educational Research Journal* **26**(3), 309–321.

Strathern, M (2005). 'Robust knowledge and fragile futures' in Ong, A and Collier, S (Eds.), *Global assemblages: Technology, politics, and ethics as anthropological problems.* Oxford: Blackwell Publishing 464–481.

Tatum Daniels, B (1999). *Why are all the black kids sitting together in the cafeteria?* New York: Basic Books (member of Perseus Books Group)

Thomas, G and Loxley, A (2001). *Deconstructing Special Education and Constructing Inclusion.* Buckingham: Open University Press.

Tierney, W and Lincoln, Y (1997). *Representation and the text: re-framing the narrative.* SUNY Press: Albany.

Timimi, S (2005). *Naughty Boys: anti-social behaviour, ADHD and the role of culture.* Basingstoke: Palgrave Macmillan.

Tomlinson, S (2006). 'Another Day, Another White Paper'. *Forum* **48**(1).

Tomlinson, S (2005). 'Race, ethnicity and education under New Labour', *Oxford Review of Education* **31**(1), 153–171.

Vincent, C (Ed.) (2003). *Social justice, education and identity.* London: RoutledgeFalmer.

Vuillamy and Webb (2000). 'The Social Construction of School Exclusion Rates: Implications for Evaluation Methodology' (Conference paper), British Educational Research Association Annual Conference, Cardiff University, September 7–10, 2000.

Walkerdine, V (1998). 'Developmental psychology and the child-centred pedagogy: the insertion of Piaget into early education' in Henriques, J *et al* (Eds.). *Changing the subject: psychology, social regulation and subjectivity.* London: Routledge 148–198.

Walkerdine, V, Lucey, H and Melody, J (2001). *Growing up girl: Psychosocial explorations of gender and class.* Hampshire: Palgrave.

REFERENCES

Ward, L (2004). 'Mother of truant sent back to prison: first parent to be jailed is inside again after daughter skips school', *Guardian online* [internet] 24 March. Available at: http://www.guardian.co.uk/uk/2004/mar/24/schools.education, [Accessed 25 May 2010].

Weiss, G and Haber, H (Eds.) (1999). *Perspectives on Embodiment*. New York: Routledge.

Wetz, J (2009). *Urban village schools: Putting relationships at the heart of secondary school organisation and design*. London: Calouste Gulbenkian Foundation.

Whitty, G (2002). *Making sense of education policy*. London: Sage.

Wiggins, G and McTighe, J (2006). *Understanding by Design: A Framework for Effecting Curricular Development and Assessment (2nd Ed)*, Association for Supervision and Curriculum Development: Alexandria, VA.

Williams, R (2010). 'Sharon Shoesmith loses appeal against dismissal' *Guardian online* [internet] 23 April. Available at: http://www.guardian.co.uk/society/2010/apr/23/sharon-shoesmith-baby-p-awaiting-verdict, [Accessed 17 May 2010].

Williams, S (2004). Domestic Science: The Education of girls at Home in Aldrich, R (Ed.), *Public or Private Education? Lessons from History*, London: Woburn Press.

Willis, P (1977). *Learning to Labour: How working-class kids get working-class jobs*. Farnborough, Hants: Saxon House, Teakfield Ltd.

Wright, C (2005). 'Black femininities go to school: how young black females navigate race and gender' in Lloyd, G (Ed.) *Problem Girls: Understanding and supporting troubled and troublesome girls and young women*. Oxon: RoutledgeFalmer 100–110.

Wright, C, Weekes, D and McGlaughlin, A (2000). *'Race', Class and Gender in Exclusion from School*. London: Falmer Press.

Wright, C, Weekes, D and McGlaughlin, A (1999). 'Gender-blind racism in the experience of schooling and identity formation', *International Journal of Inclusive Education* 3(4), 293–307.

Youth Justice Board 'ONSET form' (2003). [internet] Available at http://www.yjb.gov.uk/NR/rdonlyres/8D130C9F-C4A7–493C-8528-DD27D44248F5/0/ReferralandScreeningForm.doc , Accessed 29 March 2009.

Zizek, S (2008). *Violence*. London: Profile Books Ltd.

Zizek, S (2000). 'Enjoy your nation as yourself!' in Back, L and Solomos, J (Eds.) *Theories of race and racism*. Oxon: Routledge 594–606.

INDEX

INDEX

Ethnography, as reflective practice, 23, 28–29, 35, 39, 170, 199
Extended body, 18, 26, 31, 40–60, 63, 76–81, 83–86, 114–115, 132–133

F
Feminism, 144
Fielding, Michael, 32, 161–162, 165, 176, 180, 199–201
Foucault, Michel, 8, 15, 18, 23, 31, 40, 43–46, 48–50, 52–53, 57, 59–61, 66, 70, 76, 79–80, 83, 89–91, 105–106, 115–117, 159–160, 162, 167, 176, 179–180, 183–184, 187, 189, 191, 194, 198–203, 210–211
Freire, Paolo, 6, 16, 40, 42–43, 57, 59–60, 66–67, 81, 100–101, 105, 107, 109–110, 115, 191–193, 195, 198–199, 201–204, 210–212

G
Gangs, 38, 55–56, 91, 104, 108, 146, 151
Gender, 14–17, 20, 42–43, 48, 54, 56, 79, 81–105
Girls, 3, 16, 55, 63, 69, 81–107
Girls, exclusion of, 93
Government conferences, 172
Governmental authoritarian power, 162, 195

H
Hart, Roger, 32, 197, 199–201, 203, 210–211
Heteronormativity, 26, 57, 81–107, 165
Hip hop, 108, 154

I
Illuminate Student Researchers Project, 197–212
Inclusion, definition of, 13–15, 45
Inclusion, exclusion from school enacted in the name of, 43
Inclusion, history of, 12–13
Inclusion, policy, 14, 27, 36, 56, 67, 161–164, 167, 188
Inclusive education in international law, 14
Inclusive education, history of, 12–13
Institutional prejudice, 20–21, 42, 54, 58–59, 61, 79, 81, 88, 96, 104, 121, 138, 140, 161–188, 191–193, 195–212

L
League tables, 10–11, 15, 49, 56, 73, 79, 112, 114, 123, 125–127, 149, 162, 175, 191
Learning disabilities, 6

Linguistic capital, 135, 203
Local authority, 1, 5, 9, 11–12, 17, 20, 22, 30–31, 33, 35–39, 42, 54, 56, 58, 60, 63, 65, 68–75, 79–80, 99–100, 118, 123–126, 128, 132–134, 140, 142, 153, 160, 165, 172–176, 184–185, 192, 196

M
Mainstream school, 8, 12, 24–25, 51, 64–65, 69–70, 72–74, 80, 89, 92–93, 97, 99, 107, 121, 124–125, 149, 153–154, 156, 162, 181, 193
Managed moves, 63–65, 68–70, 74, 80, 89–90, 94, 101, 105, 127–128, 135–136, 152
Mental health, of young people, 97
Meritocracy, 110, 113–114, 116–117, 122, 124, 193
Multi-agency support planning meetings, 1

N
Nader, Laura, 15, 20–21, 23, 25, 28, 31–32, 37–38, 53, 61, 113, 115–116, 144, 160, 165, 188, 196, 198, 200, 203, 210–212
Narrative, 1, 4–5, 12, 17, 24–26, 33–34, 38, 70, 72, 76, 88, 90, 99, 104, 109, 118, 120–121, 130, 135, 144, 156, 164, 173, 177, 196, 211
Neoliberalism, 110, 162
Neoliberalism and marketisation of schooling, 15–16, 112, 117
New Labour government, 12, 56, 75, 161, 181

O
Ofsted, 10, 14, 40, 49, 69, 90, 114, 125, 172, 186–187, 200
Orwell, George, 4, 182
Osler, Audrey, 12–13, 15–17, 19, 21–22, 50–51, 56, 84–87, 90–92, 94, 96, 99, 102, 106, 130, 144–146, 149, 151–152, 158, 175, 191

P
Parents, blaming of, 10, 118
Pathologisation, 138, 140
Permanent exclusion as a critical incident, 1, 79, 104, 122, 192
Permanent exclusion as a policy, 63–79, 116–133
Persistent disruptive behaviour, 10, 18, 129, 131, 156
Policy community, 21–24, 27–28, 33, 36, 38–39, 41, 48, 163–164
Policy of inclusion, 27, 75, 161

INDEX